Understanding China

The series will provide you with in-depth information on China's social, cultural and economic aspects. It covers a broad variety of topics, from economics and history to law, philosophy, cultural geography and regional politics, and offers a wealth of materials for researchers, doctoral students, and experienced practitioners.

Laya Li

The Inflation Mechanism and Expectations

Evidence from China

知识产权出版社 有限责任公司
Intellectual Property Publishing House Co., Ltd.

Springer

Laya Li
Hangzhou, Zhejiang, China

Translated by
Lei Huang
Guangzhou, Guangdong, China

ISSN 2196-3134 ISSN 2196-3142 (electronic)
Understanding China
ISBN 978-981-97-2569-4 ISBN 978-981-97-2570-0 (eBook)
https://doi.org/10.1007/978-981-97-2570-0

Jointly published with Intellectual Property Publishing House
The print edition is not for sale in China (Mainland). Customers from China (Mainland) please order the print book from: Intellectual Property Publishing House.
ISBN of the Co-Publisher's edition: 978-7-5130-6793-5

The publication of this book is supported by the Chinese Fund for the Humanities and Social Sciences

Proofread by William Hickey

This Springer imprint is published by the registered company Springer Nature Singapore Pte Ltd.
The registered company address is: 152 Beach Road, #21-01/04 Gateway East, Singapore 189721, Singapore

Preface to the Second Edition

Thanks to the Intellectual Property Press for republishing my book *Inflation Mechanism and Expectations*. I take this opportunity to revise the textual omissions and typographical errors in the original edition by reducing colloquial words and unifying mathematical symbols in some chapters. More explanations have been added to the original text in few places to enable readers to understand better the original text. No modification has been applied to the concepts, viewpoints, conclusions, framework and mathematical derivation method of the original theory so that the original feature of the theoretical system can be maintained.

The core theory of this book is the theory of sticky expectations. With the process of reform and opening up, expectations played a critical role in China's economy in 1988. Based on China's practice at that time, I found that the expectations of the Chinese people were not rational and were characterized by stickiness and mutability (sudden change). Meanwhile, being discontent of the unrealistic assumptions of the rational expectations theory and its inability in explaining many practical problems, I believe that the rational expectations theory should not be applied to explain China's economic practice and guide China's economic policy. A new theory of expectations contraposing to the stickiness and mutability of the rational expectations theory must be established. This is the authentic motive of the birth of the theory of sticky expectations. In view of the similar sticky expectations theory initiated by Western economists around 2000, I call the theory of sticky expectations proposed in this book the Chinese Theory of Sticky Expectations to reflect the differentiation.

There exists high similarities in the theory of sticky expectations regarding the assumptions, concepts, conclusions and thoughts between the Chinese and Western economic theory circles. It can be concluded that though the research objects of economic theories might be differed, the theories abstracted from practice could possibly be identical. The more profound the theory is, the more it can reveal the common law behind different phenomena through different appearances of reality.

Therefore, several important research contents in this book and similar studies and trends in Western economic theory circles will be introduced, so that readers can understand the ideological context of these studies, in order to facilitate their in-depth research.

I. Sticky Expectations

The establishment of any theoretical system requires assumptions, which are the foundation of the theoretical edifice, the essence of the theoretical system, and the starting point and foothold of theoretical innovation. The innovation of any theoretical system is primarily the innovation of assumptions or hypothesis.

(I) Assumption of Heterogeneous Expectations

The heterogeneity of expectations is a hot topic in current economic theory and the basis of the management theory of expectations. Many economic phenomena are related to the heterogeneity of expectations and can be interpreted by such heterogeneity.

The first assumption of the Chinese theory of sticky expectations is the assumption of heterogeneity of expectations, which can be referred in the assumption of the Black Box and the Gray Box discussed in Sect. 10.2 of Chap. 10 of this book: "1. The Assumption of the Black Box and the Gray Box. What most economic actors employ to anticipate the future on the basis of the gathered information is the Black Box model. Since exploration of the relationship between inputs and outputs is their sole concern regardless of a particular structure, the model finally turns out to be merely a Black Box for economic actors. The relationship between inputs and outputs might potentially be identified based upon the actors' experiences which also might be modified in accordance with their judgments about the future. People with professional economic educational backgrounds are to a certain extent acquainted with the variable relation of economic issues as well as with the model structures. Therefore, the models they utilize could partially reflect the reality despite the certain gap between the models and reality. These models are accordingly referred to as the Gray Box." In this assumption, the economic actors are divided into two groups. One group is the vast majority of people (the public), who do not understand the model structure of the economic system and use the Black Box assumptions to predict the future. The other group consists of people with specialized economic education (experts), who have a certain level of knowledge about the relationship between variables and the structure of models in economic problems, they therefore employ the Gray Box assumption to predict the future.

The relationship between inputs and outputs of the Black Box model is influenced by two factors: first, it can be obtained from their experiences, which is consistent with the assumption of the adaptive expectations that can be derived from previous information. The second is to modify expectations with future judgments, which is not identical with the adaptive expectations. In 1988, the public judged that inflation would rise rapidly in the future, and thus made a major revision to their original expectations and consequently generated mutability in inflation expectations of the public.

The following will be a contrast of the discussion on the heterogeneity of expectations of Western economic theories. According to Western economic theorists, Roberts (1998) was the first to establish the assumption of Heterogeneous Expectations. He divided economic men into two groups: those who adopted adaptive expectations and those who adopted rational expectations. People who adopted adaptive expectations learned from those who adopted rational expectations, but learning takes time. Under this condition, it took quite a long time for expectations to be rational, which were in fact sticky expectations. The model constructed by Gali and Gertler (1999) also adopts the assumption of heterogeneous expectations. This model is a mixture of forward expectations (rational expectations) and backward expectations (adaptive expectations). It acknowledges that firms have different expectations, with some firms being forward-looking and others being backward-looking. Carroll (2003, 2005) also divided economic actors into two groups: the expertise and the public. Carroll (2003, 2005) found that expertise's expectations were more accurate and surpassed the public expectations. Moreover, public expectations tended to trace expectations of expertise.

Currently, the economic theory circles are still in the ascendant to the research of the heterogeneous expectations with a more detailed classification of economic actors. For example, Coibion et al. (2018b) separated economic actors into three groups: expertise, enterprise firms and households to study the different impacts of the central bank's expectation management on these three groups of people.

The theoretical significance of the research on assumption of heterogeneous expectations is that it breaks through the assumption of homogeneous expectations of the theory of rational expectations, lays the foundation for management theory of expectations, and provides a new perspective for central bank policy making. The combination of learning process and information transmission process offers an economic mechanism for the tardy spread of information among people, which is an innovation on the theory of learning.

(II) Assumption of Rational Inattention

The second assumption of the Chinese theory of sticky expectations (refer to Sect. 10.2 of Chap. 10 of this book) is: "2. The assumption of the Marginal Cost (MC) of information equals the Marginal Revenue (MR) of a decision. Economic actors must spend time, money and other resources on collecting information. The outlays for these resources finally become costs, namely, the costs of achieving information. Though the more information collected, the more accurate the expectations. The cost of information collection also positively correlates with the increase of the quantity of that information collected. It becomes unworthy if the cost of information collection exceeds the benefit generated by a correct decision. As a result, a rational economic actor will definitely cease further efforts in information collection once a certain quantity is gathered."

Let's contrast the argument of the theory of rational inattention. Before formally proposing this theory, Nobel laureate Christopher Sims (2003, 1998) had given a classic exposition of the assumption of rational inattention: "Because individuals have many things to think about in limited time, they can devote only limited intellectual resources to the tasks of data-gathering and analysis. We know from personal experience that many data that we could look up daily, and that are in principle relevant to our optimal economic decision-making, do not in fact influence our behavior, except when they change dramatically, or perhaps when we occasionally set aside some time to re-assess our portfolio." Levy et al. (2005) pointed out in the study of price change information that "The essence of the idea of rational inattention is that processing price change information is not a costless activity." "If the costs of processing price change information exceed the benefits, consumers may rationally choose to be inattentive to such price change information and therefore, not react to the price changes."

The idea of the Chinese theory of Sticky Expectations that economic actors only collect part of the information and give up the rest is consistent with the idea of the theory of rational inattention that economic actors only pay attention to part of the information and neglects the rest. Further more, the Chinese theory of Sticky Expectations includes time as a single item in the information cost, which corresponds to Sims' limited attention of economic actors. An economic actor allocates a finite amount of time to different pieces of information is equivalent to spreading a finite amount of attention to different pieces of information.

The theoretical significance of the research on this assumption is as follows: although economists have been concerning the assumption of complete and incomplete information, and caring about the assumption of information with cost and free information, they have not yet distinguished the information available and the information actually employed when economic actors make decisions. This assumption does distinguish the differences between the information available and the information actually utilized in decision-making of an economic actor, and holds that the marginal cost of obtaining information is equal to the marginal benefit of the decision. This is in contrast to the theory of rational expectations, which emphasizes that economic actors make full use of all available information. This assumption injects a new content into the incomplete information assumption of the theory of bounded rationality and is also an evolution of its theory of information cost. Moreover, this assumption refines the idea of information cost in the theory of bounded rationality and holds that information cost is not only related to money, but also to time of people. Time is limited for an individual, who can only concentrate on limited aspects, not everything. Since time is so scarce and the ability to process information is limited, information updating will be a slow process for an economic actor, thus imposing stickiness on expectations.

(III) Assumption of Sticky Information

There is a statement in Sect. 10.3 of Chap. 10 of this book: "Due to the comparatively high costs of gathering information in China, especially the delay in the publication of information, which consumes a long time for economic actors to collect. Correspondingly, no significant change will take place in these short-run expectations because of little change in information collected by economic actors." This is the germ of the third assumption of the Chinese theory of Sticky Expectations. This idea was formalized on page 52 of my 1995 book *Inflation and Uncertainty* as the third assumption: "3. Information Delay Assumption. The dissemination and availability of information are not necessarily synchronized with economic variables. In general equilibrium theory, information has no concept of time, or information is instantaneous regardless of delay in time dimension. In economic reality, there is a lag between the date of publication of information and the changes in the economic variables it reflects, and this is especially true in China. Meanwhile, in collecting the existing information, economic actors not only need to pay the costs, but also need to spend time. The time delay of information means that expectations do not change instantly in the short-run. The cost and time delay of information cause the economic actors to spend a longer time on collecting new information, and it is thus difficult to make instantaneous reaction to the changes of economic variables, so that expectations become sticky. Of course, once required information is gathered, economic actors will react quickly and adjust their expectations as quickly as possible."

By contrast, Mankiw and Reis (2002) put forward the core idea of sticky information theory as follows: "when making price decisions, because of either costs of acquiring information or costs to reoptimization, we assumed that each period only a fraction of the population updates itself on the current state of the economy and computes optimal prices based on that information. The rest of the population continues to set prices based on old plans and outdated information." Reis (2006) pointed out that, because there is a cost to acquiring and processing information when economic actors make expectations and decisions, one does not frequently update information and plans. While expectations are rational, they are not updated very often. Economic actors will be in the state of inattention in the intermediate stage of updating information.

It can be seen that the concept of information delay is not only consistent with the concept of sticky information in the ideological sense, but also close to the expiration of sticky information in the expression.

The theoretical significance of the research on this assumption is that the adaptation of delay information is a breakthrough to the assumption of the theory of rational expectations utilizing prevailing information. It enriches the concept of incomplete information and generates a new perspective for interpreting inflation inertia and policy persistence.

(IV) The Assumption of Learning of Expectations

The Assumption of Learning of Expectations of the Chinese theory of Sticky Expectations has been proposed in Sect. 10.2 of Chap. 10 of this book stating that people with Black Box assumptions will learn from those with Gray Box assumption. "Meanwhile, the learning behaviors associated with the expectation can further accelerate the acceptance by the public of the expectation results from any Gray Box assumptions so that a general expectation is shaped. It could finally be concluded that the correct expectations of a few could result in widespread public consensus through the dissemination of the learning behaviors." In Sect. 10.3 of Chap. 10, it states that the "formation process of expectations" is also involving learning: "(3) learning from others as well as from their own errors in the past." On page 52 of *Inflation and Uncertainty*, it is more clearly stated that: "4. The Assumption of Learning of Expectations. This assumption can be divided into two parts. Firstly, economic actors learn from the expectation experience and constantly correct the errors. Secondly, they learn from others and imitate the expectation behavior of others. Imitations of expectations of others can help to reduce information costs and delays in time."

Carroll (2003, 2005) believes that public expectations will follow expert expectations. Fuster et al. (2019) studied different house price expectations of the public and found that "individuals differ in their preferences over available information sources." "However, individuals display substantial disagreement on which piece of information to use: 45.5% chose the forecast of housing experts, 28% chose the past one-year home price change, and 22% chose the past ten-year home price change. The remaining 4.5% reported to prefer no information at all."

When proposing the learning assumption in Sect. 10.2 of Chap. 10, it is pointed out that: "Owing to the learning behaviors associated with this assumption, the probability of a normal distribution of expectations will be enhanced. Additionally, the variance in such a normal distribution will become lesser attributing to the learning behavior. The function of expectations will consequently be refined. The combination of a larger expectation with a smaller variance could better explain the concentration of the distribution." Can the variance of the information distribution be reduced by decreasing the cost of information? This is still a question being explored by economists and viewpoints are varied. Fuster et al. (2019) noted that, "These papers tend to find that when individuals are provided with objective statistics, the dispersion in expectations decreases, thereby providing suggestive support for costly information acquisition models. Extrapolating from these findings, one might conclude that as information becomes easier to access (for instance, due to the Internet), disagreement in expectations should decrease. However, these studies ignore a crucial aspect of the real world: individuals choose which information sources to consult, and where they look for information can be even more important than how frequently they look for information." "Using an innovative experimental setup measuring agents' choice, valuation and use of information, this paper attempts to understand the role of information frictions in explaining the heterogeneity in consumers' expectations. Our main empirical result is that with endogenous information acquisition, lowering the cost of information does not cause lower cross-sectional dispersion in expectations, because respondents choose to look at different pieces of information."

It is discussed in Sect. 10.2 of Chap. 10 that: "There exists a feature in the geographical distribution of the learning assumption of expectations: the rural person learns from the urban person, small cities from big ones, and the interior from the coastal areas. Such a feature helps to illustrate the rationality of economic actors who hold that expectations of people in coastal and large urban areas are generally more accurate than those of their counterparts in the interior, small urban and rural areas. This suggests that economic actors would be willing to learn from them to gain greater revenue at lower costs." In the age of the Internet, such spatial and geographic differences related to expectations will diminish. In spatial geography, the combination of the learning process of expectation and process of information dissemination is still worth exploring.

In page 55 of *Inflation and Uncertainty*, it is pointed out that: "Of course, if some new important information is added during the social transmission process of expectations, such news will be spreading more widely, which may also lead to mutation in expectations." "There is a new factor in the China's economy causing mutations in expectations, that is speculative capital. Speculators are sensitive to expectations and react to changes in government policy rapidly. Expectations of the entire economy can be influenced by expectations of the speculators." This can be illustrated by the American Financial Crisis in 2008, which did spread over many countries and regions in the world in a very short period of time. For the kind of explosive and shocking news causing tremendous public concerns, the learning process of expectations and the information dissemination process can become extremely fast, leading to a mutation in expectations.

The theoretical significance of the learning assumption of expectations is that since expectations results of the Gray Box assumption are gradually accepted by the public, the learning of expectations cannot be completed in a short period of time under normal circumstances, which is a breakthrough to the rapid learning assumption of the theory of rational expectations.

The combination of the learning process and the process of information dissemination provides an economic mechanism for the slow spread of information among people and spatial geography under normal circumstances. The expectation mutation caused by rapid spreading of information of tremendous public concerns through the learning process of expectations and process of information dissemination is also considered a theoretical innovation.

In conclusion, in the Chinese theory of Sticky Expectations, partial information is used to substitute complete information in the second assumption, delayed information is used to replace current information in the third assumption replaces, and learning from others is set in the fourth assumption. All these assumptions are believed to lead a reduction in the information cost. These methods of information cost reduction of the Chinese theory of Sticky Expectations are deemed to be innovations of the theory of information cost.

(V) False Expectations are Unsustainable

The Assumption of Unsustainable False Expectations is proposed in Sect. 10.2 of Chap. 10: "Economic actors learn not only from others, but also from practice. Once an expectation is found to be wrong, economic actors typically have it modified to match the reality. Therefore, a false expectation would not be sustainable in the long-run. The trial-and-error method adopted by economic actors will enable their expectations to move around the trends of accuracy. As a result, expectation becomes consistent with reality in the long-run. This is why we do not rely on the role of expectation when a long-run analysis is conducted. Nonetheless, an expectation can potentially deviate from reality in the short-run." The trial-and-error approach is defined in Sect. 10.5 of Chap. 10 as follows: "Therefore, in facing uncertainty in the real world, economic actors tend to explore carefully from the existing expectations and gradually adjust to reach some optimal points."

The Gray Box assumption defined in Sect. 10.2 of Chap. 10 is: "People with professional economic educational backgrounds are to a certain extent acquainted with the variable relation of economic issues as well as with the model structures. Therefore, the models they utilize could partially reflect the reality despite the certain gap between the models and reality. These models are accordingly referred to as the Gray Box." If the Gray Box model can use "a certain extent acquainted with the variable relation of economic issues as well as with the model structures" to conduct trial-and-error, efficiency of search will be thus enhanced. This is a topic worthy of study, with reference to the adaptive learning model (Evans and Honkapohja, 2001). The adaptive learning model assumes that economic actors understand the model structure but not the model parameters. It is neither a Black Box model (since the model structure is known) nor a White Box model (since the model parameters are unknown), it can therefore be regarded as a Gray Box model. Under certain conditions, the adaptive learning model can converge expectations of economic actors to rational expectations.

(VI) Formation Process of Sticky Expectations

The "Formation Process of Expectations" in Sect. 10.3 of Chap. 10 points out that: "The formation process of sticky expectations is as follows: the economic actors utilize the information attainable under cost constraints to anticipate the future value of the economic variables. Such expectations will be formulated by overlapping the following activities of the economic actors i.e. (1) following experiences; (2) relying upon newly existing phenomena; (3) learning from others as well as from their own errors in the past." Expectations based on experience and new information are similar to the Bayesian Estimation in mathematical terms. It is stated in the last part of this section that: If expectations formulated from the Gray Box model are agreeable to the majorities, the formula for the formation of sticky expectations can also be expressed in a mathematical expectation formula, which is coincident with the formula used to express the formation of rational expectations. However, this may not be consistent with reality. There may be systematic errors in the short-run, which indicate inconsistency with rational expectations. Nonetheless, in the long-run, the results generated from this formula are consistent with those from rational expectations.

The formation process of expectations is still a dominant research area at present. Yellen (2016), former chair of the Federal Reserve System, pointed out, "Perhaps most importantly, we need to know more about the manner in which inflation expectations are formed and how monetary policy influences them." Coibion et al. (2018a) carried out studies on how expectations are formed in firms. They surveyed 3000 New Zealand firms about their macroeconomic beliefs and expectations and found that firms update their beliefs in a Bayesian approach when new information about the economy is provided. Francesco et al. (2019) studied how inflation expectations are formed by consumers. They found that in order to form general inflation expectations, consumers rely on the price changes they face in daily procurement. Specifically, the frequency and size of price changes, rather than their share of spending, matter to individuals' inflation expectations. Therefore, the frequency and magnitude of grocery price changes that consumers are personally exposed to, should be incorporated into formation models of expectations. A central bank's policy based on expectations according to core inflation, which excludes food prices, can lead to systemic errors.

(VII) Explanation of Stickiness and Mutation of Expectation by Uncertainty

According to the Chinese theory of Sticky Expectations, expectations possess two fundamental properties: first, expectations are sticky; second, expectations are uncertain. Uncertainty of Expectations in Sect. 10.5 of Chap. 10 explains the stickiness and mutability of expectations in terms of uncertainty: "On one hand, expectation is stable owing to its stickiness; however, on the other hand, expectation is unstable because of its uncertainty. At present, it is still difficult for us to comprehend when and under what condition such expectation stickiness can be modified and a greater change appears." "Meanwhile, it is precisely because of the uncertainty of the objective world that economic actors realize that their expectations are not necessarily entirely accurate. Even so, economic actors will not easily alternate their expectations unless they realize that the established expectations are false and such falseness is caused by systematic errors. However, investigation of such falsehoods would be a time-consuming process. Therefore, in facing uncertainty in the real world, economic actors tend to explore carefully from the existing expectations and gradually adjust to reach some optimal points. Adjustment of expectations will thus appear to be relatively tardy." "There are two main causes for economic fluctuations, i.e. the shock of uncertainty of the real world as well as the shock of uncertainty of expectations on the economy. The economy would be substantially influenced in case the two causes are combined. For example, in 1988 the slogan of "Breakthrough of Price Reform" did trigger people to sharply raise their expectations of price levels. Such a sudden change in expectations turned out to be uncertain and unpredictable in advance and had a relatively huge impact upon the China economy in 1988."

It is still a meaningful research topic to study the impact of uncertainty on expectations. Fuster et al. (2019) stated, "Third, we show that an individual's prior uncertainty is correlated with behavior at each stage of the expectation formation process. Somewhat surprisingly, individuals with low prior uncertainty have a higher willingness to pay for information, spend more time processing the displayed information, and incorporate the information more strongly in their beliefs." This also means that individuals with a high prior uncertainty have a lower willingness to pay for information and spend less time processing the displayed information. In this way, individuals with high prior uncertainty adjust their expectations more slowly, while individuals with low prior uncertainty act more quickly in this regard.

The theory of rational inattention, theory of sticky information and theory of sticky expectations in Western economics only study the stickiness of expectations, not their mutability. In the real economy, mutability of expectations may occur. For example, the collapse of Lehman Brothers in September 2008 triggered an expectation mutation and generated financial panic, which led to the financial crisis in the United States, and serious consequences followed. Therefore, the study of expectation mutation not only carries theoretical significance, but also bears strong practical significance. On page 163 in the book *A Research on the Theoretical Basis of Macro-prudential Management*, the author points out: "Although expectation mutation does not occur frequently, and expectations demonstrate stickiness more often, the behaviors of economic actors in rational inattention, sticky information and sticky expectations will be identical to decision makers in a spider web model, who would only passively follow the previous period or earlier outdated information without the factor of expectation mutation. A rational economic actor, on the other hand, will learn from his mistakes and does not repeat the same mistakes over and over again." On page 148 of the same book, it is pointed out that: "One of the most important tasks in preventing and defusing systemic risks is to prevent and defuse financial panics. Financial panics are moments of expectation mutation. Stabilizing expectations and preventing expectation mutation are critical measures to prevent and resolve financial panic. Therefore, management of expectations constitutes an important cornerstone of the theoretical foundation of macro-prudential management." On page 150, the author claims: "Stickiness of sticky expectations corresponds to the accumulation of systematic risk, while the mutation feature of sticky expectations corresponds to the outbreak of systematic risk. It is more practical to employ the theory of Sticky Expectations rather than the theory of Rational Expectations to explain the formation and outbreak of systematic risks.

(VIII) Interpretation of Pro-cyclical Behavior and Countercyclical Regulation by Theory of Sticky Expectations

After the 2008 US financial crisis, pro-cyclical behavior and countercyclical regulation have become hot research topics in economic theory circles.

Although the word pro-cyclical is not adopted, one's pro-cyclical behavior is explained in Sect. 10.6 of Chap. 10 in terms of sticky expectations. "1. Expectation is an important factor in inducing inflation. Because of the sticky nature of expectations, in the initial phase of inflation, the shock of an increase in the money supply on the increase of product prices becomes tardy, which creates a false prosperous phenomen on with market prosperity, brisk trades, economic growth and income rise. Consequently, when the economy enters the track of inflation, the government observes only the boom in the economy without taking actions to control inflation." "2. The expectations of inflation will stick to a higher level when inflation has been rising for a certain period of time, which in turn prevents inflation from falling and which indeed helps to push up inflation." "3. When the economy touches the trough and expectations are finally driven down, the expectation trap effect emerges once again. At this point, the government attempts to stimulate the economy by increasing the money supply, however, all extra money will be absorbed by the expectation trap and turned into a backlog of inventory funds."

In Sect. 11.5 of Chap. 11, it is argued that: "One method can be called a countercyclical measure. Aggregate demand must be dropped down when it runs over aggregate supply. Aggregate demand should be otherwise stimulated in case it runs below aggregate supply. This is called "cutting high and filling low". "But countercyclical financial and fiscal policies are also problematic. The impact of the money supply on the economy unfolds over a period of time, the lagging of which is also influenced by expectation, and as that change of expectation remains uncertain, all of this may lead to a dislocated temporal reaction. This can be illustrated as the lag of money supply causing a delay in effectiveness on the monetary stimulus or on the restraining measures. The monetary expansion policy that attempts to push up the aggregate demand may only take effect when this phase of aggregate demand contraction has passed and the aggregate demand expansion has arrived. This acts as a stimulus to the expansion of economic activity, thereby exacerbating economic fluctuations." "Another problem with the countercyclical measure is that when stimulating economic growth, the government tends to stimulate aggregate supply to surpass its potential level due to the effect of expectations and price stickiness, resulting in a sharp increase in supply but not the price level. If the government is addicted to this way, a new round of inflation may then occur." "Because of the potential risks in countercyclical policies mentioned above, Chinese economists are now turning to a negative approach to tackle with the constantly changing environments. This is what was being discussed earlier, that is, regulating the money supply and rationing on the basis of a constant and stable economic growth rate." "It is believed that to stabilize the speed of economic growth, we need to first stabilize the growth rate of the money supply. That is, to stabilize the economic growth rate by in- turn stabilizing the growth rate of the money supply." "Given the uncertainty and the role of the internal expansion mechanism in the economic system, we can also adopt both countercyclical planning policy and fiscal policy, integrating them with the financial policy for stabilizing the money supply so as to eliminate fluctuations in the economic system as much as possible. This is a macroeconomic management measure with a financial policy as the core, supplemented by planning and fiscal policy."

II. Policy Rules

Policy rules include instrumental rules and targeting rules. This section introduces the instrumental rules of the Chinese theory of Sticky Expectations.

(I) Theoretical Foundations of Policy Rules

1. Equilibrium of money supply and demand. It is mentioned in Sect. 7.3 "The Determination of the Money Supply" of Chap. 7 that: "The equilibrium point of the short-run money supply and its demand is the intersection of the short-run money demand and supply function." The quantity demanded for money is determined by the real interest rate and the growth rate of national income. "As per plan arrangement of the Chinese government over the years, it is started from determining the growth rate of *NI* (i.e., from determining the growth rate of national income). That is to firstly set the growth rate of national income, and then arrange the money supply to ensure that growth rate. This is reasonable from the views of the traditional planned economy." "This issue will be further discussed in Chap. 9 of this book. The contents concerning the relationship between the product market and money market of this chapter constitute the theoretical foundation of Chap. 9."

2. Problems encountered in discretionary decision-making. "The Regulation Rules and Economic Expectations" discussed in Sect. 9.2 of Chap. 9 states: "The basic rule of government regulation is that if prices rise too high, and the government considers aggregate demand to be greater than aggregate supply, the planning and banking systems will be required to tighten their policies. At this point, the planning system will contract the planned output Q_t^*, and the banking system will reduce the supply of new money ΔM_t^s. Similarly, if the government considers the growth rate is too high, or the shortage gap is too large, it will require the planning and banking systems to tighten the economy for narrowing the gap between aggregate demand and aggregate supply." "Conversely, if the government believes the growth rate is too low, it will require the planning system and the banking system to deregulate. Accordingly, the planning system will increase the planned output Q_t^*, while the banking system will increase the supply of new money ΔM_t^s." Here, regulation rules

are the rules based on which the Chinese government makes discretionary decisions. The policy variables determined by regulation rules are exogenous variables, which are determined by the government in reference to other economic variables, not by other economic variables. In contrast, policy variables determined by policy rules are endogenous and determined by other variables in the economic system.

It can be seen that the regulation rules of the Chinese government are similar to the discretionary decisions of the central banks of Western countries based on the Phillips Curve, in which the government takes a trade-off between the inflation rate and the economic growth rate. Although the Chinese government does not regulate the economy based on a Phillips Curve derived from statistical data, the regulation rules of the Chinese government illustrate that the Chinese government empirically believes that inflation is positively correlated with economic growth, that is, inflation can be cut down through dropping the economic growth rate.

In Sect. 9.2 of Chap. 9, the empirical relationship between the two is theoretically analyzed and the problems encountered in this empirical relationship are discovered.

It is pointed out in Section 2 that: "According to the theoretical analysis in this book, the relationship between the economic growth rate and inflation will be uncertain in the short-run when economic expectations are involved. With low inflation expectations, higher growth can coexist with lower inflation, as what happened from 1984 to 1987. When inflation expectations are high, the growth rate of the price level will be significantly higher than the economic growth rate, as the case in 1988. Due to the lack of in-depth theoretical analysis and sufficient understanding, the economic expectations become quite uncertain, and it is difficult to include expectation as an independent variable in the model. Consequently, it becomes problematic to determine the quantitative relationship between the price level and the economic growth rate, which can only be solved with the development of the theory of expectations. Therefore, the discretionary decision of the government is still likened "to crossing the river by feeling the stones". Only after determining the upper limit of tolerable inflation can the economy be gradually adjusted to maintain the corresponding growth rate. It can be stated that the emergence of economic expectations has led to more hardships in economic regulation." It can be found that the uncertainty of the relationship between economic growth rate and inflation in the short term comes from the uncertainty of expectations, which leads to the failure of traditional regulation rules, that is, the failure of the discretionary decision method. This explanation is different from the Western economic theory circles that the change of the Phillips Curve leads to the invalidation of discretionary decision. Western theorists believe that under the role of rational expectations or adaptive expectations, the Phillips Curve tends to be vertical, so the discretionary decision fails.

What can be done to remove the uncertainty of expectations? This will be studied in Chap. 11 of this book.

3. Research on China's Phillips Curve. In Sect. 9.2 of Chap. 9, the author tries to use statistical data to derive the Chinese Phillips Curve model, that is, "Can the relationship between economic growth rate and inflation growth rate be described mathematically?" However, the attempt failed, a failure I attribute to the "uncertainty about the relationship between the pace of economic growth and inflation in

the short-run." Later, I present a theoretical model of the Phillips Curve in Sect. 16.2 of Chap. 16 in my book *Inflation and Uncertainty*. In Sect. 16.3 of the same Chapter, an asymmetric Phillips Curve regression model is also presented. The characteristic of this regression model is that, when the regression analysis of inflation rate and economic growth rate in each rising or falling period is conducted, it can be found out that there is a positive correlation between inflation rate and economic growth rate in each period. Moreover, when economic growth is in the rising period, the corresponding inflation rate is low, while a relative higher inflation rate is corresponding to economic growth in its declining stage. I explain this nonlinear relationship in terms of sticky expectations and cost-push inflation. In Section 3 of this chapter, it is pointed out that: "The double-value mapping relationship between inflation and economic growth bears great theoretical and practical significance. From a theoretical point of view, this further confirms the sticky nature of expectations, reveals the internal relationship between inflation and economic growth, and reveals the seemingly non-existent Phillips Curve. From a practical point of view, this will help to formulate anti-inflation policies."

(II) Theoretical Forms of Policy Rules

In Sect. 9.8 of Chap. 9, "The Form of Policy Rules" states: "Both the planned output Q_t^* and planned money supply M_t^s are generally regarded as exogenous variables. Because of the inclusion of policy rules, Q_t^* and M_t^s will change accordingly to these rules in this chapter, so that Q_t^* and M_t^s become endogenous variables, which are defined by other variables within the economic system." "Other variables" here means excessive aggregate demand in theory. Since it is hard to measure excessive aggregate demand, the subsequent argument in this section shows that Q_t^* and M_t^s are in fact determined by the rate of inflation P_t. According to the formula $\Delta P_t = \lambda(D_t - S_t)$ given in Sect. 9.1 of Chap. 9 and relevant explanations: "The greater aggregate demand is then the aggregate supply, the greater the increase in the price level." It can be seen that when excessive aggregate demand is positive, P_t rises. When excessive aggregate demand is negative, P_t drops. For the convenience of measurement, the policy rule function is represented by $Q_t^* = f_1(P_t)$ and $M_t^s = f_2(P_t)$. When P_t increases, both Q_t^* and M_t^s decrease. When P_t decreases, both Q_t^* and M_t^s increase.

The policy rules of this theory only change the policy variables of regulation rules from exogenous to endogenous. The theoretical implication of such a change is that government policy-making is governed by rules. However, this section only puts forward the theoretical form of policy rules, and the specific form of policy rule function has not been given. It is pointed out in Sect. 9.8 of Chap. 9 that: "Policy rule only analyzes the change direction of both Q_t^* and M_t^s and the directive signals they follow, but not specific amounts and the length of such changes."

In particular, $M_t^s = f_2(P_t)$ represents a quantitative monetary policy rule. Here, the government determines the tightness of the money supply according to the inflation rate. $Q_t^* = f_1(P_t)$ denotes a policy rule in which government determines the planned output. This is the characteristic of China's economic regulation.

It is stated in Sect. 9.1 of Chap. 9 that government regulation will attempt to "make an effort to narrow the gap between aggregate supply and aggregate demand as small as possible." Both government regulation rules and policy rules are for achieving this goal.

(III) The Relationship Between Policy Rules and Enterprise Cycle

In Sect. 9.9 of Chap. 9, the theoretical relationship between policy rules and the enterprise cycle has been analyzed: "When inflation falls for a while, the government policy rule will again stimulate economic growth. Thus, an economic cycle is completed. The turning point in this cycle is the government policy rule. It remains uncertain as for how long inflation will last before the policy rule takes effect to drive down inflation since it is more influenced by factors external to the economic system per se. However, when the real aggregate supply has reached its upper boundary, and the continuous increase in aggregate demand can no longer cause the real supply to rise, but all turns into increased inflation, the government will then face the pressure of public demand to pull down inflation, and the policy rule will thus take effect." It is demonstrated in this section that in the presence of a positive output gap (real aggregate supply is greater than potential aggregate supply), inflation rises. When there is a negative output gap (real aggregate supply is smaller than its potential level), inflation falls.

(IV) The Relationship Between Policy Rules and Policy Transparency

In Sect. 11.4 "Policy Information Transmission and Policy Rules" of Chap. 11, it is stated that "If the government follows an open set of policy rules and unswervingly implements them, the policy rules themselves will provide the public with more information about the process of government policy making, which in turn helps to reduce the uncertainty of public expectations. It can also prevent policymakers from changing their original intentions and improve the credibility of these policies." This statement links policy rules with policy transparency, taking policy rules as a tool for the government to convey information to the public as well as a tool for constraining policy making and improving government credibility. The idea was advanced in its time.

(V) The Smoothing Operation of Policy

In Chap. 11 of this book, it is proposed that due to the uncertainty of the economic system, the stickiness of expectations and the time lag of the effect of the policy, the policy should be introduced evenly, which should be adjusted gradually and be consistent on directions when any changes take place. Such a policy implementation is called as policy smoothing operation, which is similar to the interest rate smoothing operation defined by Western economic theorists. Policy smoothing operation is a basic regulation rule. The central bank should adopt the smoothing operation policy when adjusting the growth rate of M2, the interest rate and the required reserve ratio.

It is stated in Sect. 11.3 of Chap. 11 that "Due to the uncertainty of the economic system and the expectation stickiness, when implementing the policy, we should try to avoid eagerness for quick results and move towards the goals step by step by breaking down the process in reasonable stages and allowing the policy to become incrementally effective. Multiple stages can also betaken for controlling inflation, which can be pulled down step by step. Because of the expectation stickiness, it can be a little stronger at the initial stage, which is conducive to pulling down higher inflation expectations of the public, but afterwards the efforts must be evenly distributed so as to gradually pull down the inflation. When stimulating aggregate supply, the same approach should be adopted step by step. This will help to stabilize economic development. It is not desirable to rapidly alter the approach of implementation, which may cause severe economic fluctuations."

It is pointed out in Sect. 11.4 of Chap. 11 that: "Due to the influence of uncertainty and the time lags between policy and action, unexpected events may be encountered in the process of policy implementation, which could make the role of policy contrary to the original plan. For instance, it may be initially to stimulate economic growth by increasing the money supply to pull out the economy from the trough, however, when the policy comes into play, the economy had already recovered in achieving its potential aggregate supply level. Hence, such policy could only stimulate the supply to surpass its potential level, resulting in inflation. Therefore, we should never attempt to achieve a goal in only one leap even if the policy rules are followed. All should be accomplished gradually in order to avoid uncertainty." This paragraph not only explains why the policy smoothing operation is in place but is also consistent with the interest rate smoothing of the Western central banks under the Taylor Rule.

In Sect. 11.5 of Chap. 11, it is pointed out that: "Both the inherent uncertainty in the economic system and the enhanced influence of expectation imposed technical difficulties on the rule of counter cyclical money supply. One way to reduce the difficulties is to adopt the trial-and-error method to gradually increase the money supply. Thus, once the problem is identified, it can be settled immediately without causing greater fluctuations. Which is to say, whether we attempt to depress or stimulate the aggregate demand, we should avoid eagerness for quick results by allowing for a transition period, so that policies gradually take effect. Although this may consume a bit more time, the implementation can be steadier, thereby avoiding a negative consequence. In a system where uncertainty still plays a critical role, the trial-and-error method is a relative satisfactory basic adjustment method, or a fundamental regulation rule." Policy trial-and-error should be in the same direction. For example, to control inflation, interest rates should be raised step by step until reaching an appropriate level. In normal years, the direction of policy trial-and-error should only fluctuate within a limited scope in consistent with the smooth line of policy.

In Sect. 17.2 of Chap. 17 in the book *Inflation and Uncertainty*, three principles for managing inflation have been proposed, namely "to control inflation with principle of firmness, stepwise and stability". When discussing the principle of firmness, it is pointed out that "the government should make it clear to the public that as long as inflation remains at a high level, such as a double-digit level, the government will adopt a tighter economic policy and implement it." This links the policy smoothing operation to Forward Guidance. The Policy Smoothing Operation informs the public the intention, direction, strength and path of the policy, and clearly announces the future trend of the policy, which is extremely consistent with the Forward Guidance. When discussing the principle of stability, this section points out that "Stability means that the policy intensity should be even, neither be too big nor too tiny. A steady decline in inflation will also help stabilize inflation expectations of the public and prevent the impact of uncertainties." It also suggests that the policy smoothing operation, which requires policy changes to be in the same direction, helps to stabilize inflation expectations of the public.

It is stated in Sect. 12.5 of Chap. 12 in this book that "Considering optimal policy alternative from a dynamic perspective should begin with a study on the decreasing path of the price level. As stated in the previous theoretical analysis, the decreasing path of the price level can be determined by the quantity of the money supply. Accordingly, the dynamic optimal policy alternative can then be transformed into an issue of manipulation of an optimal money supply." "Obviously, the optimal money supply U^* is a complex function which should not be followed by the banks to inject money. However, the theoretical curve of U^* can be used as a reference for banks to determine their own money supply so that the real money supply will fluctuate around such a theoretical curve, or by not deviating too far away." The Pontryagin's Maximum Principle is adopted in this section to solve the dynamic optimal problem. To make the real money supply fluctuate around the theoretical curve is on one hand a smoothing operation, and on the other hand, a dynamic optimal operation.

From pages 97 to 106 in the book *Inflation and Uncertainty*, the stochastic quadratic optimal control method is adopted to study on how to minimize the reduction of the economic growth rate while minimizing the inflation rate during a planning period. This is a stochastic dynamic optimal control model, which requires the combination of the Kalman Filter and the Deterministic Optimal Control Method. It is found out that in the deterministic part of the model, the control variables take exactly the same value in each period. After adding random factors to the model, the spread between the value of the control variable in each period and the value in the deterministic model becomes very small. This shows that in the model, the dynamic optimal control is a uniform smooth operation.

The central banks of Western countries generally implement the interest rate smoothing operation under the Taylor Rule. Such operation is characterized by prudence, gradual, fine tuning and uniform directional, which is similar to the above-mentioned policy smoothing operation to be called the Policy Interest Rate Gradualism. Since the 1960s, Western economic theorists have been discussing the interest rate smoothing operation, and it has also attracted concerns of some well-known economists.

Barro (1988) states: "In this paper I explore the behavior of monetary policy that is consistent with an objective of interest rate smoothing. I argue that such an objective appears reasonable, and leads in a theoretical model to well defined behavior for the monetary base and the price level. Furthermore, this behavior for money and prices provides testable hypotheses about these variables under a regime where the monetary authority targets nominal interest rates."

Clarida, Gali and Gertler (1999) put forward interest rate smoothing operations as an important issue in monetary policy theory in Sect. 5.2. They point out that the optimal interest rate calculated by most models is much more volatile than the central bank's smoothing interest rate. They also mention the three theoretical explanations for this, but still argue that "in general, understanding why interest rate smoothing occurred in practice is an important unsolved issue." The unsolved theoretical problem they raised has led to a boom in the quest of interest rate smoothing.

Woodford (2003a) states: "This paper considers the desirability of the observed tendency of central banks to adjust interest rates only gradually in response to changes in economic conditions. It shows, in the context of a simple model of optimizing private-sector behaviour, that assignment of an interest rate smoothing objective to the central bank may be desirable, even when reduction of the magnitude of interest rate changes is not a social objective in itself. This is because a response of policy to 'irrelevant' lagged variables may be desirable owing to the way it steers private-sector expectations of future policy." Woodford's view that interest rate smoothing can guide public expectations about future policy is the same as that of the Forward Guidance, which is consistent with our view that policy smoothing operation can help stabilize public expectations.

Nakata and Schmidt (2019) state that "Our analysis provides a novel rationale for policy rate gradualism. In a liquidity trap, a gradualist central bank keeps the policy rate low for longer than is warranted by the dynamics of output and inflation alone, mimicking a key feature of the optimal commitment policy. This low-for-long policy creates a transitory boom in future inflation and output, which damps the declines of inflation and real activity during the liquidity trap via expectations." "A discretionary central bank that is only concerned with output and inflation stabilization will find itself unable to credibly commit to keep the policy rate low, for it has an incentive to renege on its past promise and increase the policy rate once the liquidity trap conditions recede. However, modifying the objective function of a discretionary central bank to include an IRS objective allows society to make low-for-long policies credible. An optimally chosen weight on the IRS objective relative to the central bank's objectives for inflation and output stabilization leads to a significant improvement in society's welfare even though society itself is not intrinsically concerned with the stabilization of changes in the policy rate."

Earlier than other counterparts, the Chinese theory of Sticky Expectations linked policy smoothing operation with stable expectations and forward guidance, and explained why it should be implemented from the perspectives of expectation stickiness, uncertainty and time lag of policy implementation.

The theoretical significance of the policy smoothing operation is that it expresses the policy intention, policy orientation, policy intensity and policy path to the public. It is an approach demonstrating policy transparency and a relatively prudent way of policy adjustment under uncertain environment in guiding public expectations. The policy smoothing operation also has the function of predictability, stabilizing the economy and expectations, and constraining the policy-making of the central bank. It can further enhance policy efficiency, reduce policy errors, maintain government credibility, and reduce the impact of uncertainty.

On top of that, policy smoothing operation also helps reduce systemic risk. In the general equilibrium theory system with uncertainty, under the assumption of perfect competition of market, investors can smooth their consumption in different periods and different situations by buying and selling assets, that is, make their consumption roughly the same in different periods and different situations. This suggests that investors are not in favour of consumption volatility and view it as a risk. By smoothing consumption, investors can promote their utility level and eliminate individual risks caused by fluctuations in their endowments. In this theoretical system, the fluctuation of the aggregate endowments of the whole society (a macroeconomic fluctuation) generate the consumption fluctuation of investors, which cannot offset each other and becomes a systemic risk. Under this theoretical system and corresponding assumptions, the optimal allocation of resources also means the optimal allocation of risk (or optimal risk sharing), that is, all investors share the aggregate endowment volatility risk, and eliminate the individual risks unrelated to such a risk. The policy smoothing operation not only helps investors to make their own consumption plans to smooth their consumption and eliminate individual risks, but also helps to stabilize the macro economy and reduce the systematic risks caused by macroeconomic fluctuations, thus helping to stabilize the financial system.

(VI) In Comparison with Western Policy Rules

It is stated in Sect. 11.4 of Chap. 11 that "Policy rules can be roughly divided into two types: feedback and no-feedback, which is similar to the closed-loop system and the open-loop system in cybernetics. Feedback policy rules will constantly adjust the strength of the policy according to the implementation and results of it, so that the goals can be achieved." In the book *The Science of Monetary Policy: A New Keynesian View*, Clarida, Gali and Gertler (1999) argued that Taylor Rule is a monetary policy rule with feedback function, which is different from Friedman's rule of fixed rate of money supply.

The rules of monetary policy proposed in this book share a common feature with the Rule of Quantity Theory of Money (the McCallum Rule) (1988) and the Taylor Rule (1993), that is, they both enable a feedback function to cool down economic growth when inflation rate rises, and vice versa.

Of course, the policy rule proposed in this book does not provide a specific form of the function, and it is merely a theoretical policy rule. And both the Quantity Theory of Money and Taylor Rule, offer a specific form of the function. The policy rule proposed in this book treats planned output as a policy instrument, which is completely different from Quantity Theory of Money and the Taylor Rule.

III. Inflation Targeting

Svensson (2010) pointed out that "Inflation targeting is a monetary policy strategy that was introduced in New Zealand in 1990. It has been very successful in stabilizing both inflation and the real economy. As of 2010 it has been adopted by around 25 industrialized and non-industrialized countries. It is characterized by (1) an announced numerical inflation target, (2) an implementation of monetary policy that gives a major role to an inflation forecast and has been called forecast targeting, and (3) a high degree of transparency and accountability). Inflation targeting is highly associated with an institutional framework that is characterized by the trinity of (1) a mandate for price stability, (2) independence, and (3) accountability for the central bank, but there are examples of highly successful inflation targeters, such as Norges Bank, that lack formal independence (although their de facto independence may still be substantial)." "These findings support the view that a well-known and credible inflation target helps to anchor the private sector's long-run inflation expectations."

The theoretical analysis of inflation targeting system was carried out in the 1990s. Svensson (1997) proposed the elastic inflation targeting system, which holds both objectives of inflation stability and output stability.

China's economic management system is different from Western countries. The People's Bank of China is not independent and no rules of accountability has been set upon this bank. However, the central bank carries duty and task on maintaining price stability and economic stability. Although the words "Inflation Targeting" are not employed in this work, the requirements of publishing of specific target values, stabilizing targets and realizing transparent policies proposed in this book are consistent with those of inflation targeting in Western countries, which can be regarded as a theoretical study of China's flexible inflation targeting system.

From pages 174 to 176 in the book *Theoretical Foundation Research on Macro-prudential Management,* the author explains that the reasonable interval theory proposed by the Chinese government in 2013 is a flexible inflation targeting system.

Targeting system is also a kind of policy rule, which is called the Targeting Rule.

(I) Dual Targeting System

1. A summary of the traditional dual targeting regulation model. The theoretical model of government economic regulation has been studied and summarized in Chap. 9 of this book. This model has also been viewed as the general theoretical model of inflation. In this general model, the government's regulatory target is theoretically the gap between aggregate demand and aggregate supply, which is however immeasurable directly. Therefore, signal regulation on the basis of the price level (including implicit inflation) and the economic growth rate is in fact a dual targeting regulation.

It is stated in Sect. 9.5 of Chap. 9 that "Stabilization of the price level is the common goal of government, the planning system, and the banking system. Therefore, it is easier to coordinate the regulations of the planning and the banking system from a perspective of stabilization of the price level. However, the goals of government economic regulation not only include stabilization of the price level, but also an appropriate economic growth rate." Such a dual targeting regulation has not yet been called a flexible inflation targeting because it has not yet involved stabilization of expectations and policy transparency. Both inflation targeting and flexible inflation targeting are aiming at stabilizing expectations and are required to be compatible with policy transparency. However, a new problem occurs with the emergence of a new factor of expectations.

2. Problems with the traditional dual targeting regulation model. It is pointed out in Sect. 9.2 "The Regulation Rules and Economic Expectations" of Chap. 9 that "the relationship between the economic growth rate and inflation will be uncertain in the short-run when economic expectations are involved." "It can be stated that the emergence of economic expectations has led to more hardships in economic regulation. If the economy is regulated according to traditional theory or experience, it is likely to gain outcomes that go contrary to wishes."

In Sect. 9.5 "Comprehensive Regulations" of Chap. 9, it is stated that "If planned output Q_t^* is coordinated with money supply M_t^s to jointly determine Q_t^* and M_t^s, the economic development will be more harmonious and less contradictory." "In modern economic life, due to the role of expectations, the demand for money becomes uncertain, which leads to the complexity of the relationship between Q_t^* and M_t^s. For example, with high inflation expectations, a certain amount of Q_t^* will require more M_t^s to support it, and vice versa. As a result, under the impact of expectations, the equilibrium between the commodity market and the money market is not stable. The equilibrium will change with the change of expectations." "In Figure 9.4, assuming that the equilibrium between the money supply M_t^s and the planned output Q_t^* without expectations is represented by line *AA*, the new equilibrium between the money supply M_t^s and the planned output Q_t^* with expectations is represented by curve *BB*. It shows that when the planned output Q_t^* or the money supply M_t^s exceeds a certain point, more amount of money supply M_t^s will be needed to support a certain amount of Q_t^* if there is an increase in inflation expectations and vice versa. However, it is difficult to accurately describe *BB* because of the uncertainty of expectations, which leads to the ambiguous relationship between M_t^s and Q_t^*. Specific measures to reduce such ambiguity will be analyzed in Chap. 11." The measures discussed in Chap. 11, namely the further proposal of the Chinese version of flexible inflation targeting on the basis of the summary of China's economic regulation model, are to release the particular targeting value to stabilize expectations through stable targeting, policy rules and policy transparency. In the case that the economy deviates from the two general targets, corresponding policies must be implemented to keep the economy to return on track, so as to stabilize economic growth and the price level to reduce the impacts of uncertainty in order to decelerate the regulatory problems caused by expectations.

3. Flexible inflation targeting. In Sect. 11.3 "Goals and Means of Policy" of Chap. 11, the Chinese version of the flexible inflation targeting system is proposed. "The policy goals should be relatively stable once they are finalized. Stable and feasible policy goals can stabilize public expectations, thus reduce the influence of uncertain factors in the economy and be conducive to sustainable economic growth. Frequent alternations of economic goals will only confuse the public and inject chaos into the economic system."

This is a discussion of stability of targets and relevant importance.

It also states in this section that, "Based on the aforesaid knowledge and the theoretical analysis of this book, it is believed that when making an anti-inflationary policy, it is advisable to aim at reducing inflation and maintaining the necessary economic growth rate, which are two incompatible but balanced targets. For example, the inflation rate can be targeted at 5% with an economic growth rate of 5%–7%, and regard them both as the two main targets of the outline of the economic plan. Moreover, we need to maintain the stability of the targets without changing them in the near and medium term. Because of the uncertainty in the economic system and the expectation stickiness, there will be errors in achieving these targets. But as long as the targets remain unchanged, these errors will be merely random. In order to achieve these two goals, macroeconomic policies such as planning policies, price policies, fiscal policies and financial policies should be coordinated attempting to minimize the incompatibility between policy instruments." This is a publication of the particular values of the two goals and a stabilization of these goals as well as an emphasis upon coordination and compatibility between policy instruments to have the goals stabilized.

It is further pointed out in this section that "Our theoretical analysis has highlighted that there is an inherent mechanism of economic expansions in China's economic system. The above two goals we have determined are only artificial lines, and should not be viewed as the red lines of any economic expansion. Policy measures should be developed to suppress economic expansion. According to the theory within this book, when aggregate demand expands, the economy overheats, and inflation rises, it is advisable to adopt a fiscal and credit tightening policy and, if necessary, a planned rationing policy to suppress aggregate demand; when aggregate demand is insufficient, a policy of easing rationing and increasing the money supply can be adopted; further fiscal policies should be implemented when an expectation trap emerges. In general, financial policy is more effective in suppressing aggregate demand, while fiscal policy is more effective in stimulating aggregate supply." This is about a case by case implementation of particular policies to maintain a goal stability.

In Sect. 11.4 "Policy Information Transmission and Policy Rules" of Chap. 11, it is emphasized that the transparency of policy rules, policy information and policy targets will be the particular supportive measures for implementing flexible inflation targeting. This will be detailed in Sect.s about transparency and communication without repeating here.

Dual targeting is the core element of the flexible inflation targeting system proposed by Western theorists in 1997. The Chinese version of the flexible inflation targeting system proposed in this book also covers the key content of dual targeting. Meanwhile, the two dual targeting systems share identical spirit essence, that is, by stabilizing the goals/targets, so as to stabilize the public expectations and economic growth, and reduce the impact of uncertain factors. Both dual targeting systems require coordinating policies and rules as well as with policy transparency. They are both forms of anticipatory management.

(2) The single targeting system

It is stated in Sect. 11.5 of Chap. 11 that "This is what was being discussed earlier, that is, regulating the money supply and rationing on the basis of a constant and stable economic growth rate, which is also known as a medium growth rate, referring to a national income growth rate of 6%. This is the so-called rule of a constant growth rate. The advantage of this rule is that it clearly discloses the target of the government's policy to the public, which helps to eliminate the uncertainties in public expectations and guide people to arrange their own economic activities inline with this target, thus lessening economic fluctuations. Because the government's target remains unchanged, both the government and the public will be able to alleviate the negative impact of these problems. People will then anticipate and coordinate their economic activities according to this target. In order to follow such rules, the government must primarily be credible and reliable without abandoning its policy commitment halfway." Although the rule of fixed growth rate discussed then is different from the fixed inflation rate of the inflation targeting system, this section argues that the rule of fixed growth rate can help "to eliminate the uncertainties in public expectations and guide people to arrange their own economic activities inline with this target, thus lessening economic fluctuations." This explanation is consistent with the spirit of inflation targeting.

(3) The multiple targeting system

In Sect. 11.3 "Goals and Means of Policy" of Chap. 11, it is pointed out that "Multiple goals should be considered in making macroeconomic policy: curbing inflation, stimulating economic growth, maintaining the balance of payments, improving economic efficiency, adjusting industrial structures, and so on and so forth. These policy goals are not entirely compatible, such as the contradiction between curbing inflation and stimulating economic growth. In the short-run, stimulating economic growth will inevitably lead to higher inflation, and curbing inflation will hurt economic growth. The previous theoretical analysis has shown the incompatibility of these two targets."

For a long time, China's monetary policy have been set around these four goals: lower inflation, a higher employment level, a certain economic growth rate and a general balance of payments.

IV. Theory of Expectations Management

The idea of expectations management in Western countries originated from the study of the liquidity trap in Japan, which was later than the theory of policy transparency and inflation targeting system. Woodford (2003b) introduced the idea of expectations management in a section of his book, pointing out that the key factor for the central bank to influence the market and prices is to manage the expectations of changes of future interest rate. Section 1.1 of Woodford (2005) is devoted to expectations management, arguing that it is not real interest rates that affect people's decisions, but expectations of future interest rates. These two papers are critical literature for the theory of expectations management and are widely cited.

Expectations management has become an important policy tool for central banks all over the world. Morris and Shin (2008) note that "The last fifteen years have seen a remarkable revolution in both the conduct of and the common understanding of monetary policy around the world." "In this view, monetary policy is-at its heart-the problem of managing and coordinating expectations in the economy. The instruments under the direct control of the central bank-such as overnight interest rates-are less important than the messages the central bank sends." Policy transparency and targeting systems both play the role of helping central bank to convey information to the public, which can be regarded as expectations management approaches. The targeting system has been introduced previously and will not be repeated here.

Though the words of expectations management are not precisely quoted in this book, the author attempts to argue that through the publications of policy goals, rules and dynamics as well as reliance upon the power and reputation of the government, transparent policies can be carried out to convey the policy information so as to guide the public to cooperate with the government to implement expectations management, and consequently to stabilize expectations to enhance policy efficiency, to reduce economic volatility, as well as decelerate the impacts of uncertainty. These thoughts are similar to expectations management ideas in Western countries. The research on expectations management in the Chinese theory of Sticky Expectations covers the following five aspects.

(I) The Liquidity Trap

The Chinese theory of Sticky Expectations proposes the concept of an expectations trap to explain the liquidity trap problem that China encountered in 1991, which was then named as the Market Sluggish by the Chinese economists. One of the hallmarks of Keynes's liquidity trap is the extremely low or even zero interest rates, and China has not yet fully implemented market interest rates up to date. Therefore, the hallmark of the Chinese theory of Sticky Expectations to adopt the concept of an expectation trap is the extremely low level of expectations stuck by the public, which is the key factor leading to the failure of monetary policy. The common feature of both traps is that once the economy has already hit its trough, expansionary monetary policy will be ineffective at stimulating growth.

In Sect. 7.5 of Chap. 7, it is stated that "An expectation trap will be born with low inflation expectations of households. At this point, much of the increase in the money supply is absorbed by the expectation trap, which neither pushes up price levels nor enhances supply. The sluggish market in 1990 can be regarded as a typical case of the expectation trap. In 1990, the many rounds of money injections by the government to stimulate the economy failed because most of the injected money was absorbed by the expectation trap and accumulated into stock capital. These money injections carried no effect upon the supply and price levels." It is further pointed out in Sect. 10.6 of Chap. 10 that "When the economy touches the trough and expectations are finally driven down, the expectation trap effect emerges once again. At this point, the government attempts to stimulate the economy by increasing the money supply, however, all extra money will be absorbed by the expectation trap and turned into a backlog of inventory funds. Consumers tend to save more because of the lower inflation expectation, or hold money to buy. A sluggish market will hence be formed. China's economy also faced such a situation in 1990."

It becomes a critical task for the government to pull the economy out of the trap and change the excessively low inflation expectations of the public once the economy falls into the expectation trap. In Sects. 11.2, 11.3 and 11.5 of Chap. 11, it states respectively that "When real supply is lower than its potential level, an expectation trap will appear when expectation sticks to a lower level, hence an increase in the money supply will not be able to propel the output level. This was reflected in China's economic practices in 1990. However, a period after an increase in the money supply, especially when money for investment explores, economic expansion will create a change in expectations due to the multiplier effect of investment. The role of monetary policy will be demonstrated at this time." "Further fiscal policies should be implemented when an expectation trap emerges." "Usually, stimulating aggregate demand will indirectly expand aggregate supply. However, when the expectation is sticking to a lower level, a direct adoption of fiscal policy would be more effective. This involves increasing government investment and consumption in order to directly stimulate aggregate supply depending on the multiplier effect of these two instruments. In 1990, when the government started to stimulate the economy, the first two rounds all relied on money injections, and the effectiveness of which was not obvious. The reason for this was that public expectations stuck to lower levels, or fell into the expectation trap. Fiscal policy was adopted in the third round to increase the government's investment and consumption, which turned out to be more fruitful." It is obvious that an increase in investment can push up the government investment and consumption through fiscal policy to change the expectations through economic expansion and thus be out of the expectation trap.

In the appendix of Krugman (1998) (pp. 188–189), Kathryn offers an excellent introduction to Krugman's theory of liquidity trap: "A liquidity trap is defined as a situation in which, because nominal interest rates are at or near zero, investors are indifferent between holding bonds and money, and as a consequence, monetary policy is ineffective at boosting demand. Under normal circumstances, monetary policy will be neutral, or ineffective, in the long-run. But if one allows for some price stickiness, in the short- run a monetary expansion may increase output and will, in any case, lead to an equiproportionate increase in prices. However, when interest rates are already 'too low', so that the economy is in a liquidity trap, monetary policy is powerless to influence output or prices (in the *IS-LM* paradigm, the *LM* curve is horizontal). It is for this reason that the traditional way out of a liquidity trap has been rely on fiscal policy (an *IS* shift)." However, Kathryn's definition of Krugman's liquidity trap is somewhat different from the original text. Krugman's original definition of liquidity trap is as follows "A liquidity trap may be defined as a situation in which conventional monetary policies have become impotent, because nominal interest rates are at or near zero: injecting monetary base into the economy has no effect, because base and bonds are viewed by the private sector as perfect substitutes."

Following the 2008 financial crisis in the United States, expectations management became a critical policy to get out of the liquidity trap. Coibion et al. (2018b) pointed out that "At the heart of these policies lies a mechanism hinging on the inflation expectations of agents: convincing them that inflation will be higher in the future should, in the absence of interest rate policy offsets due to the zero bound, lower their perceptions of current real interest rates and therefore induce households and firms to increase their spending today. Higher expected inflation can also lead firms to immediately raise their prices in anticipation of rapidly declining relative prices, and workers may similarly bargain for larger nominal wage increases. Thus, policies directly impacting agents' inflation expectations can be used to stabilize economic conditions when traditional policy tools are limited." Hagedorn et al. (2018) noted: "As a response to the decline in economic activity during the Great Recession, the monetary authority lowered the nominal interest rate to zero in an attempt to stimulate output and employment. Having reached the limit of conventional monetary policy (the zero lower bound) and in the face of high unemployment and low output, the monetary authority attempted to provide further accommodation by announcing its forecast of future policy rates. In the liquidity trap, this 'forward guidance' has become one of the main new tools for the monetary authority to conduct policy."

Introducing the concept of sticky expectations into a Keynesian liquidity trap is an innovation of the Chinese theory of Sticky Expectations, similar to Krugman (1998) introduced the concept of rational expectations into Keynesian liquidity trap. Just like Krugman (1998), the Chinese theory of Sticky Expectations also believes that the core problem of liquidity trap is expectations and confidence. It also holds that economic actors in the liquidity trap do not necessarily hold cash, and that fiscal policy is more effective in getting out of the liquidity trap.

(II) Coordinating Expectations

Morris and Shin (2008) summarized the theoretical model of management of expectations and held that a core concept of this model is coordinating expectations, the idea that central banks should command the authority to make the public understand policies of the central banks and take similar actions.

Expectations of the economic actors in coordinating expectations are heterogeneous, which are the first assumption of the Chinese theory of Sticky Expectations. In Sect. 11.5 of Chap. 11 of this book, the concept of coordinating expectations is put forward: "The advantage of this rule is that it clearly discloses the target of the government's policy to the public, which helps to eliminate the uncertainties in public expectations and guide people to arrange their own economic activities in line with this target, thus lessening economic fluctuations. Because the government's target remains unchanged, both the government and the public will be able to alleviate the negative impact of these problems. People will then anticipate and coordinate their economic activities according to this target. In order to follow such rules, the government must primarily be credible and reliable without abandoning its policy commitment halfway."

Here, "People will then anticipate and coordinate their economic activities according to this target" denotes the idea of coordinating expectations, which is equivalent to the same action in the sunspot metaphor model of expectations management described by Morris and Shin (2008). "[It] clearly discloses the target of the government's policy to the public" includes the meaning of making the public know and understand, which is identical to the public knowledge and unified understanding of the sunspot metaphor model. "The government must primarily be credible and reliable" is the primary condition for coordinating expectations, which is equivalent to the authority requirement of the sunspot metaphor model. Therefore, the thought of coordinating expectations in the Chinese theory of Sticky Expectations is similar to the thought of coordinating expectations in the sunspot metaphor model described by Morris and Shin (2008).

(III) Transparency and Communication

Transparency and communication have become an important theoretical research topic. Transparency and communication are two sides of the same coin. Literature reviews of both transparency and communication can be referred to Cruijsen and Eijffinger (2007) and Blinder et al. (2008) respectively.

Cruijsen and Eijffinger (2007) pointed out that the idea of transparency was first proposed by Cukierman and Meltzer (1986). Blinder et al. (2008) summarized three important developments in the evolution of transparency and communication ideas: "Notice the progression here: from Brunner's 1981 lament about central bankers' refusal to communicate, to Blinder's 1996 argument that more communication would enhance the effectiveness of monetary policy, to Woodford's 2001 claims that the essence of monetary policy is the art of managing expectations and that this was already received wisdom. Woodford probably exaggerated that last point. But the view that monetary policy is, at least in part, about managing expectations is by now standard fare both in academia and in central banking circles. It is no exaggeration to call this a revolution in thinking."

Prior to the mid-1990s, very few papers were published on transparency in Western countries. After that, the transparency and communication policy of central banks gradually became a hot topic in Western economic circles. Meanwhile, Western central banks began to abandon policy formulation and implementation in dark box and surprise. Policy implementation became more and more transparent.

Since the twenty-first century, Western economic theorists have segmented the transparency policies of central banks into different categories and constructed indexes to measure them. The transparency idea in the Chinese theory of Sticky Expectations can also be divided into different categories.

1. Transparency of rules. It is stated in Sect. 11.2 of Chap. 11 that "[to] enable an effective policy, the direction of expectation should be consistent with the policy goals. When the direction is inconsistent, effectiveness of policy will be crippled or even invalidated. It is obvious that a clear set of policy rules should be required to align the change of the expectation direction with that of the policy goals." This is consistent with Blinder's 1996 argument that communication would improve the effectiveness of monetary policy.

In Sect. 11.4 of Chap. 11, it is argued that "If the government follows an open set of policy rules and unswervingly implements them, the policy rules themselves will provide the public with more information about the process of government policy making, which in turn helps to reduce the uncertainty of public expectations. It can also prevent policymakers from changing their original intentions and improve the credibility of these policies."

2. Transparency of goals. It is argued in Sect. 11.5 of Chap. 11 that "The advantage of this rule is that it clearly discloses the target of the government's policy to the public, which helps to eliminate the uncertainties in public expectations and guide people to arrange their own economic activities in line with this target, thus lessening economic fluctuations. Because the government's target remains unchanged, both the government and the public will be able to alleviate the negative impact of these problems. People will then anticipate and coordinate their economic activities according to this target. In order to follow such rules, the government must primarily be credible and reliable without abandoning its policy commitment halfway."

3. Transparency of policy dynamics. On page 355 of *Inflation and Uncertainty*, the author points out that "The government should make it clear to the public that as long as inflation remains at a high level, such as a double- digit level, the government will adopt a tighter economic policy and have it implemented." This statement is not only about the policy transparency and communication between the central bank, but also concerned with Forward Guidance.

4. Transparency of policy implementation. As mentioned earlier, a policy smoothing operation is also a transparent policy.

5. Communication. In Sect. 11.4 "Policy Information Transmission and Policy Rules" of Chap. 11, it is stated that "[the] critical point is that, how can the government make the public aware of its targets as well as the measures to achieve these targets. Moreover, how can the government convince the public that the government is determined and able to achieve these targets without giving up halfway." This is in fact a communication problem between central banks. The problem raised in this book still remained a problem that economic theorists concern and attempt to solve.

Blinder et al. (2008) noted that: "Finally, nearly all the research to date has focused on central bank communication with financial markets. It is time to pay more attention to communication with the general public. While this will pose new challenges to researchers, in particular with regard to data availability, the issues are at least as important, as it is the general public that gives central banks their democratic legitimacy, and hence their independence, and as the general public's inflation expectations eventually feed into the actual evolution of inflation, e.g. through corresponding wage claims and savings, investment and consumption decisions, and thus determine whether a central bank is able to achieve its policy objectives."

In the last section of their paper, Coibion et al. (2019) pointed out that: "Since many expectations channels run through households and firms, central banks could also aim to affect economic conditions via direct communications to the public. In this paper, we present new evidence that such communications can change expectations by economically significant magnitudes: simple messages about the central bank's inflation target have implications about real interest rates that dwarf those typically found for monetary policy announcements. However, we find that the effectiveness of these messages to the public is significantly dampened when transmitted via news media: households effectively dismiss much of the information content when presented to them in the form of a news article. This suggests that, if central banks want to add direct communications to the public as a new policy tool, they will have to find new ways to reach the public without relying on traditional media."

It can be seen from the above that it is not only transparent but also communication to clearly inform the public about policy goals, policy rules and policy dynamics. The previous discussion also shows that transparency and communication can stabilize expectations, enhance policy credibility, improve policy efficiency, reduce economic fluctuations and reduce the impact of uncertainties. This is also the theoretical significance of studying transparency and communication.

(IV) Stability of Expectations

An important task of expectations management is to stabilize expectations. Cœuré (2019), European Central Bank (ECB) Executive Board member, argued that "[stable] inflation expectations at levels consistent with price stability provide an important nominal anchor for the economy. They reduce inflation persistence and curb harmful macroeconomic volatility." "[stable] inflation expectations play a crucial role for the effectiveness of monetary policy." The fundamental purpose of inflation targeting is to anchor the public's inflation expectations.

In Chap. 11, the author attempts to argue that through the publications of policy goals, rules and means as well as reliance upon the power and reputation of the government, transparent policies can be carried out to convey the policy information so as to guide the public to cooperate with the government to implement expectations management, and consequently to stabilize expectations to enhance policy efficiency, to reduce economic volatility, as well as decelerate the impacts of uncertainty.

It is pointed out in Sect. 11.2 of Chap. 11 that "[to] enable an effective policy, the direction of expectation should be consistent with the policy goals. When the direction is inconsistent, effectiveness of policy will be crippled or even invalidated. It is obvious that a clear set of policy rules should be required to align the change of the expectation direction with that of the policy goals." This attempts to validate policy by guiding expectations on the direction of policy objectives through clear policy rules, which are also a form of policy transparency. The fundamental purpose of expectations management is to make the direction changes of expectations be consistent with that of policy goals.

In Section 3 of the same chapter, the author states that: "[the] policy goals should be relatively stable once they are finalized. Stable and feasible policy goals can stabilize public expectations, thus reduce the influence of uncertain factors in the economy and be conducive to sustainable economic growth. Frequent alternations of economic goals will only confuse the public and inject chaos into the economic system." This is to stabilize expectations, eliminate uncertainties in public expectations and reduce economic fluctuations by making policy goals public and constant.

It is further argued in Sect. 11.4 of Chap. 11 that "If the government follows an open set of policy rules and unswervingly implements them, the policy rules themselves will provide the public with more information about the process of government policy making, which in turn helps to reduce the uncertainty of public expectations. It can also prevent policymakers from changing their original intentions and improve the credibility of these policies." "Once the policy is formulated, it will not be modified if nothing special happens so as to reduce the public uncertainty and stabilize the public expectations." This requires the government to inform the public the policy goals, including the instruments to achieve them. That is, it requires the government's policies to be transparent. Meanwhile, through stability of policy rules and policies to stabilize expectations, reduce the uncertainty of public expectations.

In Sect. 11.5 of Chap. 11, it is argued that "The advantage of this rule is that it clearly discloses the target of the government's policy to the public, which helps to eliminate the uncertainties in public expectations and guide people to arrange their own economic activities inline with this target, thus lessening economic fluctuations. Because the government's target remains unchanged, both the government and the public will be able to alleviate the negative impact of these problems. People will then anticipate and coordinate their economic activities according to this target. In order to follow such rules, the government must primarily be credible and reliable without abandoning its policy commitment halfway." This requires credibility from the government.

Since 2007, the Chinese government has emphasized the stabilization of expectations. How can we stabilize expectations? No one is quite sure. The above discussion shows that the Chinese Theory of Sticky Expectations has provided four approaches to stabilize expectations long ago. The first is transparency of policy, which aims at informing the public of the policy rules, policy goals and policy instruments, as well as the government's confidence and determination; the second is stability of policy goals; third, stability of policy rules; fourth, stability of policy. For the effectiveness of these four approaches, the primary requirement relies on the credibility of the government. In addition, the policy smoothing operation described earlier is also an approach to stabilize expectations.

(V) Forward Guidance

Forward Guidance is a new development in the research of expectations management. It is a crucial policy tool adopted by Western central banks in recent years. However, there has not yet been any unified definition of Forward Guidance. A concise and authoritative definition is that the central bank clearly announces the future trend of monetary policy (Woodford, 2012). According to the definition of the Bank of England (2013), there exist three kinds of forward guidance. One is open instruction: it is too flexible and easy to be misunderstood. For instance, interest rates are not expected to rise above current levels for some time to come. The second is time-dependent guidance: it is too rigid without credibility. For example, interest rates are not expected to rise above current levels until a particular date in the future. The third is state-dependent guidance: policy change is related to particular economic index value in the future. For example, interest rates are not expected to rise above current levels until unemployment or economic growth reaches a certain level. At present, Western central banks generally rely upon state-dependent guidance.

Although forward guidance has been widely recognized by the economic theorists in Western countries, it is still controversial, and its role has been denied by some economists especially in incomplete markets. Hagedorn et al. (2018) states "To summarize, in incomplete markets models the effect of forward guidance operates through a distributional channel—induced by movements in prices, wages, and interest rates—and an inter-temporal substitution channel. We find that both channels are muted when markets are incomplete in the presence of the empirically relevant nominal rigidities and a partially nominal government budget, implying the overall ineffectiveness of forward guidance. The theoretical arguments for our findings are quite general, so that we conclude that forward guidance is not a powerful monetary policy tool, even in a liquidity trap."

In Sect. 11.4 "Policy Information Transmission and Policy Rules" of Chap. 11, it is stated that "The critical point is that, how can the government make the public aware of its targets as well as the measures to achieve these targets. Moreover, how can the government convince the public that the government is determined and able to achieve these targets without giving up halfway." The argument of "how can the government make the public aware of its targets as well as the measures to achieve these targets" is close to what forward guidance means by "central bank clearly announces the future trend of monetary policy."

On page 355 of *Inflation and Uncertainty*, the author offers a state-dependent guidance similar to the one currently adopted by Western central banks, which links tighter policy changes to double-digit inflation rate with particular economic indicators in the future. "The government should make it clear to the public that as long as inflation remains at a high level, such as a double-digit level, the government will adopt a tighter economic policy and have it implemented."

The idea of a policy smoothing operation has been introduced previously, which is relatively in tune with the idea of forward guidance, and will not be repeated here.

The thought of forward guidance in the Chinese theory of Sticky Expectations is just a germ of thought, because except for the frequent discussion of the policy smoothing operation, other ideas of forward guidance have only been briefly mentioned without any further analysis. But the idea of forward guidance has been embedded in the logic of the theory of sticky expectations. It is argued in the assumption of Black Box assumption of the Chinese theory of Sticky Expectations that "[the] relationship between inputs and outputs might potentially be identified based upon the actors' experiences which also might be modified in accordance with their judgments about the future." This assumption indicates that the central bank can influence the public's anticipation on the future by explicitly announcing the future trend of monetary policy, so as to guide or change the public's expectations.

V. Pricing Rules of Firms

In discussing the definition of sticky prices in the Introduction of this book, it is stated that "Economic contracts guarantee buyers to purchase any quantity of goods at the agreed prices at the time when contracts are signed. These types of contracts may allow prices to change with the change in production costs in the future, but not with the change in demand. In the case of higher inflation, since a change in planned prices fall behind the change in the production costs, many enterprises are unable to buy products at planned prices as planned but at negotiated prices set by the sellers following the markup on change in costs. The common practice of transforming planned prices into negotiated prices reflects the mutual acceptance between buyers and sellers regarding the pricing principle of a markup on the production costs." In Sect. 8.5 of Chap. 8 of this book, the basic principles for firms to set prices have been proposed: "[however], things will be different once inflation turns worse. In this case, enterprises would further markup the proportion of price rise caused by inflation expectations on the original price, which will appear to change more quickly without sticking to any certain price level. Nonetheless, the core price will generally remain stable in case such an expectation markup is ignored."

The firm's pricing criterion of Gali and Gertler (1999) is an important achievement of the New Keynesian economic theory. Sheedy Kevin (2005) expressed Gali and

Gertler's criterion as: "[these] firms do not maximize profit when they choose a new price, but instead simply revise prices that were optimal in the past by adding on a correction for inflation that has occurred recently." This pricing criterion of Gali and Gertler (1999) has become the most popular theoretical explanation of inflation inertia in the theory of sticky prices, where the pricing criterion of the Chinese Theory of Sticky Expectations is similar, except that it will ignore the changes of inflation in case it does not change too much, reflecting the thought of rational negligence.

The theoretical significance of the firm's pricing criterion lies in its organic integration of both the theory of sticky prices and the theory of sticky expectations. Such an integration reveals the change relationship between the price stickiness on a micro level and the general price level on a macro level, which denotes a new meaning to the theory of cost-push inflation.

VI. Conclusion

Although the Chinese Theory of Sticky Expectations has been constructed for nearly 30 years, it still possesses explanatory power for real economic problems. Here, I conclude the theory with an argument from another of my book *Studies on the Theoretical Foundations of Macro-prudential Management* (p.171): "Rational inattention, sticky information and theory of sticky expectations are all new schools of economic thoughts emerged in the Western economic world after the twenty-first century. They are all possessing features of nonlinear stickiness. Based on the research of incomplete information of the bounded rationality theory, these new economic thoughts further substitute partial information with overall information, past information with current information, and identical expectations with non-identical expectations, so as to narrow the search scope to avoid heavy information cost and lengthy information search time. These thoughts effectively escaped from problems of Information Explosion and Combinatorial Explosion to tie theories with reality. The Chinese theory of Sticky Expectations share the same characteristics above-mentioned."

"Based upon innovation of methodology, these three new theories and the Chinese theory of Sticky Expectations all conducted theoretical innovations. They broke the framework of neoclassical economic theory, denied their fundamental premise conditions such as complete information and expectations homogeneity in an attempt to construct a new theoretical framework to comprehend the economic behavior of people, and to interpret the mechanism of economic performance. For example, these theories can well explain why people's behavior follow inertia, and why people rely more upon experiences (inertia) rather than on current information in making optimal decisions (rationality). Consequently, economic actors are potentially generating errors in their decision makings, even systematic mistakes, which might lead to economic crisis. On the basis of the above discussions, we can explain the formation and evolution of the 2008 financial crisis in the United States. For example, we can explain why people tended to purchase houses regardless of their income, and smart bankers stuck to the myth that housing prices will only rise not fall, and finally which created a bubble in the US real estate industry under the common inertia of people. It is such an inertia that drove the US economy into the abyss." "The Chinese theory of Sticky Expectations can further explain the behavioral mechanism of unexpected changes in people's expectations in financial panic, explain the Minsky moment from the perspective of the theory of expectations, and explain the suddenness and nonlinearity of outbreak of crisis."

All references mentioned in this preface can be referred to references II of this book.

Wenzhou, China
01, November 2019

Laya Li

Preface of the Original Edition

In 1988, I undertook a research project on *The Chinese Inflation Problems* funded by the National Social Science Foundation. This book is one of the achievements of this project.

After 1978, China's study of economic theory witnessed a brand-new situation. The Chinese economists broke through the rules and regulations set by the Soviet political economy textbooks, began to practice on the basis of reality, and gradually adopted new ideas, new means, and new theories to analyze and solve new problems in practice. We finally realize that in the past several hundred years the development of human social economic theory, especially in the past hundred years after the birth of Karl Marx's economic theory, the study of world economic theory has tended to be scientific and practical. So far, the theoretical knowledge of economic science accumulated by economists has contributed exactly as much to the development of human society as natural science has. At the same time, we realize that there are still many crucial problems to be solved in the study of economic theory, among which the problem of inflation is particularly noticeable. No matter whether it is in socialist countries or in capitalist countries, inflation is a comprehensive issue affecting normal economic growth and a recurrent disease in the economic system.

Although mankind has mastered nuclear technology in the microcosmic world and possesses space flight capability of sending men to the moon, we have not yet fully understood the relevant issues within inflation, let alone find an effective approach to eliminating inflation without affecting normal economic growth. We also realize that only by inheriting the essence of human social and economic theories on the basis of previous studies on inflation, especially by absorbing the latest achievements of economic theories, can we further deepen our understanding of the issues of inflation and construct a set of inflation theories inline with China's economic practice.

The above cognition is the commencing spot of the research of this book and also the basic ideas guiding the research. We will face China's economic practice and absorb the essence of human economic research so as to conform to the trend of world economic theoretical research to forge a new path of theoretical research. This is the mission granted to our generation by history. It is the wish of the older generation of economists as well as the call of economic reform presented to us.

Inflation is the core issue of macroeconomic research. Exploration of inflation is no different from making a systematic investigation of macroeconomic research. Similarly, setting up a theory for studying inflation is similar to setting up macroeconomic theory in China, which is still in its infancy. Since theory lags behind practice, we have to bear a double burden in the research of inflation. Consequently, this book will take inflation as a core issue on the basis of studying macroeconomic theory.

The research in this book focuses on the analysis of economic problems from the economic system and adheres to the fundamental research methodology of Karl Marx's economic theory. The economic system is the fundamental factor that determines economic phenomenon. The recurring inflation in China's economy has close domestic relations with its economic system. In the long-run, only a thorough reform of the current system can eliminate the very root of inflation. However, neither reforming the system nor managing of inflation can be accomplished overnight. Nonetheless, the theoretical research in managing inflation in the near and medium term revealed that quantitative analysis has a more practical value. Therefore, this book will study the mechanism of interest on the basis of ownership and the quantitative relationship between variables on the basis of the mechanism of interest. The focus of this book is on the quantitative relationship between the variables of inflation, that is, the mechanisms of inflation.

The book also focuses on absorbing the theoretical viewpoints and research methodology of scientific value in Western economics. For instance, equilibrium theory, disequilibrium theory, and expectation theory all occupy a critical position in this book. In fact, the early research of equilibrium and disequilibrium theory has been discovered in Karl Marx's economic theory. Both the equilibrium theory developed from Walras and the disequilibrium theory developed in the 1970s are the common wealth of human economic theory. Various economic theory schools can express their theoretical views by means of the analytical framework endowed by equilibrium theory or disequilibrium theory. The comprehensive equilibrium theory pursued by socialist countries for a long time and the shortage theory developed during the reform period can be regarded as a specific school of equilibrium theory and disequilibrium theory. It should be pointed out that disequilibrium theory is not an anti-equilibrium theory. Disequilibrium theory is developed on the basis of equilibrium theory and includes equilibrium theory as its core component.

China implements a planned commodity economy. In a commodity market, planning and market function simultaneously. Planning in both the labor and capital market still play a decisive role. Therefore, a paradigm of disequilibrium theory should be recommended in studying China's real economic problems especially the problem of inflation. The research of disequilibrium theory and model used to be my research focus when I was a visiting scholar at Stanford University from 1989 to 1990. It was the research of this period that prompted me to further study China's macroeconomic theory especially inflation theory from a disequilibrium perspective. As a result, the disequilibrium analysis method forms the basis of the methodology of this book.

Expectation theory has played an important role in the development of Western economics in recent decades and constitutes a core content of Western economic theory. It is of great theoretical and practical significance to include expectation factors in China's economic theory. Based on the reality of China, the author constructs the Sticky Expectations Theory, which is different from the Adaptive Expectations Theory and the Rational Expectations Theory in the Western world. The basic feature of the sticky expectations theory is that expectations are neither completely rigid nor completely elastic. With the help of the sticky expectations theory, this book analyzes and explains a series of problems in China's macroeconomic theory, especially the problem of inflation. Consequently, the theoretical characteristics of this book will rely upon the sticky expectations theory per se and the employment of the sticky expectations theory to explain the problem of inflation and other economic problems.

Although this is a purely academic work, the theoretical research is based upon practical economic problems, especially the problem of inflation. The motto of this book is that theory originates from practice, but it is superior to practice and must be applied to practice. A series of problems have emerged since the reform, especially inflation since 1984 and the sluggish market since 1989, have posed severe challenges to China's economic theory study. In 1988, serious inflation incurred while the monetary growth rate was not significantly different from that of previous years, and in 1990, there was significantly sluggish market when the monetary growth rate was not very different from that of previous years. It has become a mystery in the study of China's economic theory. On the one hand, household income increases, and on the other hand, the consumer market is sluggish; on the one hand, the money supply is expanded, and on the other, production is hurdled; on the one hand, underlying inflationary pressures are rising, while on the other hand, inflation is at its lowest level in recent years. From the theoretical to the policy world, we have never been more puzzled by the economic problems in a reality like this.

Traditional theories are unable to interpret these new problems, while the new theories need to be tested in practice. Economic theory is at a historical turning point of connecting the past with the future. Therefore, this book attempts to answer these questions systematically on the basis of its own established macroeconomic theory. In early 1989, I analyzed inflation from the perspective of expectations. My views remain unchanged and are further developed in this book. The more we debate, the clearer the truth becomes, but in more cases, the more time elapses, the clearer the truth becomes. I am expecting practice to test whether the explanations of inflation and other economic problems in this book are appropriate.

The research commences with basic macroeconomic theory. In the process of basic theory research, the behavior mechanism of inflation is analyzed step by step, and finally a theoretical model to explain inflation is derived. The policy propositions of managing inflation are proposed from this theoretical model. This book takes aggregate supply and aggregate demand as the two pillars of the logical structure of macroeconomic theory as well as the core content of inflation theory. Inflation is the gap between aggregate demand and aggregate supply. Therefore, the research of the process of inflation is to study the operational process of aggregate supply and aggregate demand. The contradiction between aggregate supply and aggregate demand constitutes the main clue of the theory of this book.

The introduction part introduces the basic propositions of the book and the empirical methodology adopted in scientific research and analyzes the significance of the expectations theory. The introduction emphasizes the importance of empirical methodology in economic science research and discusses some characteristics of the employment of this methodology.

Chapter 1[1] focuses on the process of transforming national income produced into national income spent from the perspective of accounting. Traditional economic theories usually regard the contradiction between the amount of national income produced and the amount of national income spent as the focus of their theoretical analysis. This chapter tries to clarify that only these two contradictions are not sufficient to analyze inflation and the main contradictions of macroeconomic problems. In particular, I highlight that the national income produced plus net export should be equal to the amount of national income spent from an accounting perspective. The gap between national income produced and national income spent provided by statistics is composed of the gap between net export and statistical discrepancy. It is neither the source of inflation nor the measure of the over-distribution of national income, let alone the gap between aggregate supply and aggregate demand. This chapter also analyzes the operation process of other economic flow and stock variables. The law of nodes and the law of networks proposed in this chapter are summarized according to the basic principles of the theory of national economic accounting. These two laws help to illustrate the identity relationship between some basic macroeconomic variables.

Chapter 2 systematically compares the three types of concepts of aggregate supply and aggregate demand, and further introduces how the two concepts are developed in disequilibrium theory. The chapter also analyzes the relationship between the effective demand defined by disequilibrium theory and the Walra demand (also the Keynesian effective demand). This chapter emphasizes the theoretical significance of the distinction between ex ante and ex postin economic research.

Chapters 1 and 2 constitute Part I of this book, which is more concerned with some basic and disagreeable theoretical problems in China. Research on inflation and other economic problems is not possible without a clear discussion of these theoretical issues. These basic theoretical problems are still extensively discussed in China. Part I constitutes the starting point and basis of the theoretical analysis of this book.

Chapter 3 analyzes the formation process of aggregate demand, the consumption function, investment function, and aggregate demand function. It also analyzes the impact of expectations on aggregate demand to establish the basic aggregate demand model and discusses the role of multiplier under resource constraints.

Chapter 4 analyzes the basic factors that determine aggregate supply, studies the basic shape of the aggregate supply function, and summarizes several factors that create the upper boundary of aggregate supply growth. The chapter distinguishes the

[1] The order of chapters in this English version has been re-numbered while the chapter order of the original Chinese version remains unchanged. The first chapter of this English version corresponds to the introduction chapter of the Chinese version and the second to the first, and so forth.

short-run aggregate supply function from the long-run aggregate supply function and points out the influence of the money illusion on aggregate supply.

Chapters 3 and 4 make up Part II of the book. This part studies the internal behavior mechanism of the formation of inflation and analyzes the various factors leading to inflation and the relationship between these factors. The contents of this part constitute the immediate foundation of the inflation theory of this book.

Chapter 5 analyzes the general inflation gap, which is a natural extension of the logical analysis of the previous two chapters. We analyze the inflation mechanisms of demand-pull inflation, cost-push inflation, expected inflation, and structural inflation. Since there have been many domestic discussions on the mechanism of demand-pull, cost-push, and structural inflation, this chapter only focuses on introducing some of the author's own insights without further analyzing these types of inflation; especially it does not make a detailed comparison of different views on these inflations. It seems to become a more popular research mode in China's economic theory research that views and theories can be derived from systematic comparison of different viewpoints. However, this book focuses on constructing the author's own theory from the perspective of a logical analysis.

Chapter 6 studies the money demand and supply and puts forward the author's own monetary theory. I argued that money acts not only on prices but also on output, and proposed a theory that under what circumstances it may act on prices and on output respectively. In particular, I propose an expectation trap effect, which holds that the increase in the money supply will be absorbed by the expectation trap. Hence, money is acting neither on prices nor on output.

Chapter 7 studies the dual-gap model of inflation. This chapter analyzes the formation mechanism of two different types of shortage gaps and their mutual relationships. The chapter also analyzes the relationship between the shortage gap and the price gap. It measures the shortage gap with disequilibrium methodology and estimates the parameters of both the aggregate demand function and aggregate supply function.

Chapter 8 studies the general model of inflation theory. This model closely integrates aggregate supply and aggregate demand in the commodity market with the money supply and demand in the money market through regulation targets and rules to establish a unified model of inflation theory.

Chapter 9 systematically summarizes the concept of sticky expectations discussed in previous chapters and puts forward the author's own sticky expectations theory. This chapter analyzes the formation process of sticky expectations, points out the characteristics of sticky expectations, and compares this theory with other expectations theories. Both sticky expectations and sticky prices are the two main theoretical tools adopted to analyze the transformation of the short-run economic fluctuations into the long-run economic trends, as well as the main theoretical features of the analysis of inflation in this book.

Chapters 5–9 form Part III of the book. This is the main body of the book, among which both Chaps. 8 and 9 are the two main chapters that finally complete the theoretical logic system.

Chapter 10 studies the policy options for managing inflation, and studies when inflation policies can stimulate the output level and when they cannot. This book focuses on theoretical policy (that is, more abstract policy) rather than concrete policy proposals.

Chapter 11 discusses the effect of inflation and the cost of managing inflation, and analyzes the static minimum costs and the dynamic optimal managing measures.

Chapters 10 and 11 make up Part IV of the book. The policy analysis in this part is the logical extension of the theoretical analysis in the previous chapters. In China, there is plenty of research on specific policies of managing inflation, but little research on policy theory. The transition from economic theory to concrete policy needs policy theory as a bridge. Research on policy theory needs to be strengthened.

A concise theoretical summary of the book can be found in Sect. 10.1 of Chap. 10, which will not be repeated here.

Upon the completion of this book, I would like to express my heartfelt thanks to Prof. Jianbai Yang, Prof. Jiapei Wu, and Prof. Jinglian Wu, the three advisors of the research team on *The Chinese Inflation Problems.* I would also like to thank my colleagues in the research team, with whom I have discussed some of the contents of this book and asked for their opinions. Co-authoring with my research team member Researcher Shuguang Zhang, Associate Researcher Zhongwei Yang, Associate Researcher Gang Fan, Dr. Dabei Zuo, and Master Yongqiang Liu, wrote a paper titled *A Research on China's Inflation Expectations*, which was published in *The Economic Daily* on March 10, 1989. Several ideas in the book have derived from this paper. I am, of course, personally responsible for any potential errors in this book.

I am grateful to the National Social Science Foundation in Beijing, whose funding made this work possible. I would like to express my gratitude to the Science Foundation of the National Information Center, which has bridged the funding gap for this project. I am grateful to the Ford Foundation, whose funding made it possible for me to carry on this research at Stanford University; I also want to acknowledge Stanford University, which provided me with outstanding research facilities that enabled the completion of some of the work in this research. I would also like to express my gratitude to my mentor and collaborator at Stanford University—Prof. Lawrence J. Lau, from whom I have learned a great deal. This has been helpful to the research of this book.

I would like to take this opportunity to express my heartfelt thanks to all the teachers who have nurtured my growth. Their generosity and wisdom encourage me to complete this academic work.

Beijing, China Laya Li
01, May 1991

Contents

Author and Translator

About the Author

Laya Li received his Ph.D. of Economics from the Chinese Academy of Social Sciences and he is the winner of Sun Yefang Economic Science Award. From March 1988 to November 1994, he worked at the National Information Center, and from August 1989 to June 1990, he was a visiting scholar at Stanford University in the United States. From March 1992 to March 1993, he was a visiting scholar at the Chinese University of Hong Kong. From January 1997 to March 2010, he worked at the Texas Legislative Budget Board and the Office of the Texas Secretary of State in the United States, engaging in data analysis and processing. From March 2010 to August 2018, he served as a full-time distinguished professor and doctoral supervisor at Huaqiao University, and in 2017, he won the fifth "Golden Sheep Award" of Financial Books. From September 2018 to August 2023, he served as a full-time distinguished professor and director of the Wenzhou Research Base of the National Laboratory for Financial and Development at Wenzhou Business College, as well as a distinguished professor at Liaocheng University. In 2020, his book *Inflation Mechanism and Expectations* was nominated for and approved by the the Chinese Academic Translation Project. From September 2023 onwards, he has served as a part-time professor at Hangzhou City University and a part-time professor at Liaocheng University.

About the Translator

Dr. Lei Huang is a professor in Guangdong University of Foreign Studies, where he used to serve as a Deputy Dean of the School of Business and the Executive Dean of the MBA Education Centre. He also acts as an Executive member of the Guangdong Society of Economics in Guangdong, China. He obtained his B.A. in English Literature from Huazhong Normal University and his Master degree in Economics from Guangxi University respectively. He was conferred his Ph.D. from the University of Technology Sydney (with EIPRS Scholarship), Australia in the field of Management.

He was a Fulbright Scholar-in-Residence in USA and a visiting professor to teach in different programs in Australia, India and Chile. Dr. Lei Huang is also an experienced practitioner in international project contracting management and he participated in the construction of various international projects for more than five years in different countries, where he served as professional interpreter, procurement manager, senior economist and assistant project manager respectively.

His research interests lie in International Business Management, Economics and Corporate Sustainability. Focusing upon these fields, his academic papers and works have been published in a wide range of national and international journals and publishers. He acts as a peer reviewer for journals such as *Journal of Business Ethics, Journal of Knowledge Management, International Journal of Innovation and Sustainable Development.*

Chapter 1
Introduction

For a considerable period, inflation has been deemed to be a forbidden zone in theoretical research in the socialist economy. Inflation is seemingly only a product of the capitalist economy. It seems that inflation never occurred in any socialist economy because it has been developed in a planned and proportionate approach. That inflation occurred over history in socialist countries has been viewed as merely a consequence of policy failure, thus accidental.

Now it's time to face reality. In this book, the internal mechanism of inflation in the socialist economy will be studied. By analyzing the quantitative relationship among differing variables of inflation, anti-inflation policies will be probed to construct a theoretical system of research on inflation. In the introduction, the basic propositions for constructing the theoretical system and a fundamental research approach of this book will be introduced.

1.1 Preliminaries for Theory Construction

The rigorous theoretical edifice rests on a few basic propositions made with cautious assumptions. Tracing back to the 4th century BC, mathematics embarked on the path of theoretical system construction, followed by natural science in the 17th century. In the 19th century, as a humanities discipline, though belatedly, economics lost no time in embarking on a similar path of truth seeking. However, economics does not include in the category of natural science after all; it possesses its own research characteristics, which are reflected in its basic propositions and theoretical structure. On top of that, different economic theories also differ in the choice of their fundamental propositions.

This book chooses the following propositions as the basic elements of its theoretical construction.

L. Li, *The Inflation Mechanism and Expectations*, Understanding China,
https://doi.org/10.1007/978-981-97-2570-0_1

Both nature and human society are cognizable, and so are the economic activities of human society. The basis for the first proposition would therefore be that the world is cognizable. Being cognizable, however, is not the same as being cognized. Human beings still faced with many things cognizable but unrecognized, which are still uncertain. These uncertainties will remain unpredictable until their internal laws are recognized.

There is a well-known saying in economics that goes, "*The past cannot be retrieved and the future is unforeseeable.*" Current economic knowledge is insufficient to explain the economic activities of the human societies, so the ability of human to predict the future economies is limited. Especially, human beings knows a little about the external factors of the economic system, which also exert huge impact on the economic system per se. Such impacts will certainly be more uncertain and more unpredictable.

In addition, there are some random variables without a fixed probability distribution in the internal and external economic system, which are very crucial and uncertain factors. Atypical example is price fluctuations in the stock market. As for natural disasters, no feasible approach has been commanded to describe the movement of such random variables.

Uncertainty of economic activities is the first basic proposition in this book, which is named as the proposition of uncertainty.

Existence determines consciousness, which in turn retroacts on existence. The economic system is a type of objective existence, which determines the human beings' consciousness—one of the components of the economic system. Meanwhile, human beings' consciousness also reacts to the economic system. Expectations are components of the human beings' consciousness in the economic system, and they function as a judgment of human beings for future economic activities. As a psychological activity of human being, expectations, though dominated by the economic system, will in turn react to the economic system.

However, consciousness is relatively independent of existence, which means that consciousness can lead or follow the changes of existence to a certain extent. Similarly, as a component of human consciousness, expectation is relatively independent of the economic system and may lead or follow the changes of this economic system. In this book, such a relative independence is defined as the stickiness of expectations, the nature of expectations will be examined in detail later.

Stickiness of expectations is the second basic proposition in this book, which is referred to as the proposition of sticky expectations.

In the economic system, human behaves rationally in two aspects: one is in pursuing maximum benefits under a certain constraint; the other is in learning constantly from experiences, and persistently adjust his own behaviors to achieve maximum benefits at minimum losses.[1]

---

[1] Rational man, by usual definition, only specifies the first aspect, and the second is implicitly included. Considering the important role of economic man's learning function in this book, the two meanings of an economic rational man are explicitly stated here.

Human's behaviors are rational, which is the third basic proposition referred to as the proposition of rational man.

Because of the uncertainty in the economic system, economic man's knowledge of economic activities is limited. The learning process of general economic man is same as the searching method in the theory of optimization. They know little about the functional expressions of the economic issues being examined, let alone the path leading to optimal values of the functions. Once a certain variable is chosen, a trial method would be applied to generate new variables based upon the most updated values of the functions. More tentative trials will be repeated in the same direction of the most updated values of the functions until no optimal values can be detected. This method is feasible to achieve the optimal point if the functions are unimodal. In the case of the multimodal functions, only a partial optimal point may be found. This method is called the trial-and-error method in economics.[2]

In the long-run, economic man can achieve his goal by using this trial- and-error method, which is the one to find the maximum value with the least information, but need a longer time. This method has been commonly adopted by governments, enterprises, and households to find the optimal targets in their economic activities. However, it should be noted that in real economic life, it may not be necessary for them to pursue optimal goals, but sub-optimal goals instead. That is, they will stop searching once a satisfactory point, instead of an optimal point, is achieved. For example, the method that the Chinese government employed to regulate economic activities can be regarded as a trial-and-error method. The government curbs the high economic growth rate, which can lead to inflation or vice versa, so as to keep the real economic growth rate fluctuating around its potential level.[3]

The learning function of rational economic man occupies an important position in the theoretical system of this book. As the rational economic man learns repeatedly

---

[2] Visually, the trial-and-error method is akin to a blind man climbing a mountain. He does not know the shape of the mountain, let alone the best path to reach the peak. Being at a certain point in the mountain, he can only test all directions to see which side is higher and then take a step towards it. Other directions will be tested again to take a step towards the other side. This process continues until there is no higher point in all directions.

[3] Kornai argued that the government's ability to control a planned economy was inadequate. He believed that shortage was a constant phenomenon in the planned economy. Portes disagreed with Kornai's view, stating that the central planned economy could roughly balance the aggregate supply and the aggregate demand by adopting the quantitative adjustment measures such as rationing. Portes also adopted the method of disequilibrium analysis to measure the supply and demand of consumer goods markets in several eastern European countries, where supportive data were achieved (refer to Ref. [23]). The views toward this issue are also controversial in China. For example, the views of professor Jinglian Wu are close to those of Portes, while views of Mr. Yining Li are more connected with those of Kornai (refer to Refs. [38, 50, 51]). Different views on this issue lead to different approaches to the economic reform, which is reflected in the question of whether to reform prices before reforming the economic system or vice versa. Prioritizing prices reform means to firstly control the aggregate demand, while reforming the economic system first may then generate difficulty in controlling the aggregate demand. Prioritizing price reforms will definitely bring on inflation, which can fail the overall economic system reform. In conclusion, only by firstly reforming the economic system to set foundations for controlling the aggregate demand can prices be reformed.

from experiences, he can control the economic growth rate in an appropriate scope in the long-run so as to keep inflation within an acceptable range. That is, the economic development per se possesses an objective law in its long-run growth trend. This law has been precisely proven by economic fluctuations.

Therefore, in the long-run, economic activities will not be influenced substantially by expectations, which fluctuate around the real economic performance. However, in the short-run, expectations do exert significant impact upon economic activities. Deviation of expectations from reality is an important factor leading to economic fluctuations in the short-run. This basic idea will be repeatedly emphasized in this book. For example, both the long- run neutral effect of money and the short-run non-neutral effect of money upon the economy will be analyzed in line with this idea.

In fact, the regression equation achieved from the regression analysis reflects the quantitative relationship between the dependent variables and the independent variables in the long-run. In each specific year, there will be more or less some deviations between the regression values and the real ones caused by diverse factors, among which expectations will be highlighted in this book. The regression equation is thus regarded as the long-run quantitative relationship among different variables. By employing the trial-and-error method, economic actors may get to comprehend such a relationship, which is expressed mathematically in the regression equation.

In conclusion, this book will highlight the short-run analysis based on the long-run analysis. In terms of time, the short-run analysis may cover a span of one year or several years. In terms of economic implications, the short- run analysis indicates that time is not long enough for enterprises to increase new fixed assets, so supply can only be increased by adding labor and raw materials under the original plant size when aggregate demand increases. Long-run analysis means that the time is long enough for enterprise to add new fixed assets or to update the existing plant size, so as to increase supply through inputting more laborers or raw materials to the new production capacity, responding to an increase in aggregate demand.

The task of economic theory is not only to explain the short-run economic fluctuations and the long-run economic development trends, but also to explain how the short-run economic fluctuations are transformed into long-run economic trends. This is a more challenging issue to be targeted by this book.

According to the principles of microeconomics, the price determining mechanism, or the market mechanism, works as follows: when demand exceeds supply, the price increases and vice versa. However, in the socialist economy, the change in the planned price is driven by the change in the production costs rather than the change in demand itself. After the economic reforms in China, products of planned prices are declining and more products with market prices are dominating the market, and thus the change in demand begins to exert significant influence on these market prices. Nonetheless, it is believed that the change in price is relatively independent of the change in demand. Such a relative independence is caused by the following factors.

1. There still exist some planned prices, which do not change with the change in demand.

2. There exist constraints of economic contracts. Economic contracts guarantee buyers to purchase any quantity of goods at the agreed prices at the time when contracts are signed. These type of contracts may allow prices to change with the change in production costs in the future, but not with the change in demand. In the case of higher inflation, since a change in planned prices fall behind the change in the production costs, many enterprises are unable to buy products at planned prices as planned but at negotiated prices set by the sellers following the markup on change in costs. The common practice of transforming planned prices into negotiated prices reflects the mutual acceptance between buyers and sellers regarding the pricing principle of a markup on the production costs.
3. There exist constraints of corporate reputation. To maintain their reputation for reasonable prices, large-scale enterprises will not set product price entirely in response to the change in demand. Though demand changes all the time, large-scale enterprises would not change their prices with the change in demand since their products are sold in large quantities. In the long- run, the principle of pricing at cost for large quantities of products will not lead to loss, which is conducive not only to internal accounting of enterprises, but also to the stability of the relationship between buyers and sellers.

In this book, the relative independence of change in planned prices to the change in demand is defined as the price stickiness. Price stickiness is the fourth basic proposition of this book—the proposition of sticky prices. After China's economic system reform, price stickiness plays an important role in explaining China's economic activities. Though planned price stickiness in China is some what different from the market price stickiness defined in Western economics, they share some similarities.

Both the stickiness of expectations and the stickiness of price dominate a critical position in the analytical process in this book, and they are employed as the basic tools to interpret short-run economic fluctuations. Each important conclusion drawn in this book is relevant to the stickiness of expectations and the stickiness of price. Therefore, the theoretical mode of inflation defined in this book can also be called the dual stickiness mode of inflation. This term reflects the basic characteristic of theoretical analysis as well as the basic perspective adopted in the analysis in this book.

This book attempts to build a set of theoretical structures of logic based on the above four basic propositions and the basic proposition (soft budget constraint) in Sect. 1.3. Nevertheless, it is still impossible for the current economic science to establish an ideal structure of pure logic that coincides with natural science, particularly as mathematics does because inductive and generalization are still adopted in theoretical system of economics. The process of construction of a theoretical system is in fact a process of elevation from the abstract to the concrete. This process begins with fundamental concepts and laws, which appear highly abstract, and afterward leads to a variety of increasingly concrete concepts and theorems until a complete system is established. Objectives of theoretical research will then be duplicated abstractly during thinking processes, which is similar to the process of a primitive cell going through fissiparity and becoming a well- developed organism. The way of creation of the classical work *Das Kapital* by Marx is a typical example of theoretical construction. In fact, this process is followed by all theoretical works in natural science.

1.2 Empirical Methods of Theories

It is worthwhile to review the historical process of research methodology in natural sciences before introducing the empirical approach of economic theory.

Tracing back to the 4th century B.C., Plato realized that knowledge needed to be interpreted through a deductive approach. The task of science was to discover (ideally) the structure of nature and to express it in a deductive system because knowledge based upon general conclusions from induction, experiment, and experiences may possibly be true, while deduction provided absolute certainty to knowledge given the right premises. Based on Plato's work, his student, Aristotle, founded the science of logic, which is still prevailing nowadays. Subsequently (about 300 B.C.), Euclid completed his book *Elements* after making use of as few axioms and postulations as possible and proved a series of geometrical theorems from the simple to the complex. The research activities accomplished by these three giants from ancient Greece exert influence on the evolution of science in several thousand years. The period is truthfully one of boasting of many illustrious names in the history of human development. As history turns the page, it should be noted that the rigorous deductive approach of contemporary mathematics textbooks gives the impression that mathematicians invent and innovate by deductive reasoning. In fact, there must be conjecture before proofing, and analysis prior to synthesizing. Yet, the academic achievements made by superstars in scientific community do not lie in introducing new results based on the existing assumptions, but in reforming the existing assumptions with their talent to update the structure of science so as to accommodate more and new knowledge.

Thousand years passed. As human history entered the 17th century, two talents—Rene Descartes (1596—1650) and Galileo Galilie (1564—1642)—figured prominently. They revolutionized the basic nature of scientific activities by choosing appropriate concepts in science, redefining the goals for scientific activities and altering methodologies in science. What they accomplished not only injected unexpected and unprecedented force into science, but also tightly combined science with mathematics, so as to synthesize theoretical science into mathematics. They provoked that all scientific branches should commence from axioms or theories as mathematics to make further deduction so as to arrive at as many results as possible. The prominence of Galileo lies in his denial of the belief that axioms or theories originated from human minds as reckoned by others, who firstly identified the movement of the world then integrated what they saw into preconceived theories. Galileo maintained that basic principles must be drawn from experiences and experiments in physics. He consented that the road taken to seek correct and fundamental principles should be focused on what existed in nature rather than what was in the minds of human beings.

Galileo pointed out that it was not true that nature firstly created the human brain and then made certain arrangements for the world to be acceptable by human wisdom. Knowledge came from observations, not from books. Galileo also realized that it might be possible that an incorrect principle was reached from experiments so that the deduction from that principle would be wrong. He accordingly suggested people check the results of inference by conducting experiments and testing basic principles. Galileo's another profound thought was that people should only provide true descriptions of the nature rather than interpreting it. In other words, the function of equations is to describe, instead of interpretation. In contrast, the Aristotelians believed that one of the tasks of science was to explain why events occurred, and the word "explain" meant uncovering the cause for phenomena. For instance, an object fell because it had weight. This explanation provided the immediate cause for falling. Furthermore, an object fell to the ground because any object had to find its natural location, which connected the ultimate cause for falling. On the contrary, Galileo chose a group of completely new and measurable concepts to be linked with equations. They included distance, time, speed, acceleration, force, mass, and weight. These concepts are now familiar and not so novel to us nowadays, but they indicated a radical reform in physics in Galileo's time (similarly, a radical reform of methodology also facing Chinese theoretical economic research today). These concepts have been proven most helpful for human efforts in understanding nature. The empirical method used by Galileo to seek description is the most profound and most effective thought in the developmental history of scientific methodology. Galileo's thought had been fully accepted by succeeding natural scientists, including Newton, who was himself a giant. Until now, the research approach in natural science still follows the course inaugurated by Galileo.

The following will be a comparison of the historical process of economic research methodology. Economics as a discipline began with *Political Arithmetic* written by William Petty, who focused on economic measurement. By the time of Adam Smith, economics had become a relatively mature system, but not yet a strict deductive system because it emphasized explanation on how the economy works. Karl Marx was attempting not only to explain how the economy works, but also to describe its working processes, which could be clearly identified in Marx's reproduction schema. Until Leon Walras's theory of general equilibrium, the focus upon describing how the economy works had surpassed that upon explaining why it works. By the 20th century, economists had made a clear distinction between the positive and normative analytical methodology. The former used descriptive methods to study the economy, while the latter tried to answer questions involving value judgments of good and bad for how the economy should work.

The research methodology adopted by Chinese economists looks chaotic currently. It is reflected in the lack of unified definitions, of generally accepted principles, and even an agreed theoretical system established through deductive inference. This situation has led to a standstill in theoretical research and controversies involved in identifying right and wrong. In recent years, economists have noticed the situation, and efforts have been made to improve the situation. The gradual adaptation of the empirical research methodology in China does signify an optimistic commencement in China's economic research path.

The empirical research methodology will be more frequently adopted in this book. Although priority is given to discussion of mutual relationship among economic variables, efforts will also be made to determine the answer to questions such as why other variables change following the change in one variable, namely, to provide explanations to mutual causation of the relationship among different variables. It is believed that description and explanation are complementary because only clear explanations can generate accurate descriptions. If, in theory, this book is viewed to focus on studying variables on the basis of ownership analysis, then in methodology, it deems to be focused upon quantitative (descriptive) exploration on the basis of qualitative (explanatory) analysis. It attempts to present the research results through deductive methodology and make efforts to test the assumptions and results of these theories. Generally speaking, it is much easier to test results of theories rather than to inspect relevant assumptions. Results from correct testing for theories do not necessarily guarantee appropriateness of assumptions. Though correct assumptions ensure proper results from deduction, the opposite situation may not be true. Nevertheless, when it is hard to verify a certain assumption and thought experiment will be the sole approach to testify its correctness, results of such deductions will have to be verified.

One basic characteristic of positive economic research is the measurability of both the research objective and relevant variables so as to ensure post verifications. In fact, the common term operability is firstly required to prioritize the measurability of variables. Western economists greatly emphasize operability since the lack of operability may indicate little significance of a theory. Therefore, operability of a theory is deemed to be a prerequisite for its practicability.

Inadequate importance has been attached to the operability of theories in economic theoretical research in China. Theoretical problems have not yet been inducted to relationship among variables. As for those being inducted to relationship among variables, such variables remain commonly immeasurable. Thus, theories themselves cannot be tested or falsified, which are far from being operable, and their practicability is largely crippled. What is the point in conducting a large amount of logical analysis on a pile of immeasurable variables?

Due to uncertainty in the economic system and the constraints of human knowledge of economics, there will naturally be some immeasurable variables in theoretical research. The development of theories requires us to deal with such measurement issues, or a step back, to approximately measure these variables. At least, key variables in the theoretical system should not include too many of those immeasurable variables. On top of that, any immeasurable variables should be viewed as exogenous instead of endogenous to the greatest extent possible. For example, it is difficult to measure factors of expectations, which were then being treated by Keynes as exogenous variables. Afterwards, economists treated expectations as endogenous variables, employing a method of extrapolative expectations and adaptive expectations. Here, on one hand, extrapolative expectations and adaptive expectations described the formation mechanism of expectations; on the other hand, they provided a way of value selection for expectation variables. At this point, expectation variables became measurable. The theory of rational expectations has further strengthened the research on the behavioral mechanisms and value selection for the expectation variables.

This book tries to avoid immeasurable variables and adopt measurable variables for the logic of its theoretical structure. Both the falsifiability and operability of theories will be consistently highlighted in this book.

1.3 The Research Objective of This Book

Reality is highly complicated. The task of theoretical research is not to "take a picture" for reality, but to remove the false premise and retain the truth, discard the coarse, and select the essence so as to abstract on the basis of perceptual knowledge, then determine the research object that represents the essential characteristics of the phenomena, and reject those non-essential characteristics. It is such an abstract objective that stands at the center of theoretical research.

Inflation is an economic phenomenon, from where this book abstracts the relationship among human beings, among substances, as well as between human beings and substances. Inflation is thus viewed as the consequence of the recombination action of these three levels. Therefore, these three composite levels, which are both distinctive and yet interrelated, become the research objectives of this book. Thus, inflation generated by these composite levels will be the research focus.

From the perspective of economic theory, the relationship among people is mainly reflected in the relationship among their interests, which is established on the basis of the production relationship formed by human beings during economic activities, especially the production activities not indicative of any type of contract. The essential attribute of production relations is ownership. The economic system on the macro level is a reflection of the production relations on the micro level.

Public ownership is a key feature of China's economic system. Although the forms of public ownership are diverse, and the meaning of public ownership is plentiful, the core characteristics of public ownership are reflected in the ownership of the means of production. Seizing on this point, we could dominate the commanding heights of problem analysis for a public ownership economy.

Generally speaking, current public ownership in China can be divided into two forms, one is ownership by the whole people and the other is collective ownership. There are possibly other forms of public ownership, which are ignored here since they carry little impact on the economy at present. The ownership by the whole people has been clearly defined as ownership by the state, which indicates that the means of production are possessed by the nation on behalf of all citizens. Nominally, under collective ownership, means of production shall not be owned by the state, but in fact, at present the local governments intervene on enterprises of collective ownership and take relatively huge economic responsibility for them. They are entitled to appoint or remove the leaders and separate part of the assets and workers of these enterprises to set up new production. They are authorized to lower taxes and increase loans for these enterprises to save them from bankruptcy in case of economic difficulties. Therefore, collective enterprises can also be regarded as enterprises owned by the local governments. From this point of view, public ownership in China can be expressed as state ownership.

At present, the basic form of state ownership is ownership by government and management by enterprises. It is a type of state ownership with separation between the two powers. This type of state ownership and the economic operational mechanism it generates will be viewed as components of the research objective in this book. In other words, it is the foundation of the study of the relationship among people.

To study the relationship among people in an economic system, we should determine the type of people because people of different types possess different interests in economic activities. The proper classification of the types of people is the foundation of the study of the relationship between them.

In Marx's economic theoretical system, two types of people, i.e. capitalists and workers, are abstractly separated. On the basis of capitalist ownership, Marx studied the interest mechanism of the capitalist economy formed by these two types of people, a series of consequences generated by such an interest mechanism were also analyzed by Marx.

In the theoretical framework of this book, three entities have also been abstractly separated. They are government, enterprises, and households.

1. The government, also known as the state, is the regulator of the economic system, which represents the overall interests of all people in the economic system. The government is also the owner of the means of production. The government is constituted by various administrative sectors.

Usually the government is further divided into the planning system, the financial system, and the banking system, which are employed by the government to regulate the economy. However, this book treats the financial system as an integral part of the planning system and regulatory system of the government is simplified to the planning system and the banking system, which correspond to the product market and money market respectively. The planning system regulates the product market and the banking system regulates the money market. The area of comprehensive balance of financial credit will not be further researched in this book since traditional economic theory has carried quite thorough research on it. However, a different perspective will be adopted to analyze the inflation problem from the comprehensive balance of the product market and money market. In so doing, it is not with an intention of ignoring the importance of the financial sector, but to integrate it into the planning system, which helps to explain in a unified manner about how the SPC (the State Planning Commission)[4] and the Ministry of Finance regulate the product market.

[4] The State Planning Commission of the People's Republic of China, referred to as the SPC (the State Planning Commission), was one of the original departments of The State Council in charge of national economic planning and market macro management. On November 16, 1952, the State Planning Commission of the Central People's Government was established, which was the predecessor of the State Planning Commission. In September 1954, the State Planning Commission of the Central People's Government was renamed the State Planning Commission of the People's Republic

2. Producers, also known as enterprise, or firms, are operators or users of the fixed assets. The role of the producers is specialized in producing goods or services. Producers are the collection of various firms.
3. Consumers include households and government consumption sectors. Households provide labor services and receive remuneration for such services, with which they may then purchase articles for daily use or savings. The function of the government consumption sectors is to provide services and to consume. This book focuses on the study of household consumption endogeneity, while government consumption is treated as an exogenous variable.

These three types of economic actors are all rational man pursuing their respective maximum interests under certain constraints, and repeatedly learn to strive for maximum benefits with minimum costs.

Particularly, producers pursue profit maximization under the cost constraint, consumers pursue utility maximization under the income constraint, and governments strive for their ultimate goal under the social cost constraint (social cost is the loss caused by achieving the goal), which represents the common interests of the entire society. Thus the third basic proposition of this book is further crystallized here.

It should be pointed out that before the economic reform, many non- economic factors were included in the production costs of the producers and political interests also included in their targets. Under special circumstances, although the profit motive was seriously criticized, enterprises were still able to manage to maximize profits under cost constraints to a certain extent. After all, political interests should have to be reflected in economic interests.

Since the means of production are owned by the state, enterprises should freely submit profits to the government, while requiring the government to assume ancillary responsibilities. So these two entities share a common interest while enterprises may also pursue their own local interests. As rational producers, in order to maximize their local interests (reflected in the maximization of profits retained by enterprises), enterprises are allowed to transfer profits from the state to retain as much profit as possible. This is mainly reflected in the refusal of enterprises to repay loans, profits, or even taxes when they run into difficulties, or force the state to offer them new loans. The state on the other hand may understand and show sympathy to the enterprises and acquiesce in their behaviors.

In addition, enterprises tend to propose a lion's share in their plans, attempting to earn more investments from the national level. There are always capital gaps to be filled by the state in the enterprise investment plans. Such behavior under a public ownership economy has been concluded by Janos Kornai as the proposition of the "soft budget constraint", which is included as the fifth basic proposition of this book. Although enterprises try to maximize profit, they also understand that the consequence of such a target may actually be the average profit of capital or

of China. In March 2003, the Restructuring Office of the State Council and some functions of the State Economic and Trade Commission were merged into SPC, which was renamed as the State Development and Reform Commission.—By the translator.

the average income of employees (concepts of these two averages are different). Particularly, what enterprises seek is to maximize their profit retention, which is consistent with the objective of maximization of the average income of the employees. The more profit retained by the enterprises, the higher the income of their employees.

However, there may be controversy in this regard because maximization of the average income of employees is often prioritized over the goal of profit maximization of the enterprises. When recognizing that its retention level is lower than the average, or the income of its employees is lower than the average, an enterprise will be prone to transfer profits from the state, that is, delaying repayment of loans and refusing to pay taxes and profits[5] so as to transfer its burden to the state. This is an internal economic mechanism in China originated from the behavior of equalizing capital profit, especially equalizing household incomes. Therefore, the proposition of "Soft Budget the word of profit transference,[6] which more accurately reflects the behavioral characteristics of enterprises pursuing the average retention level, or the average income level of employees under the "soft budget constraints".

The relationship between human beings and substances studied in this book does not refer to the relationship of the utilization of the means of production by human beings, but to human's estimation or expectation of the future value of economic variables (such as output, money supply, increases in the price level, and so forth). The expectation outcomes will influence the changes of their behaviors, which in turn will lead to the change in the choice of the economic variables. The change of materials leads to the change of human expectations, which in turn will affect the change of substances. This denotes the relationship between human beings and substances. Thus, the intermediate link between human beings and substances will be human expectations. As a result, the focus of the study of the relationship between human beings and substances is to study the expectation behavior of human beings and the mutual relationship between human expectations and economic variables. In the next section of this chapter, the significance of incorporating proposition of expectations into economic theory research will be discussed.

The relationship among substances is reflected in the intricate integration between commodity flows and capital flows. It is easier to be measured and analyzed empirically comparing the relationships among people beings as well as human beings and substances. The next chapter of this book will analyze in detail the relationship between substances in the economic system, that is, material flow and capital flow and their mutual relationship. A particular focus will be placed upon the relationship

[5] This is different from the behavior of enterprises pursuing average profit in the market economy, where enterprises earn average profit through capital flow among sectors. However, in a planned economy, enterprises rely on the "Soft Budget Constraint" to achieve average profit. There is a difference between the two situations since average profit is relative to capital while average income is concerned with employees.

[6] ProfiT transference can be understood as follows: the revenue of a enterprise is certain as set as g, the operating cost is $C + V$, and the profit is $M1 + M2$, among which $M1$ is retained by the enterprise and $M2$ is turned over to the state. In the case that a enterprise believes that $M1$ is lower than the average profit retention level, it will make efforts to seek compensation from $M2$ or even from other types of national income. Such compensation is called the profit transference.

between the amount of national income produced and the amount of national income spent because these two concepts are closely associated with the theory of inflation. Only by understanding clearly the specific processes of how the amount of national income produced is transformed into the amount of national income spent can the operational process and the internal mechanism of inflation be clearly interpreted. This book will study the relationship among capital flows and material flows from the perspective of national economic accounting, and then discuss the limitations of an ex post analysis, so as to lay a foundation for the clues of the theoretical research of this book.

1.4 The Theoretical Significance of Expectation Proposition

Expectations are anticipations of the future values of economic variables related to current decisions. Inflation expectations are therefore regarded as anticipations of future inflation.

In the 19th century, expectations did not seem to have drawn the attention of economists but things changed radically in the 20th century. In Keynes's classical work *The General Theory of Employment, Interest, and Money*, the concept of expectations has been placed at the heart of his economic theory. In the third chapter of this book, the aggregate demand function and aggregate supply function are defined with expectations as the basic concept; the fifth chapter examines expectations and employment and the twelfth Chapter deals with the situation of long-run expectations. Following Keynes, the theory of expectations continues to attract the attention of economists, so expectations are studied as endogenous variables of the economic system. In the early 1970s, because the Keynesian economic theory failed to explain the problem of "stagflation", the theory of rational expectations came to play on the stage of Western economic research, attracting more attention.

In view of the course of development of Western economics, the theory of expectations has been emphasized twice, and both are all related to economic crisis and theoretical crisis in reality. The first crisis happened after the Great Depression, in the late 1920s, which could not be explained by traditional economic theories until Keynes proposed the theory of insufficient effective demand on the basis of the concept of expectation. The theory of rational expectations was propelled secondly with stagflation of the early 1970s. The role of expectations was then promoted to the extreme in the theory of rational expectations. In conclusion, there used to be a profound practical background for the introduction of the concept of expectations into Western economic theory. Its occurrence and development is by no means accidental but in fact the inexorable outcome of the theoretical development per se.

The operational mechanism of China's economy is completely different from that of Western economies, which should not be simply imitated to solve China's practical economic problems. Nevertheless, it does not mean that nothing useful could be learned from Western economics. For example, since there is no content about expectations in traditional economic theory in China, it becomes helpful for us to absorb some contents of this theory to enrich the economic theory of China. Unfortunately, it has been ignored for too long a time. It is safe to state that the introduction of the expectation factor into economic theory in China is not the result of learning from Western economics, but is completely a compelled output due to solving practical economic problems in China, and is the result of practice on repeated calls to do so. Particularly, the anabatic increase in inflation after 1984 attracted the attention of economists to the theory of expectations. Moreover, the sudden acceleration of inflation in 1988, and the sharp decrease in inflation in 1990 were difficult to explain by the quantity of money supply alone, which forced Chinese economists to re-examine the economic theory itself based upon reality. This process led to the inauguration of the theory of expectations in China. Although not powerful at present, the theory of expectations will be certainly growing gradually and triggering profound transformation in China's current economic theory.

The significance of the theory of expectations is also indicated in expanding the scope of traditional economic theory, which is restricted to the three constructs of humanity, finance and materiality, manifesting themselves as four equilibriums, namely, the human equilibrium, financial equilibrium, material equilibrium as well as equilibrium of the balance of payments. Human beings herein are regarded as the factors of production, whose output depends on the quantity of the labor input. In this case, both human psychological activities and reaction to the economic system are excluded from the scope of this research. Therefore, by introducing the expectation factors into the economic theory, we will observe not only the determination of existence to consciousness, but also the reaction of consciousness to existence will be observed. In other words, based on the concept of expectations, not only can the decisive influence of the four equilibriums on human expectations be found, but also the impacts of human expectations on the four equilibriums can be detected in turn. Consequently, following the changes of human expectations, the original equilibrium will be broken through or transformed into a new equilibrium.

Both the concepts of ex ante and ex post have been adopted in traditional economic theory. For instance, the planning balance is an ex ante concept. However, the foothold of traditional theoretical analysis is an ex post analysis. With the concept of expectation, such a foothold will be shifted to the concept of ex ante. Therefore, aggregate supply and aggregate demand analyzed in this book will be ex ante analysis. The necessity and significance of distinguishing between the ex ante analysis and the ex post analysis will be further explained in the next chapter.

It should be noted that the emphasis on expectations in this book does not mean that they are the variables determining all activities in the economic system, let alone that inflation is entirely caused by expectations. The author believes that expectations are parts of the crucial variables in the economic system, the influence of which is reflected through the changes of other variables. Without the objective existence of the economic system, there will be no subjective factor of expectations. On the contrary, the changes of an economic system could not be thoroughly interpreted without the subjective factor of expectations. It can be derived from the analysis that inflation is triggered by a variety of factors, and the factor of expectations is only one of them. Expectations alone will be unable to explain the formation mechanism of inflation; without expectations, the various phenomena of inflation in recent years will not be illustrated. Thus, the focus on the analysis of inflation from the perspective of expectations does not necessarily mean that it takes no account of the impacts of other variables on inflation.

1.5 The Definition of Inflation

This book defines inflation as a sustained increase in the price level, both explicitly and implicitly. Inflation means an increase in the prices of products, and it does not mean the price of money.[7] The explicit price level means the GNP (Gross National Product) deflator,[8] which reflects the overall price level and includes both the prices of goods and services. The implicit price level means shortages, which denotes that money cannot buy what is demanded.

Another definition of inflation will also be applied in this book. It is defined as the difference between aggregate demand and aggregate supply, that is, inflation equals the gap between aggregate demand and aggregate supply (also called excess aggregate demand, a definition to be introduced later).

The first definition of inflation is better at reflecting the rate of inflation, while the second is better at reflecting the quantity of inflation. Subsequent analysis will prove that these two definitions are essentially consistent.

Through the second definition, inflation will be linked with some important variables in the economic system and be regarded as a syndrome of it. Generally speaking, aggregate demand and aggregate supply will be employed correspondingly as the horizontal coordinates and the vertical coordinates of the theoretical analysis respectively to analyze the trajectory of inflation. *Macroeconomics and Expectations*, therefore, would have possibly been a plausible title for this book. The current title, of course, is more appropriate to convey a research focus.

Inflation and paper money are relevant. An economic system with paper money will possibly experience inflation. Therefore, inflation is a common phenomenon regardless of it being a socialist country or a capitalist country. But inflation is not just a phenomenon for paper money. In China, enterprises and public institutions usually use checks for procurement. This kind of check is also a type of money to be used for bank transfers and settlements, or often called credit money. Such credit money is commonly used by households in Western countries, which can cause prices to increase. From a more broad perspective, the increase in bank loans will induce an increase in paper and credit money supply since bank loans can also be regarded

[7] The contents in the next and other chapters will show that measuring monetary inflation is difficult. The use of immeasurable definitions is not conducive to theoretical construction. In fact, excessive money supply and increasing prices are two aspects of a problem. The former is the cause, and the latter the effect. This book defines inflation in terms of convenience of measurement, which is considered more consistent with the development of economic theory.

[8] Sometimes, the term general social retail price index is also used, which is more timely and accurate, but reflects relatively narrow on reality.

as a kind of money. Therefore, to understand the relationship between inflation and money, we should study not only the relationship between inflation and paper money, but also the relationship between inflation and credit money as well as bank loans.

Because of the close relationship between inflation and money, the translation of the word "inflation" into Chinese literally means "monetary inflation". As currency stands for money, inflation is therefore viewed as "the money that is inflated" or "monetary inflation". It may make sense from a classical economic point of view since classical economists believed that money only works on product prices. However, from the perspective of modern economics, money not only works on product prices, but also on output. And in the short-run, money would possibly work neither on prices nor output. Therefore, it is not appropriate to define inflation only from a perspective of inflation of money. This question will be explored further later, thus monetary inflation will not be used to define inflation. If inflation must be defined in monetary terms, it is better to define inflation as a sustained depreciation of money. Depreciation of money and an increase in price level are two sides of the same coin. But depreciation of money can hardly reflect shortages, or the implicit increase in the price level. It is not comprehensive to define inflation by depreciation of money in China. It points out that the standard definition of inflation in economic theory circles in China and abroad is still controversial, and the definition chosen in this book is the only one commonly used in economic theory circles.

Part I
Theoretical Foundation of Inflation

Chapter 2
Analysis on Flow and Stock Variables in the Economic System

The physical objects of study in this book are the main economic flow variables and stock variables of the national economic system and their economic and technological relations. The focus of the study is on inflation caused by these relations. The study commences with the exploration and measurement of the object, that is to say, we must be firstly acquainted with the basic flow variables and stock variables existing in the national economic system, where they are from, where they are heading, how they are transforming, how the flow variables are transformed into the stock variables, what are the identical relationships among the macro economic variables, and so forth. The national economy to a certain extent is similar to the human body. The economic flow variables and stock variables and their relationship during the economic process in the social economy can be studied through the measures of the physiological anatomy. Only through in-depth research on the physiological structure of the economics organism and its operational pattern can the economic mechanism be correctly revealed, the quantitative characteristics and relations of the economic mechanism be described, and the operational rules of the economic system be seized.

2.1 Where to Start

There exists two entrances to the interior of the economic system: one is the gross product, and the other is net product.

Karl Marx entered the economic system from the gross product. Based on the theory of the Two-fold Character of Labor, he scientifically divided commodity value into three parts C, V and M, divided social production into two parts, including the production of as the means of production and production of consumption goods, established his famous reproduction chart, and revealed the laws that must be followed by the performance of the economic system.

L. Li, *The Inflation Mechanism and Expectations*, Understanding China,
https://doi.org/10.1007/978-981-97-2570-0_2

To study the economic system from the perspective of the gross social product is actually to divide the economic system into two components: The first is the compensation for the original value, and the second is the creation of the new value. The study on the first component is to inquire into the technical connections between different sectors, which then become the research content of the first quadrant of the input-output table. The study on the second component is to examine how newly created value is consumed and invested in the reproduction process, which is an examination of the economic connections between different sectors. The core problem of social reproduction is the problem of realization, i.e., how to compensate goods in value and how to substitute goods in use value, which can be solved thoroughly only on this basis.

Since Adam Smith, Western economics has basically studied the economic system from the perspective of the net product. Although this approach is able to explain how newly created value is consumed and reinvested in the production process, the technical connection of the social economy is excluded from the research object, and the problem of realization of social reproduction cannot be solved completely.

This book analyzes the internal structure of the economic system from the perspective of the gross social product. It is well known that at the entrance to science, as at the entrance to hell, the demand must be made: *Qui si convien lasciare ogni sospetto, Ogni vilta convien che quisia morta.* [From Dante, *Divina Commedia*: Here must all distrust be left; All cowardice must here be dead.]

2.2 Law of Nodes and Law of Networks

In studying circuits, Kirchhoff's Law(KCL, Gustav Robert Kirchhoff, 1824-1887) states that the amount of current flowing into a node is equal to that of current flowing out of that node. This is not only a natural phenomenon, but also applicable to an economy.

In the economic sector, income and expenditure are equal; expenditure depends on income. Income can be thus regarded as the inflow of a sector, with expenditure as the outflow. If a sector is treated as a node, then the inflow must equal the outflow. This is called the law of node.

A sector must follow the node law to possess inflow and outflow, and the outflow of one node will become the inflow of other nodes, so all nodes are connected by inflow and outflow to constitute a network. In the economic system, this is referred to as the law of network.[1]

---

[1] This book describes the law of node and the law of network from the perspective of national economic accounting. These two laws are the abstract representation of the principle of sector balance of payment in the national income accounting theory. Based on these two laws, we can easily prove the identical relationship between some macroeconomic variables, such as the national income spent equals the sum of the national income produced and the net export.

It is important to note that savings and cash in hand in a sector are viewed as expenditure, which is the source of revenue of banks. On the contrary, the debt of a sector is regarded as its revenue.

The law of node and the law of network are the two basic laws of the performance of national economy; They are also two sharp scalpels for dissection of the national economy. The national economic system looks very complex, with various internal flows criss-crossing and with intricate relationships, but as long as commencing from the gross product with these two scalpels, the national economy can be methodically analyzed, laying the foundation for the subsequent theoretical analysis.

2.3 Specific Description of Circulation of Flow and Stock Variables

There are four types of flow variables in the performance of national economy: (1) product flow; (2) fund flow; (3) people flow; and (4) information flow. The first three kinds of flows possess their own stock.

Product flow can be divided into physical goods and services based on their forms of existence. The production and consumption of physical goods can be separated, while services should be produced and consumed simultaneously, as they are mutually inclusive. In addition, physical products may enjoy corresponding stock, while services may not. This is also a crucial difference between the physical goods and services.

Physical goods can be further divided into current assets and fixed assets according to their forms of circulation. Current assets are physical products used and circulated only once. Fixed assets are physical products utilized for a long time span, whose value incrementally participates in circulation.

Money flow can be separated from the fund flow. In the sense of political economy, fund and money are strictly differentiated and cannot be confused. This book only studies the circulation, not the creation of value, so no strict distinction between fund and money will be drawn.

Various materials in the national economy are constituted by these aforesaid components, each of which functions differently. Here we focus on the circulation of the physical products and fund.

The moment of their entering the market can be viewed as the starting point of the circulation of the physical goods, while the ending point is when they reach the hands of the users. Two types of users are discussed here. The first is the consumer, who directly consumes and ends the circulation of the physical goods, which no longer enter the field of production or circulation. The second is the producer, who buys the physical goods for production, and the goods purchased will re-enter the production cycle. Two approaches have been adopted to describe the circulation of physical goods. One is to describe the product with the dimension of the physical properties, such as how many tons of coal are produced and consumed. The circulation is shown in Figure 2.1. The other is from the value dimension of the product itself, as shown in Figure 2.2.

The above is an analysis of the circulation of a certain type of physical product. In the circular flow of the national economy, circulation involves tens of thousands of kinds of products. The well-known input-output analysis method, which is not further introduced here, can comprehensively demonstrate the circulation of these products and their relationships.

From the perspective of the circulation process of physical goods, inventory can be divided into three categories. The first category is the inventory in the production process, that is, inventory of work-in-process and inventory of finished good. The second category is the inventory in circulation and the third is the inventory with the

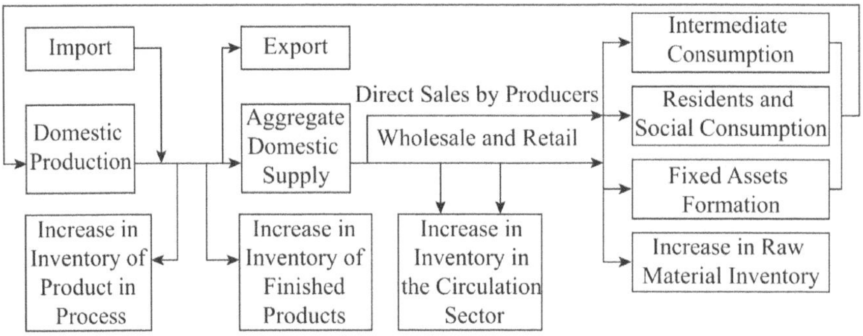

Fig. 2.1 The physical circulation of a single product

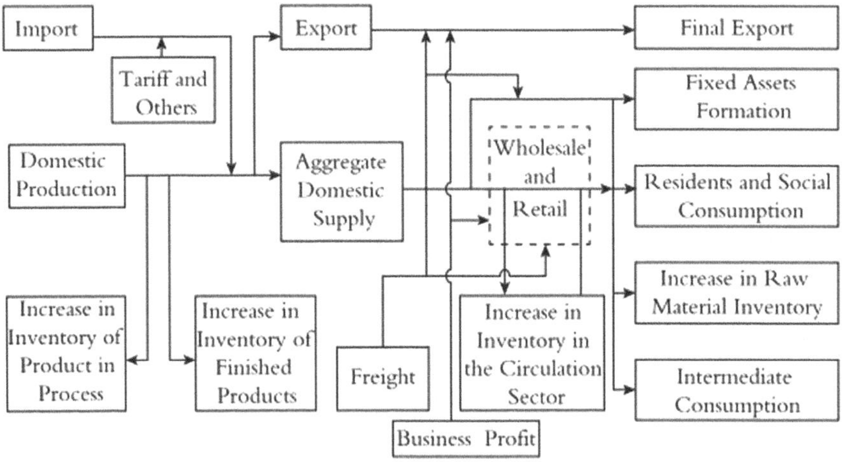

Fig. 2.2 The value circulation of a single product

final user. The increase and decrease of these three kinds of inventory reflect different situations in the national economic circulation, which will be analyzed later.

The following will be the examination on the circulation process of the fund flow.

The compensation funds are ignored here to clearly reflect the core process of redistribution from accumulated funds to real investment funds. The input- output table is employed here to analyze the source and use of funds and the circulation of funds among various sectors, as shown in Table 2.1.

The rows in Table 2.1 indicate where the funds are used and the columns indicate their sources of revenue. Corresponding to the division of the input-output table, this table can also be divided into three quadrants: the intermediate expenditure and the intermediate input are the first quadrant, reflecting the fund flow relationship between sectors; the cross section of the final expenditure and the intermediate input constitutes the second quadrant, reflecting the final use of the funds; the cross section of the intermediate expenditure and the initial input constitutes the third quadrant, reflecting the initial input source of the funds, which is the amount of national income produced plus the foreign investment.

As can be observed from Table 2.1, the original disposable income of the initial investment is 2,070 domestically and 34 abroad, totaling 2,104. The final expenditure of foreigners is 34, domestic consumption 1,395, accumulation of fixed assets 334, and accumulation of current assets 341, totaling 2,104. The above clearly shows that the amount of national income produced plus foreign inputs is equal to the amount of national income spent plus the amount spent abroad. This is an important identical relation in fund flow and a crucial foundation for theoretical analysis. The national economic accounting in China is following such a fundamental relation. Thus, it is incorrect to regard the difference between the national income produced and the national income spent as the difference between aggregate supply and demand. Here, the first quadrant (sector fund flow) is functioning as an intermediate process for the final input quadrant (the third quadrant) to transform into the final expenditure quadrant (the second quadrant). Therefore, the table reflect show the seven economic sectors transform their initial income (initial input including income from abroad and Original Disposable Income) into final utilization through criss-cross redistribution channels upon ending of the original distribution process. This table in fact reflects the hub and gate functions performed by the redistribution sectors such as the fiscal and financial sectors in the fund operation channel, which reflects their ability in controlling and regulating the direction and scale of fund flows. Since it is able to reflect the domestic fund flow interweaving the circulation of foreign exchange capital, this table is considered to comprehensively disclose the performance of funds in an economy.

As can be seen from Table 2.1, the income and expenditure of funds in each sector are equal. This is a typical application of the law of nodes and the law of networks. If there is a change in income and expenditure relationship in one sector, the income and expenditure relationship of other sectors will be influenced, thus generating a series of influences on the entire economic system. It is similar to the direct consumption and indirect consumption in the input–output table, and these influences can also be defined as direct influence and indirect influence.

Table 2.1 The input–output type fund flow

Physical products		Intermediate expenditure							Final expenditure				Aggregate expenditure
		Services		Households	Public institutions	Fiscal	Finance	Other redistributions	Foreign	Consumption	Accumulation of fixed assets	Accumulation of Current Assets	
Intermediate input	Physical Products	–	–	–	95	275	105	30	25	–	210	315	1055
	Services	–	–	–	15	100	30	10	–	–	39	26	220
	Households	–	–	–	140	115	40	10	–	877	60	–	1242
	Public Institution	–	–	–	–	80	35	13	3	518	25	–	784
	Fiscal	108	5	110	449	–	–	–	6	–	–	–	603
	Finance	92	10	35	75	33	–	–	–	–	–	–	220
	Other Redistributions	40	5	10	8	–	10	–	–	–	–	–	63
sInitial Input	Foreign Original Disposable Income	30 785	200	2 1085	2	–	–	–	–	–	–	–	34 2070
Total Income		1055	220	1242	784	603	220	63	34	1395	334	341	

Stone argued that it was possible to establish an input-output system for income and expenditure accounting for each sector if the necessary information was available. This issue was discussed at a conference of the research planning agency of the World Bank in 1978. In the Soviet Union, the distribution of national income, especially the redistribution process, was included in the expanded input–output table. What needs to be done here is just an experiment, which attempts to be helpful for a clear analysis of the fund flow at least. The contents will not be clearly understood if the method is only described in pure words. Thus, the input-output model can be imitated in this regard to easily transform relevant data into a mathematical model to analyze the direct and indirect influences of those sectors mentioned above, namely

$$AX + Y = X$$

where, A is the direct consumption coefficient matrix (completely defined by imitating the method in the input-output method); X is the column vector of the aggregate expenditure of each sector; Y is the column vector of final expenditure of each sector. From the above equation, we have

$$(I - A)X = Y$$

where, I is the identity matrix.

Then

$$X = (I - A)^{-1}Y$$

where, $(I - A)^{-1}$ is the inverse matrix of $(I - A)$.

Given the final expenditure of each sector, its total output can be counted by multiplying it to $(I - A)^{-1}$. Thus, a variety of economic analysis can be conducted, such as calculating the impact of investment on variables such as the national income: $(I - A)^{-1}$ here is equivalent to the broad multiplier matrix of investment. A is the direct influence matrix (corresponding to the direct consumption matrix in the input–output model), $\left[(I - A)^{-1} - I\right]$ is called the complete influence matrix (corresponding to the complete consumption matrix in the input–output model).

It should be pointed out that although this analytical method possesses certain practical value, its utilization is substantially constraint because economic relations between sectors are far less stable than that of the technical relations, particularly in times of inflation.[2] Special caution should betaken in using this method. It does a better job of simulating situations in one year than predicting situations in the next. In particular, the concept of the broad multiplier contains much more information than the pure multiplier commonly used in macroeconomic theory.

---

[2] The constant price method can be adopted to partially eliminate the effects of inflation.

2.4 Overall Description of Circulation of Flow and Stock Variables

The overall description of the circulation process of economic flow and stock variables requires the organic combination of the product flow and fund flow as well as the flow and stock. Let's start with a circulation diagram that reflects the fund and product flows in a high degree of generalization, as shown in Figure 2.3.

As you can see from Figure 2.3, product flow has three branches. The first branch is converted into fund flow after the initial distribution, then becomes final use through the intricate redistribution channels (as shown in Table 2.1), which is then decomposed into accumulation and consumption, and finally returns to the starting point. The second branch alone constitutes a compensation cycle. The third branch constitutes an import-export cycle through foreign countries. In the latter two branches, the flow of products is accompanied by the flow of funds in opposite directions.

In the operation of fund flow, in addition to the above three circulations related to the operation of product flow, there are two external fund flow processes connected with foreign countries. One is the cycle composed of foreign fund income and expenditure. The other is the one-way operation of fund between accumulation and foreign countries. If the net value of a loan lent to foreign countries is positive, it means that fund outflows abroad; if it is negative, it means that fund inflows domestically. This final one-way operation of fund plays a role in balancing foreign and domestic payments.

The operational process of the national economy described in Figure 2.3 also fully follows the law of node and the law of network. If each box is viewed as a node, the inflow of each node will be equal to its outflow, forming a network relationship between nodes.

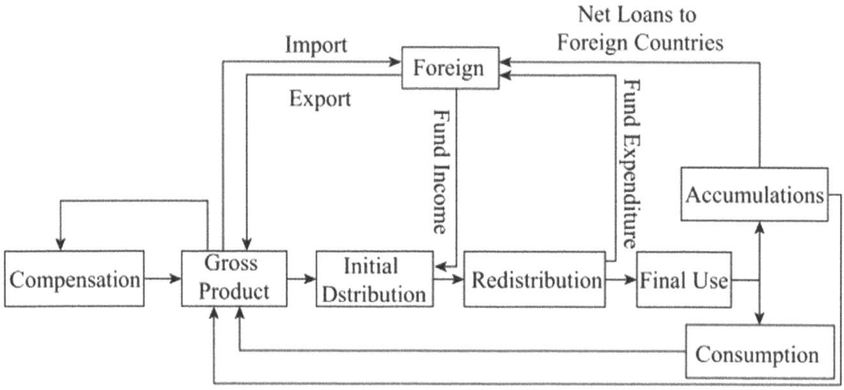

Fig. 2.3 Circulation of the macroeconomic aggregate

Next, Figure 2.3 is further refined and production conditions such as fixed assets, financial assets, and liabilities are also included to fabricate a more complicated operation chart of the national economy, as shown in Figure 2.4.

The first stage are production conditions, which are a set of measurement indices reflecting on the stock and describing the conditions of national economic circulation. The measurement index can be further separated into three categories, the first is the labor force index; the second is the national wealth index; the third is the financial index.

The second stage is the production and the initial distribution process. The inclusion of the service sector in the field of production here is inconsistent with the statistical coverage of the national income prior to 1991. In the second stage, the production and initial distribution process will be described by drawing support from the input–output table.

The third stage is the redistribution and final utilization situation, where three redistribution subsystems, including financial, fiscal and other transfer payments are established. Through these three subsystems of redistribution, the original household income from the initial distribution and the social net income will be decomposed into the personal consumption fund, the social consumption fund, the non-productive accumulation fund, the productive fixed assets accumulation fund, and the reserve fund. These five categories of funds will then be merged into the consumption fund and accumulation fund to reflect the final utilization of the national income. At the same time, the compensation fund generated in the production stage and adjusted in the redistribution stage is also classified as a category, which, combined with the final utilization of the national income, reflects the ultimate utilization of the annual gross social output after distribution and redistribution. Integrating with the production conditions of the previous year, such ultimate utilization will deem to be the production conditions for the next circulation. Figure 2.4 provides a comprehensive description of the commencement, production, distribution, redistribution, and final utilization of the national economic circulation.

Furthermore, Figure 2.4 can be reflected more accurately in detail in the form of a matrix. However, two critical problems should be solved by doing so. The first is the connection between the fund flow and the product flow and the second is the connection between the flow variables and the stock variables. In Figure 2.4, both of these connections are simply reflected by lines, which are not rigorous. These two connection problems are satisfactorily solved in the matrix of national economic circulation designed in this book. This matrix perfectly conforms to the law of nodes and the law of networks in the case that each row and corresponding column in the entire matrix are viewed as a node, as shown in Table 2.2.

In Table 2.2, each row in the matrix and its corresponding column is called an account: the row represents the income and the column represents the expenditure. For example, if the third row reflects the income of the physical product sector, then the third column will present its expenditure. Income and expenditure are balanced in every account here.

In Table 2.2, row 1-2 and corresponding columns reflect the production conditions, where the tangible assets include the fixed assets and current assets. Row 3-6

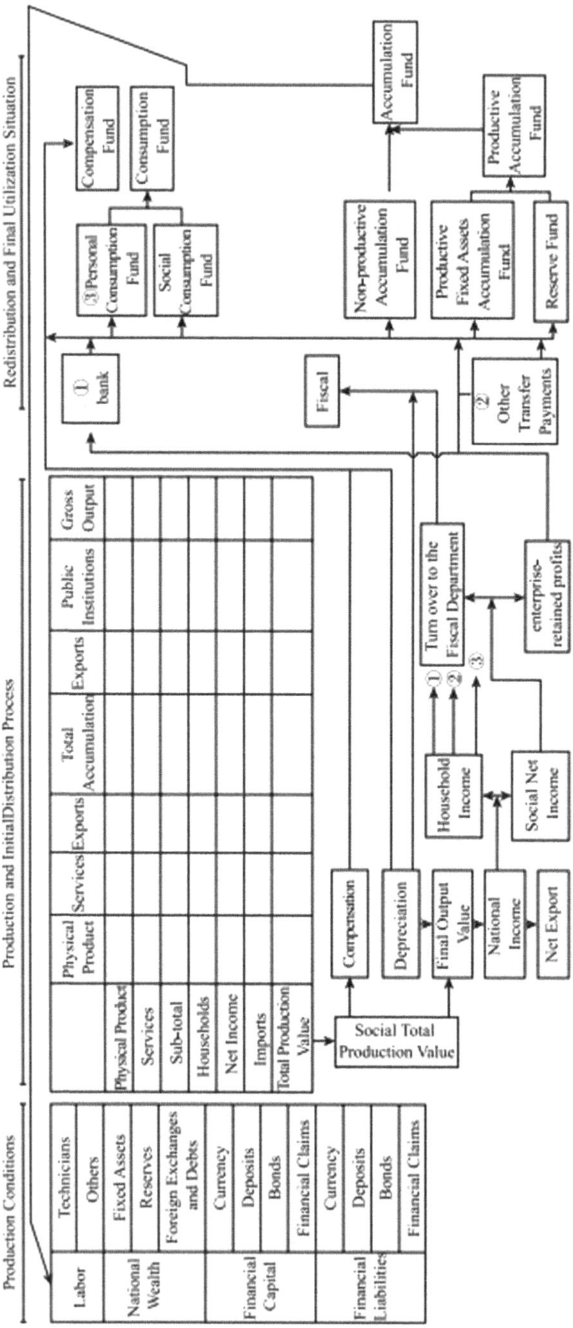

Fig. 2.4 Decomposition of macroeconomic indicators

Table 2.2 General circular flow of macro-economy

Item			S.N	1	2	3	4	5	6	7	8	9	10
Initial Balance Sheet		Financial assets	1	–	–	–	–	–	–	–	–	–	–
		Tangible assets	2	–	–	–	–	–	–	–	–	–	–
Production	Commodity	Physical products	3	–	–	–	–	1320	120	–	–	–	–
		Services	4	–	–	–	–	120	10	–	–	–	–
	Sector	Physical products	5	–	–	3115	45	–	–	–	–	–	–
		Services	6	–	–	–	480	–	–	–	–	–	–
Distribution	Depreciation		7	–	–	–	–	190	40	–	–	–	–
	Initial Income of households		8	–	–	–	–	935	150	–	–	–	–
	Net social income		9	–	–	–	–	595	160	–	–	–	–
Redistribution	Physical products		10	–	–	–	–		–	190	–	595	–
	Services		11	–	–	–	–	–	–	40	–	160	–
	Households		12	–	–	–	–	–	–	–	1085	–	–
	Public institutions		13	–	–	–	–	–	–	–	–	–	95
	Fiscal		14	–	–	–	–	–	–	–	–	–	275
	Credit		15	–	–	–	–	–	–	–	–	–	105
	Other redistributions		16	–	–	–	–	–	–	–	–	–	30
Consumption	Households		17	–	–	–	–	–	–	–	–	–	–
	Public institutions		18	–	–	–	–	–	–	–	–	–	–
Accumulations	Productive investment	Fixed Assets	19	–	–	–	–	–	–	–	–	–	210
		Current Assets	20	–	–	–	–	–	–	–	–	–	315
	Non-productive investment	Households	21	–	–	–	–	–	–	–	–	–	–
		Public institutions	22	–	–	–	–	–	–	–	–	–	–

(continued)

Table 2.2 (continued)

Item		S.N	1	2	3	4	5	6	7	8	9	10
Foreign Countries		23	–	–	180	–	–	–	–	–	–	25
Re-evaluation		24	–	–	–	–	–	–	–	–	–	–
Ending balance sheet	Financial assets	–	–	–	–	–	–	–	–	–	–	
	Tangible assets	–	–	–	–	–	–	–	–	–	–	
Total		27	–	–	3295	525	3160	480	230	1085	755	1055

and corresponding columns are uv type input-output tables describing the production process. Row 7-9 and corresponding columns represent the initial distribution process. Row 10-16 and corresponding columns represent the redistribution process. Row 17-22 and corresponding columns reflect the final utilization process, which is separated into consumption and accumulation (or investment). Row 23 and corresponding columns are foreign accounts, reflecting the balance of imports and exports (product flow) and foreign exchange funds (fund flow). Row 24 and the corresponding column is the revaluation, which adjusts the value of the financial assets (e.g. changes in value of shares in the stock market) and the fixed assets (e.g. to reflect obsolescence on fixed assets). Row 25-26 and corresponding columns reflect the new production conditions at the end of the year, which constitute the starting point of the national economic circulation for the incoming year.

In Table 2.2, the investment account (or accumulation account) is a pivot account that performs both functions by connecting product flow and fund flow as well as the flow and stock variables.

Table 2.2 shows the operation mechanism of the national economy: based on the initial production conditions, the current period of production is carried out through labor inputs. Two flows are generated through the production activities: one is the product flow, consisting of C_1 (net compensation), C_2 (depreciation), V (original household income) and M (social net income), C_1 also constitutes the technical and economic links between the sectors, and the rest constitutes the original distribution. The second flow generated in the production process is the import and export flow.

Upon the completion of the production and initial distribution process, the operation of fund flow follows. C_2 , V and M, formed in the initial distribution process, will finally be transformed into the final utilization, namely the formation of the consumption fund and accumulation fund. This occurs after passing through the intricate redistribution channels by interweaving the inflow and outflow of foreign capital. The final utilization is equal in quantity to the initial input. The core of fund operation revolves around how the net income provided by the production sector can be transformed into the accumulation fund of the public institutions and the households as well as the investment fund of the production sector through the redistribution process. Consequently, after the adjustment of the revaluation, the new investment and the production conditions of the previous period will constitute the production conditions at the end of the period, so as to initiate a new circulation.

Several important components in Table 2.2 will be introduced in detail as follows:

The initial distribution formed in the production process (row 7-9), and the initial income source that constitutes the redistribution (column 7-9) and the initial income circulated in the redistribution channel will be turned into final expenditure through the regulatory gates established by the fiscal and credit sectors.

The relationship between income and expenditure in the foreign account is relatively a special case because it is designed by viewing Foreign Countries as the main body. Consequently, the domestic expenditure to any foreign country will be recorded as income, while the domestic income from a foreign country is recorded as an expenditure in this account.

The process of product flow and fund flow reflected in Table 2.2 is similar to the mechanism of blood circulation in a human body. Product flow constitutes the veins, fund flow constitutes the arteries, and the fiscal and financial redistribution constitutes the heart of this circulatory system. Under control of the heartbeats, products in the veins flow into the consumer and production market, which will then be converted into fund flow via the heart. The heart beats will accordingly drive the fund flow back to the arteries, which connect thousands of enterprises and households as the cells. The fund here will be transformed into product flows into the veins, to start a new round of circulation. At the same time, there is also a micro-circulation of the compensation process, which involves an exchange of products and funds. However, the fund circulation at this point does not go through the heart but circulate directly between businesses. The general term *extracorporeal circulation of fund* is in fact a kind of micro-circulation.

2.5 Balance and Imbalance of National Economic Circulation

The above description of the national economic circulation is based on the actual income and expenditure as the premise, which is an ante post description method. According to this method, the income and expenditure of each sector, and the national economy as a whole, are in balance, as such, no imbalance problem exists in this case. Accordingly, it is sure that the flow and stock variables as well as their relationship in the national economy are described and measured here from the perspective of national economic accounting.[3]

This book, however, deals with inflation, which is essentially the consequence of an imbalance circulation in the national economy. How do we find out the breakthrough leading to such an imbalance? This is the question to be explored later.

The time dimension of describing the problem should have to be altered from ex post to ex ante in order to discover the breakthrough. Only by commencing from an ex ante analysis can the many imbalance phenomena in the national economic circulation be discovered. These imbalance phenomena used to be disguised by increases in the price level and forced savings from the ex post perspective. Under such a circumstance, the imbalance disappeared, substituted by the sectoral balance of payments.

---

[3] Usually, when a bank's credit balance sheet is analyzed,only the fact that income equals expenditure, but not the size of over money supply, can be observed. The deficit on the balance sheet of finance can also be detected but its impact on over money supply will be disguised once such a deficit is absorbed by the balance sheet of the bank. The same is true for the financial and material balance. If the initial income distribution is regarded as the final outcome of the commodity, then it will also be in the same amount as the final utilization of the fund. Therefore, the method in this chapter provides the ins and outs of fund and product flow and their mutual transformation process, but does not provide the expansion process of the fund flow and the gap between fund and product.

To analyze the circulation of the national economy from the ex ante perspective is to analyze how many products can be produced and how much loans should be increased accordingly under the conditions of production, especially under the conditions of financial assets, at the end of the current year. The output level here reflects the potential supply and the increased loans represent the potential demand. The potential supply and demand are not necessarily balanced here because it is unreliable to calculate output levels and loan levels in this period according to the economic relations of the previous period. Further, it remains unknown whether there is a balance of funds and products in the previous period. On top of that, the economic relationship in the previous period (especially the fund relationship shown in Table 2.1) was not stable, which was quite different from the relative stability of the technical relationship between sectors. As a consequence, it is perfectly possible to obtain imbalance results in the implementation.

One of the research emphases of this book is to analyze the changing characteristics of economic relations between sectors and search for their inherent regularity. However, due to the influence of uncertain factors and the role of expectations, such inherent regularity is not extremely precise, and it can only be expressed as a trend.

Economic relations between sectors largely reflect on the inter-sectoral interest relations, that is to say, the relationship between human beings backdropped against the relationship between substances. It is a critical approach to analyze economic relations through analyzing the relationship between human beings, especially their interest relationships. For example, in the initial distribution, the interest relationship between households and enterprises is reflected in the proportion of household income and social net income. The process of transforming the initial income into the final utilization is also a process of interest conflict and coordination among households, enterprises and government sectors.

The ex post analysis is useful because it can precisely reflect the final outcome of these interest conflicts and their coordination—the economic relations between sectors—the intricate income and expenditure flows between sectors, and the flow and stock variables and their relationship. Nonetheless, the ex post analysis is also limited because it cannot mirror the cause and motivation of such interest conflicts, let alone the influence of uncertainty and expectation factors on the national economic circulation.

If the ex post analysis is equivalent to a physiological dissection, then the exante analysis will be similar to seeking the physiological mechanism. The analysis of the physiological mechanism is based on the physiological dissection. If the contents of this chapter are equivalent to anatomy, then the contents of the rest of this book will be corresponding to physiology, pathology, diagnostics, and pharmacology in the medical world.

The basic proposition for theoretical construction suggested in the introduction and the process of circulation of the national economy described with the ante post method form the primary foundation of this book. Later in this book, the formation of national income produced and its transformation into national income spent discussed in this chapter will be used as the fundamentals for the analysis of the functions of various interest mechanisms, expectation, and other factors during such transformation processes. How these functions lead to inflation will also be explored at the same time. Namely, given the real amount of national income produced (in constant prices), how the nominal value (in current prices) will be inflated with the expansion of the national income spent.

In fact, traditional economic theory has discussed the problem of excessive distribution of national income. It is precisely because of the discussion of this problem that economists pay attention to macroeconomic theory, so much that the traditional comprehensive balance theory of national economy is gradually transformed into pure macroeconomic theory. In practice, such a transformation also meets with the needs of the transition from the traditional planned economy to the planned commodity economy.

Excessive distribution of national income can only exist in value forms, not physical forms. No matter how it is distributed, the physical products will never change with the patterns of distribution. However, its nominal value can indeed change with the patterns of distribution. To be more precise, the amount of national income produced (which represents the physical form of the national income) calculated at the previous year's prices plus the value of net exports may not be equal to the amount of national income spent at current prices (which represents the value form of the national income). This gap between the two will be reflected as the excessive distribution of national income. The gap is bridged by changes in the nominal value of national income produced, that is, the difference between the national income produced in current prices plus the value of net exports must equal the national income spent in current prices.

It is clear that the problem of excessive distribution of national income can only be discussed within the scope of national economic accounting. Since the excessive distribution of national income only reflects the price gap, not the shortage gap, the latter cannot be measured with the national economic accounting system, and thus cannot be analyzed. Therefore, the introduction of the concept of aggregate supply and aggregate demand will carry theoretical and practical significance. Within the theoretical framework of aggregate supply and aggregate demand, it is possible to measure and analyze the price gap and shortage gap simultaneously.

In conclusion, the theoretical task of this book is not only to analyze the problem of excessive distribution of national income, but also to analyze the shortage problem beyond the scope of excessive distribution of national income. This book will integrate these two problems in the gap between the aggregate demand and aggregate supply to solve them within a unified logical framework.

Chapter 3
Basic Concepts of Aggregate Supply and Aggregate Demand

A few years ago, Chinese economics began to use aggregate supply and aggregate demand to replace the traditional analysis of national income produced and national income spent, which is an in-depth development of the macroeconomic theory. At present, these two concepts are more frequently utilized in China, but meanwhile they are causing more chaos. It seems that the current domestic economic theory circles only accepted these two terminologies nominally but not the original definition of them. Because of disagreements on understanding these two concepts, confusion arose in practice, leading to some meaningless arguments.

This book regards inflation as the intersection of the theory of aggregate supply and aggregate demand.It naturally becomes the first task to define these two aggregate, and how to define them also becomes the first problem encountered in the course of theoretical analysis. Since the aggregate supply and aggregate demand model was introduced from Western economics, it is certain that the most convenient approach is to follow their original definitions. This approach is conducive to the exchange of Chinese economic theory with the rest of the world and the integration of Chinese economic theory into the development trend of contemporary international economic theory. There is no need to redefine these two concepts, so that more analytical efforts can be directed to the methodology of theoretical research, the ability of theory to describe reality, and the structure of theory per se. Promoting the development of theory is better than being tangled in disputes over definitions of terminologies.[1]

[1] Introducing definitions from Western economics is different from introducing Western economic theory. Generally speaking, definitions are more universally applicable to different sets of theories. This is obvious in the natural sciences. It must be applicable to the study of economic theory.

L. Li, *The Inflation Mechanism and Expectations*, Understanding China,
https://doi.org/10.1007/978-981-97-2570-0_3

3.1 Walras's Definition of Aggregate Supply and Aggregate Demand

Walras defined aggregate supply and aggregate demand through aggregating the supply and demand of n individual markets. Here, a simple example will be employed to illustrate Walras's concept of aggregate supply and aggregate demand as well as the related Walras's Law.

The simplest general equilibrium economic system is a pure exchange economic system. In such an economic system, all economic actors possess some commodities (called economic goods) for consumption or exchange at the beginning, which can be defined as the initial endowment. It is further assumed that no production activity exists in the economic system, and economic actors only consume and exchange.

Each consumer h initially possesses economic goods in an amount of $\overline{x}^k$, which is an n dimensional vector of economic goods. The consumer faces the price vector P. Under the following budget constraints

$$P'x^k = P'\overline{x}^k \tag{3.1}$$

The consumer will choose a consumption vector x^k to maximize the utility function. It is assumed here that all income of the consumer will be spent on consumption with no accumulation. In this identity, $P'x^k$ represents the total consumption of consumer h, and $P'x^k$ represents the total income of consumer h.

In this pure exchange economic system, all consumer budget constraints are added up to obtain

$$\sum_h P'x^k = P'\overline{x}^k \tag{3.2}$$

In equation (3.2), the term on the left represents the aggregate demand, while the term on the right represents the aggregate supply in the economic system. Clearly, there exists the following laws in this economic system:

Walras's Law is aggregate demand must equal aggregate supply in any price system. It is a very profound economic law, even in a more complex general equilibrium economy. Thus, some fundamental propositions concerned with the general equilibrium theory will be introduced on the basis of this law. These fundamental propositions have become the basic principles in modern economic theory or constituted the basic controversial arguments.

1. The principle of rigid budget constraint. Total income must equal aggregate expenditure in any economic system. This principle provides the basic framework for a subsequent economic analysis and constitutes the basic principle for the theory of national economic accounting. However, it remains controversial for individual economic actors. Though the general equilibrium theory confirms its validity for individual economic actors, it is invalidated in disequilibrium theory.

For example, enterprises as producers in socialist economies are no longer subject to this principle since they face softness of budget constraint. This proposition is deeply analyzed by János Kornai in his book *Economics of Shortage*, which is not covered here.

2. The principle of price mechanism. In a typical market system, the price of a commodity is the function of the gap between the quantity supplied and quantity demanded. When quantity supplied exceeds quantity demanded, the price falls and vice versa. When quantity supplied equals quantity demanded, price remains unchanged. It is called the equilibrium price.

In the general equilibrium theory, although aggregate supply is equal to aggregate demand under any set of prices, such set of prices cannot guarantee that the quantity supplied of each commodity is equal to the quantity demanded. Only the equilibrium price can ensure the equivalence of the two.

In disequilibrium theory, price is no longer a function of the gap between quantity supplied and quantity demanded because price is determined by external conditions, which are exogenous variables, or called the price rigidity. The typical market disequilibrium theory is to study the economic performance process under the condition of price rigidity.

3. The principle of consumer behavior. This principle is expressed as how the consumer maximizes one's utility function under the budget constraints.

This principle is universally consent with various economic theories.

4. The principle of producer behavior. This principle is expressed as how the producer maximizes one's profit function under cost constraints. The earliest disequilibrium theory first challenged this principle, arguing that the producer may not necessarily pursue profit maximization when considering costs and adjusting expenses. This constituted the cost adjustment model in the early disequilibrium theory. Disequilibrium theory developed in the later days focuses on the two problems of price rigidity and the softness of budget constraints.

Walras's theoretical system possesses three functions, namely, descriptive, explanatory and evaluative. The system describes economic activities as a set of equations. In Walras's theory, three basic elements such as price, supply, and demand are measurable or calculable. Walras explained the performance process of the market economy under the assumptions of the above basic principles. The typical general equilibrium theory will not directly propose on how the economic process should performance. However, in fact, the theory explains that resources can be optimally allocated in an equilibrated market economy. Therefore, maintaining an equilibrium situation becomes the value orientation in practice guided by theory.

Although the assumptions of Walras are different from real economic life, the contribution of this theoretical system to the axiomatization of theoretical development should not be underestimated. On the basis of this theory, economists in the later days have constructed the most rigorous deductive system in economics, which is a magnificent milestone from experience to science.

One of the striking weaknesses of Walras's system is that it is based on the barter system. So far, economists have not yet succeeded in dragging money into this system. It is hence difficult to discuss inflation in a theoretical system. However, money has been successfully integrated into the macroeconomic model based on Walras's general equilibrium theory. The *IS-LM* model is an example in this regard. Therefore, Walras's theory system is still of theoretical significance to the study of inflation. Especially the general equilibrium theory has become the theoretical foundation for the modern Keynesian school of economics, the monetarism, the rational expectations and the supply-side school. These theories can be collectively called the equilibrium theory, which constitutes the mainstream economic school in the modern Western world. Disequilibrium theory exists symmetrically with the equilibrium theory.

3.2 Keynes's Definition of Aggregate Supply and Aggregate Demand

If Walras's definition of aggregate supply and aggregate demand is considered a classical definition, then Keynes's definition will be viewed as a modern definition. The fundamental difference between the two is that Keynes integrated the factor of expectations into the definition of aggregate supply and aggregate demand. Take a look at Keynes's original words about the definition of aggregate supply and aggregate demand. In the third chapter of the *General Theory of Employment Interest and Money*, Keynes pointed out, "the aggregate supply price of the output of a given amount of employment is the expectation of proceeds which will just make it worth the while of the entrepreneurs to give that employment."[2] "Let Z be the aggregate supply price of the output from employing N men, the relationship between Z and N being written $Z = \Phi(N)$, which can be called the *aggregate supply function*. Similarly, let D be the proceeds which entrepreneurs expect to receive from the employment of N men, the relationship between D and N being written $D = f(N)$, which can be called the *aggregate demand function*."[2] "The value of D at the point of the aggregate demand function, where it is intersected by the aggregate supply function, will be called *the effective demand*. Since this is then the substance of the General Theory of Employment …".[2]

The definitions of aggregate supply and aggregate demand used in the modern macroeconomic theory are usually based on Keynesian definitions that include expectations.

The Keynesian economic theory takes the market economy as the premise and serves the capitalist economic system. Therefore, it is not feasible to attempt to copy Keynesian economic theory to solve China's current economic problems. However, it is meaningful for Keynes to integrate a factor of expectations into the definitions of aggregate supply and aggregate demand and set it as the fundamental for macroeconomic analysis. This should not be rejected. Since terminologies of aggregate supply and aggregate demand have been introduced in China, it is only natural to import the

---

[2] See reference I [37], pages 24–26.

modern definitions of both at the same time. Otherwise, what is the significance of introducing these two terminologies?

After the integration of the factor of expectations, aggregate supply and aggregate demand are no longer necessarily equal in the Keynesian theoretical system, but may not be equal.[3] Keynes attributed inadequate effective demand to a psychological propensity to consume, a psychological preference for flexibility, and a psychological expectation of future returns on assets. The psychological propensity to consume causes the consumption growth to lag behind the income growth, thus leading to insufficient consumption demand. The other two psychological factors tend to lower the expected profit rates and be out of line with the interest rate, thus resulting in insufficient investment demand. More broadly, savings and desired investments are unequal, generating a disequilibrium situation in the economic system. To maintain the economic equilibrium, the government should take responsibility for investment and implement a range of macroeconomic policy measures to raise investment expectations of entrepreneurs and stimulate household consumptions.

In the beginning, it was believed the key point of the Keynesian revolution was that investments did not equal savings. Since both Say's Law and Walras's Law hold that supply creates its own demand, savings and investments must be equal. It took a great deal of courage for Keynes to overturn this dogma. From today's point of view, it is probably fair to attribute the Keynesian revolution to the prominent position he gave to uncertainty and expectations in economic analysis. However, "despite the leading role given to expectations in his work, Keynes did not really address the question of how expectations are formed. Moreover, since his treatment was theoretical and discursive rather than analytical and empirical, his notion of expectations was a long way from an operational concept."[4]

Different interpretations of Keynesian theory have resulted in two different Keynesian schools in Cambridge Massachusetts and Cambridge British.The former is based on the equilibrium theory, while the latter tends to be in favor of disequilibrium theory.

3.3 Definitions of Aggregate Supply and Aggregate Demand in National Economic Accounting

The aggregate supply and aggregate demand defined by Walras and Keynes are both from the perspective of theoretical analysis. However, there is another definition of aggregate supply and aggregate demand from the perspective of accounting, which imitates Keynes's definition in format, but in essence, it is defined according to the fundamental principles of national economic accounting.

---

[3] Expectation is not the decisive factor that leads to the inequality between ex ante aggregate supply and aggregate demand and ex post aggregate supply and aggregate demand. Such inequality is caused by other factors such as price rigidity, which will also be discussed later.

[4] Refer to the original English text of reference I [41].

The fundamental principle of national economic accounting is that income must be matched by expenditure. For a country, aggregate income must equal aggregate expenditure. These are the Law of Nodes and Networks analyzed earlier. According to this basic principle, the aggregate supply defined from the perspective of national accounting must be equal to the aggregate demand. In accordance with this definition, aggregate demand and aggregate supply can be expressed as

$$\text{Aggregate Demand} = \text{Consumption} + \text{Investment} + \text{Exports}$$
$$\text{Aggregate Supply} = \text{Consumption} + \text{Savings} + \text{Imports}$$

Since aggregate demand equals aggregate supply, there is

$$\text{Investments} - \text{Savings} = \text{Imports} - \text{Exports}$$

It is the Dual-Gap model. When investments surpass savings, imports must be greater than exports. When investments run lower than savings, imports must be less than exports.

It should be noted that in Table 2.1 of Chapter 2, the aggregate demand equals the final expenditure, and the aggregate supply equals initial inputs, where the final expenditure equals the initial inputs.

The object of the national economic accounting system must be the facts that already occurred. Therefore, consumption, investment, savings, imports, and exports are all the results of economic activities that occurred. Consequently, the aggregate supply and aggregate demand are also the results of economic activities accomplished. The concise value of such aggregate supply and aggregate demand can be computed by ordinary statistical methods, which is similar to measuring national income and gross national product. In fact, for a closed economic system, the following equation holds

$$\text{Gross National Product(or National Income)} = \text{Aggregate Demand} = \text{Aggregate Supply}$$

For an open economic system, there is

$$\text{Gross National Product(or National Income)} + \text{Net Exports} = \text{Aggregate Demand} = \text{Aggregate Supply}$$

Western macroeconomic textbooks generally contain particular chapters to introduce the national economic accounting system, and explain the definition of aggregate supply and aggregate demand from this perspective. However, prior to the formal theoretical analysis, they all return to Keynes's definition of ex ante aggregate supply and aggregate demand so as to introduce the aggregate demand function and the aggregate supply function. The previous chapter has introduced some basic knowledge of the national economic accounting, which will be the foundation for further analysis relying on the ex ante method.

At present, the domestic discussion on the statistical dimension of aggregate supply and aggregate demand indicators is in fact an attempt to adopt the ex post statistical accounting method to calculate ex ante aggregate supply and aggregate demand defined by Keynes. This discussion helps us to understand the basic two concepts, but no concrete calculation method has yet been improved. There has not yet been any effective method available to calculate ex ante aggregate supply and aggregate demand directly from the ex post statistical results. A fundamental difficulty here is how to calculate the forced savings, which is closely related to expectations and hard to measure directly.

Although ex post aggregate supply and aggregate demand defined from the perspective of national accounting can be computed, it contains not much analytical significance theoretically. This is not the kind of ex ante aggregate supply and aggregate demand indicators anticipated by economists. This point has been already explained in the previous chapter.

3.4 Differentiations Among Three Definitions of Aggregate Supply and Aggregate Demand

Differences among these three definitions of aggregate supply and aggregate demand can be observed from the above definitions. Following will be further discussions on that

1. The difference between ex ante and ex post. Walras's definitions of aggregate supply and aggregate demand, which ignore the time dimension, are instantaneous and can be called aggregate supply and aggregate demand in the event. Aggregate supply and aggregate demand in Keynes's eyes have not yet occurred, or are desired, which can be called ex ante aggregate supply and aggregate demand. The definitions given by the national economic accounting are ex post, since aggregate supply and aggregate demand have already taken place. Thus, these three definitions are fundamentally differed by the time dimension they adopted.
2. The difference between specific numerical values and the functional forms. Aggregate supply and aggregate demand defined by the national economic accounting, namely ex post aggregate supply and aggregate demand, is with a basic expression in specific statistical data while the basic expression of ex ante and in the event aggregate supply and aggregate demand and are both in the functional forms. Only when the parameters and external variable values of the function are given can the two function values of aggregate supply and aggregate demand be calculated. Therefore, the key to calculate ex ante and in the event aggregate supply and aggregate demand is not to determine the statistical caliber, but to determine the function form, to estimate the parameters of the function and to select the variables of the function.

3. The difference between equivalence and nonequivalence. Under whatever price level, aggregate supply must equal aggregate demand for both ex post and in the event aggregate supply aggregate and aggregate demand. However, this may not necessarily be applicable to ex ante aggregate supply and demand. Generally speaking, there will only be a single consequence from the three potential relationships between aggregate supply and aggregate demand, namely, aggregate supply being greater than, less than, or equal to aggregate demand. Just because of this, only aggregate supply and aggregate demand possesses general significance in theoretical analysis. Comparatively speaking, since aggregate supply must be equal to aggregate demand for in the event and ex post aggregate supply and aggregate demand, they bear less theoretical significance. Therefore, the nature of ex ante aggregate demand and supply will be of particular significance to disequilibrium theory. In the equilibrium theory, price is perfectly elastic and extremely sensitive to the gap between ex ante supply and demand, which can be instantly adjusted along with the change of price. Moreover, the market can only transact when the gap is fully adjusted. As a result, price for both supply and demand ex ante and ex post will tend to converge on the equilibrium price, which forms the foundation of the equilibrium theory. On the contrary, with price rigidity, the gap cannot be adjusted instantly as in disequilibrium theory, and market transaction can only be completed under the disequilibrium price. Consequently, ex ante may be inconsistent with ex post in aggregate supply and aggregate demand. Thus, the measurement of aggregate demand and aggregate supply would be problematic and consequently shock the foundation of traditional equilibrium theory.

3.5 Potential Aggregate Supply

The potential aggregate supply is also a concept frequently used in macroeconomic theoretical analysis, which reflects the "average" production capacity of the economy and society from the quantitative perspective and reflects the normal production capacity determined by the technical condition of the economic society from the qualitative perspective. Western economic theory usually defines a potential aggregate supply as the output level produced on the basis of potential employment levels and current capital stock. It can be expressed in a production function as follows:

$$Y = f(L, K)$$

This function shows that the output level Y of the economy depends on the employment level L and capital K. If L^* is the potential employment level, the potential quantity of aggregate supply will be

$$Y^* = f\left(L^*, K\right)$$

Western economic theory defines potential employment level as the number of jobs that the entire population would choose under various existing incentives. It means that if everyone can find a job at prevailing real wage rate, then the total amount of jobs equals the level of potential employment. Nonetheless, the real employment level can be higher, equal to, or lower than potential employment.

It can be inferred from the above analysis that the concept of potential employment is used in Western economic theories to reflect the "average" production capacity of an economy, which should not be blindly copied in China. For a long time, China has implemented the policy of low wages and high employment, and has customarily defined those who are temporarily unable to work as laid-off. In fact, this kind of laid-off terminology can also be interpreted as temporary unemployment. Currently, a new terminology "on-the-job unemployment" has been adopted in China's economic theory circles to explain a situation that the workload declined due to insufficient productive capacity without firing employees in enterprise firms. Thus, potential employment cannot be employed to define the "average" productive capacity in an economy, which may possibly be substituted by the concept of "on-the-job unemployment". However, "on-the-job unemployment" is not measurable directly in practice, which causes inconvenience. Relatively speaking, the operating (utilization) rate of fixed assets is easier to measure, and it can also reflect the situation of "on-the-job unemployment" (under the current economic system in China). If the operating rate of a fixed asset matching with its normal design capacity is regarded as the potential operational rate, then there will be

$$Y^* = f\left(L, K^*\right)$$

where, Y^* is the potential aggregate supply; K^* is the potential operating rate.

The problem now becomes how to aggregate the potential operating rates of different machines and plants? This is a very complicated job without any ready-made statistical indicators to refer at present. Furthermore, understanding of normal design capability remains problematic. Some new processes and equipment, in accordance with the prevailing domestic technical conditions, are still unable to reach its technical design capacity. However, this should not be interpreted as underproduction under the circumstance of "on-the-job unemployment".

A simple way to approximate the potential aggregate supply is to conduct a regression (regression over time) analysis on ex post aggregate supply over the sample period, defining the regression line as the potential aggregate supply.[5] This is shown in Fig. 3.1.

The solid curve in Fig. 3.1 is ex post aggregate supply, and the broken line represents the regression line, which is the potential aggregate supply for each corresponding year. However, the following points should be noted when this method is adopted: (1) when the sample period expands or shrinks, the parameters of the regression line will change correspondingly, followed by the change in the annual regression

[5] The learning function of economic man mentioned above provides a theoretical basis for explaining this method.

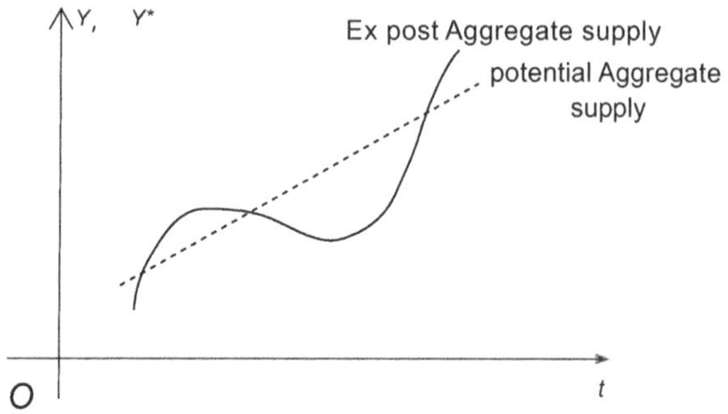

Fig. 3.1 Potential aggregate supply

value. (2) When the economy is overheating for a long period, the potential aggregate supply obtained from the regression line will be higher than the real potential aggregate supply. This is especially important for a country like China. The common solution to both problems is to use as large a sample period as possible, which will help alleviate these problems, though not possible to solve them fundamentally. Despite these problems, the potential aggregate supply defined on the regression line can be approximately corresponding to the potential aggregate supply defined by the on-the-job unemployment or operating rate, of fixed assets.

It is very convenient to use potential aggregate supply in the long-run analysis. It shows that in the long-run of economic change, aggregate supply depends on two critical variables, namely labor force and fixed assets as well as the social economic and technical conditions. This simplifies the analysis of the problem. Therefore, in the long-run analysis, potential aggregate supply can also be directly defined as

$$\overline{Y} = f(L, K)$$

It means that potential aggregate supply Y is the regression of ex post aggregate supply Y with respect to L and K. The following two expressions are thus established

$$L^* = \frac{\overline{Y}}{L}, \ K^* = \frac{\overline{Y}}{K}$$

where, L^* can be regarded as the potential employment level defined above; K^* is the potential operating rate.

The potential aggregate supply obtained by linear regression of ex post aggregate supply with respect to time t is quantitatively different from that obtained by regression of ex post aggregate supply with respect to L and K, but it is essentially the same in reflecting the "average" production capacity in the economy.

In this book, the concept of potential aggregate supply can be generally understood as the "average" productive capacity of an economy. The particular measurement must be disclosed when a quantitative analysis is conducted, that is, whether to use ex post aggregate supply as a regression over time, or over L and K.

A concept worth analyzing is the socio-economic and technological conditions involved in the definition of potential aggregate supply, which refer to not only natural science and technological conditions, but also the management level, institutional and policy environment, and so forth. This was evident after the promotion of the new household contract responsibility system in rural areas after 1978 because output increased significantly without substantial expansion in inputs. In this book, socio-economic and technological conditions are treated as external conditions, which will not be analyzed in particular. However, it does not mean that they are not important. Specialized books may be required to study these issues.

3.6 Measurement of Aggregate Supply and Aggregate Demand

It is not difficult to measure and ex post aggregate demand. It can be done through the prevailing gross national product (GNP) and the value of imports and exports (This is applicable to the dual gap model only. If the triple gap model is involved, the volume of inflow and outflow of capital must be considered, the gap between them is viewed as the third gap). Presently, Walras's general equilibrium theory is still in its theoretical stage, so it is not necessary to directly measure its aggregate supply and aggregate demand. On the contrary, aggregate supply and aggregate demand defined by Keynes are common concepts in modern economic theory, which is concerned with an issue of measurement because it attempts to study the operational process of economy through the descriptive methodology. That is to say, the methodology of variable analysis in modern economic theory is emphasized in the study of the quantitative relations of various variables in the operational process of the economy. In order to do that, these variables are firstly required to be measurable. Otherwise, no quantitative relationship between these variables can be explored. The problem herein is that Keynes's definitions are all related to expectations, an unmeasurable psychological factor imposing difficulties on the measurement of aggregate supply and aggregate demand. It therefore becomes significant to take a look at how Western economists are solving this problem.

The methodology of the Keynesian school tries to integrate Keynesian theory into the equilibrium framework of Walras. Since the aggregate supply equals the aggregate demand, the potential aggregate supply as well as equals the ex post aggregate supply when the economic system reaches equilibrium, they are hence all measurable.

Let's start with a simple Keynesian model.

1. The equilibrium conditions in the product market.

$$S(Y) = I(r)$$

where, $S(Y)$ is the savings function determined by income Y. $I(r)$ is the investment function determined by the interest rate r, which essentially means that equilibrium will be achieved when the aggregate demand level, namely the sum of the consumption expenditure as an income function and the investment expenditure as an interest rate function, is precisely adequate to purchase the current output level. This can also be explicitly expressed as $Y = C(Y) + I(r)$.

2. The equilibrium conditions in the money market.

$$\overline{M} = kPY + L(r)$$

where, M is the current quantity of money supply; P is the price level; k is the coefficient and kPY is the quantity of money to meet the demand for transactions and contingency; $L(r)$ is the demand for speculative balance determined by the interest rate.

3. The equilibrium conditions in the labor market.

$$N^S\left(\frac{W}{P}\right) = N^D\left(\frac{W}{P}\right)$$

where, $N^S(W/P)$ stands for the supply of labor, which is a function of real wage W/P; $N^D(W/P)$ is the demand for labor, also a function of real wage W/P.

4. The production function.

$$Y = Y(N, K)$$

where, N represents the number of labors; K is the fixed assets.

A simple Keynesian model can be derived from the four equations aforementioned. Income Y, consumption C, investment I, savings S, and interest rate r are simultaneously determined by the equilibrium in both the product and money markets. This decision process can be illustrated by the *IS-LM* diagram.

Let's take a look firstly at $S(Y) = I(r)$. In this equation, Y and r are both independent variables, and dependent variable S equals dependent variable I. Y lies on the horizontal axis and r on the vertical axis, I as the inverse of Y, and S as the inverse of r. A 45° line is drawn between I and S as shown in Fig. 3.2.

In Fig. 3.2, the *IS* curve is derived as per $I(r) = S(Y)$ by corresponding different r to different Y. Specifically, it can be expressed as I_1 is obtained from the $I(r)$ curve corresponding to r_1, S_1 from the corresponding 45° line (that is, $I(r) = S(Y)$), and Y_1 from the $S(Y)$ corresponding to S_1. The point inside the coordinate rY is determined by R_1 and Y_1. Similarly, Y_2 can be obtained from r_2.

Now, Let's look at $\overline{M} = kPY + L(r)$. The unknown variables are still Y and r, which are viewed as the horizontal and vertical axis respectively. Draw a coordinate in the opposite direction of the Y axis, where the money supply M is indicated. Then draw a coordinate in the opposite direction of the r axis and plot a 45° line in the coordinate in the reverse direction of Y and r represented by AB, where A coincides with M as shown in Fig. 3.3.

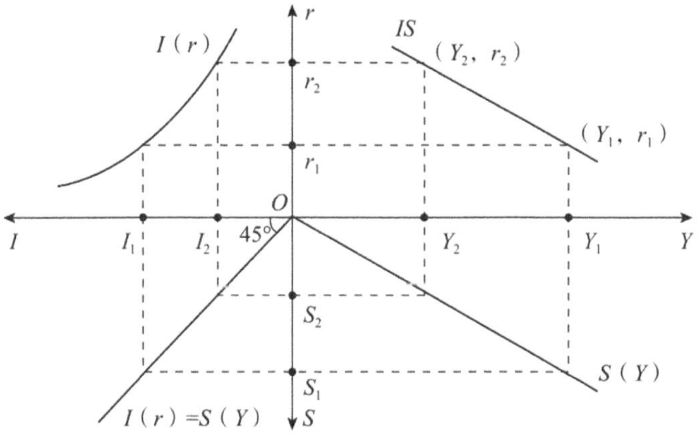

Fig. 3.2 The IS curve

Fig. 3.3 The *LM* curve

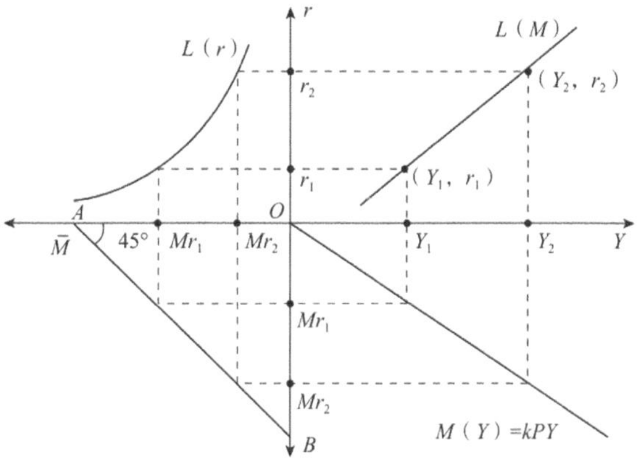

In Fig. 3.3, Mr_1 is obtained when r_1 corresponds to L (r). The difference between $\overline{M}$ and Mr_1 (i.e. the line segment from M to Mr_1) represents the money demand corresponding to the kPY [since $kPY = \overline{M} - L(r)$, then $\overline{M} = kPY + L(r)$]. Through the 45° line, AB corresponds to MY_1, MY_1 corresponds to Y_1 through kPY, so a point (Y_1, R_1) is obtained on the Yr quadrant. Similarly, Y_2 can be achieved from r_2. The *LM* curve will therefore be derived by connecting these points.

The *IS* curve represents the equilibrium conditions of the product market, while the *LM* curve represents the equilibrium conditions of the money market. Consequently, the intersection of the *IS* curve and *LM* curve will indicate the common equilibrium conditions of both the product and money markets. This can be illustrated in Fig. 3.4.

When both the money and product markets reach a common equilibrium condition, point (r; Y) will be accordingly determined, where Y represents the output level and r the interest rate. From the output level Y and the known amount of fixed assets, employment level N can be identified by the inverse function of $Y = Y$ (N, K). If

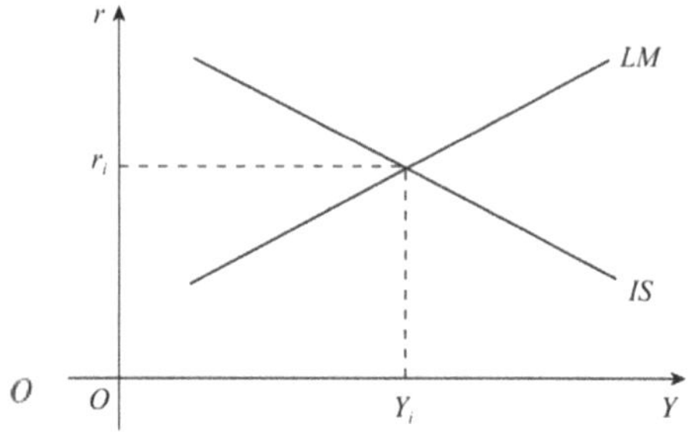

Fig. 3.4 Simultaneous Equilibrium of the Product and Money Markets

this employment level is exactly the equilibrium point in the labor market, then all the three markets reach equilibrium simultaneously. Nonetheless, the equilibrium employment in the labor market is determined by the real wage level *W/P*, where *W* is the nominal wage and *P* the price level. If the current employment level is the equilibrium point, the price level can be consequently derived simply by taking the fixed money wages in history as a constant.

The simultaneous equilibrium conditions for all three markets are shown in Fig. 3.5. In the Keynesian model, the employment level *N* determined by the simultaneous equilibrium of both the money and product markets is not necessarily the equilibrium point of employment in the labor market. So unemployment may also incur under such a circumstance.

The *IS*-*LM* model represents a relatively simple deductive theory system in modern economic theory. All variables in this model are measurable or computable. However, it should be noted that these variables could be measured only when the model is at its equilibrium. Its disequilibrium will make these measurements impossible and thus invalidate the basis of any theoretical analysis.

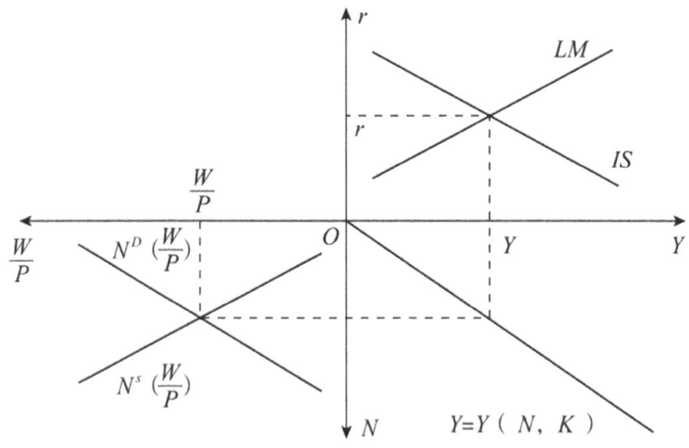

Fig. 3.5 Equilibrium in Three Markets

The *IS-LM* model relies on the assumption that prices are perfectly elastic. In the labor market, disequilibrium (unemployment) arises from rigidity of the wage rate. From this perspective, the Keynesian economic theory is not a general theory but a special variant of classical economic theory. The critical influences of uncertainty on the economic system proposed by Keynes have been filtered out by the assumptions of the Keynesian theory itself.

Equilibrium can only be treated as a theoretical abstraction in a market economy since there exists only disequilibrium not equilibrium in real life. As a result, the general equilibrium theoretical model can only be employed to describe approximately the disequilibrium situation through the equilibrium mode. The measurement problem must be solved preferentially in the case that the disequilibrium situation is taken as the descriptive object of the model because no other problem can be tackled unless such a measurement problem is settled.

The disequilibrium phenomenon is more obvious in the traditional socialist economy than in the market economy, so a direct adaptation of the equilibrium structure becomes inapplicable. Consequently, it becomes a critical theoretical task to explore the measurement approach of the aggregate supply and aggregate demand under the disequilibrium situation.

The general disequilibrium model is as follows

$$D = B_1'X_1 + u_1,\ u_1 \sim N\left(0, \sigma_1^2\right).$$

$$S = B_2'X_2 + u_2,\ u_2 \sim N\left(0, \sigma_2^2\right).$$

$$Q = \min(D, S)$$

where, B_1 and B_2 are undetermined parameter vectors; X_1 and X_2 are variable vectors; u_1 and u_2 are random error terms. Q is the market transaction volume; D is the demand and S is the supply; Q is determined by the smaller side of D and S. Q is measurable here but not D and S, which would possibly be indirectly measured through Q on the basis of the disequilibrium method.

In 1974, Maddala and Nelson invented the classical estimation method of this disequilibrium model (called *M-N* algorithm),thus solving the measurement problem of D and S under disequilibrium conditions.[6] So the *M-N* algorithm has been viewed as the most important milestone in the history of disequilibrium theory by the school of disequilibrium economics. The foundation of the entire disequilibrium theory could not be established without this paper. It can also be seen here how great of importance Western economic theories have attached to the measurability of economic variables because the significance of theoretical research may be substantially minimized or even become meaningless with the lack of such an attribute. In this perspective, Western economic theory did inherit the tradition of Galileo and strive to approach the natural science research methodology.

[6] See reference I [21].

3.7 Excess Aggregate Demand

Aggregate supply equals aggregate demand under equilibrium so the gap between the two is eliminated. This is however not applicable in a disequilibrium situation. Based on equilibrium, no gap exists in the Keynesian *IS-LM* model. However, it is also obvious in this model that the simultaneous equilibrium in the product and money market does not guarantee the equilibrium of the labor market. Thus, it becomes meaningful to study the gap between aggregate supply and aggregate demand only when the problem is studied on the basis of disequilibrium. Usually, the gap between aggregate demand and aggregate supply is defined as an excess aggregate demand (in this book,it is generally assumed that its value is greater than zero.Of course, there are also cases of less than or equal to zero), and its expression is

$$\text{Excess Aggregate Demand} = \text{Aggregate demand} - \text{Aggregate supply}$$

The concept of excess aggregate demand already exists in Walras's general equilibrium theory, where it equals zero at any given set of prices.

In modern economic theory, excess aggregate demand can exist in two forms: one is ex ante, which is shown as the gap between ex ante aggregate demand and aggregate supply; the other is ex post, which manifests itself in increased prices and forced savings.

In a typical market economy, excess aggregate demand is fully translated into price rises in the absence of price controls. However, in a typical planned economy, prices are not determined by the forces of supply and demand, so excess aggregate demand is translated entirely into forced savings. In an economy between these two extremes, excess aggregate demand will be translated into a rise in prices and forced savings.

Inflation, as defined in this book, is essentially excess aggregate demand. As a result, in studying inflation, we should stay not only the increase in the price level, but also forced savings or shortages. Since it is the sum of the price level gap and shortage gap, excess aggregate demand can be regarded as the double gap model of inflation, namely

$$\text{Inflation} = \text{Price Level Gap} + \text{Shortage Gap}$$

Excess aggregate demand, namely inflation, will be determined accordingly given ex ante aggregate supply and ex ante aggregate demand.

At this point, there will be a tradeoff between the price level gap and shortage gap, that is, the shortage gap will shrink corresponding to an escalating price level gap and vice versa. Such a tradeoff is precisely the core research of this book. Therefore, the main body of this book can be divided into two layers. The first layer will deal with the research on what variables determine both the aggregate demand function and the aggregate supply function, as well as what values of these variables generate the excess aggregate demand. In the second layer, what variables determine the price rise and the shortage will be explored given a positive value of the excess aggregate demand.

In a static sense, the economic system is still in its equilibrium if the inflation gap is exactly equal to the price level gap. The gap between ex ante aggregate demand and ex post aggregate supply is bridged by adjustment of the price level. The economic disequilibrium appears only when part or the entire inflation gap becomes the shortage gap. In view of the real economic context in China, its inflation problem will be analyzed by the disequilibrium analysis method.

3.8 Latest Developments of Conceptual Research on Supply and Demand

The theory of disequilibrium expands the scope of the definition of supply and demand, and economists begin to consider deeper connotations in these concepts. The new knowledge about supply and demand also plays an important role in the construction of inflation theory in this book. The new research progress in this respect will be introduced as follows.

Assume three kinds of products exist in the economic system: consumer goods X_1, labor supply X_2 and the real money balance X_M ($X_M = M/P_1$), where M is the money balance; P_1 is the prices of consumer goods; T is the total labor force available. The consumer utility function is then

$$U = X_1^{\alpha}(T - X_2)^{\beta} X_M^{\gamma}$$

The consumer budget constraint is

$$P_1 X_1 + M = P_2 X_2 + \overline{M}$$

where, P_1 is the price of X_1; P_2 is the price of X_2; $\overline{M}$ is the money held by the consumer at the beginning of the period (the beginning of the transaction); M is the balanced amount with the consumer after the transaction (the end of the transaction).

For the sake of discussion and without loss of generality, the budget constraint can be simplified as

$$P_2 X_2 = P_1 X_M + P_1 X_1$$

Assuming the initial money held by the consumer is set as zero, that is, $\overline{M} = 0$, and since $X_M = M/P_1$, therefore $P_1 X_M = M$.

Under these simplified budget constraints, the Walrasian demand function for consumer goods, the labor supply function and the money balance function can be obtained by maximizing the utility function. These methods are shown as follows

The Lagrangian function is

$$\overline{U} = X_1^{\alpha}(T - X_2)^{\beta} X_M^{\gamma} + \lambda(P_2 X_2 - P_1 X_M - P_1 X_1)$$

The first-order partial derivatives of this function are

$$\frac{\partial \overline{U}}{\partial X_2} = -\beta X_1^{\alpha}(T - X_2)^{\beta - 1} X_M^{\gamma} + \lambda P_2 = 0$$

$$\frac{\partial \overline{U}}{\partial X_1} = \alpha X_1^{\alpha - 1}(T - X_2)^{\beta} X_M^{\gamma} - \lambda P_1 = 0$$

Therefore

$$\widetilde{X_1} = \frac{\alpha P_2 T}{P_1(\alpha + \beta + \gamma)}$$
$$\widetilde{X_2} = \frac{(\alpha + \gamma)T}{(\alpha + \beta + \gamma)}$$
$$\widetilde{X_M} = \frac{\gamma P_2 T}{P_1(\alpha + \beta + \gamma)}$$

Above are the three Walrasian functions constructed in accordance with the assumptions of the general equilibrium theory. Under assumptions of disequilibrium theory, the consumer's labor supply is constrained by rationing, there will be $\overline{X}_2 < \tilde{X}_2$ (it can be interpreted as that the labor X_2 the consumer sells in the labor market now is a given number, which is smaller than the desired labor supply X_2 under the current price), as a result, the utility function is now becoming

$$U = X_1^{\alpha}\left(T - \overline{X_2}\right)^{\beta} X_M^{\gamma}$$

The budget constraint is

$$P_2 \overline{X}_2 = P_1 X_M + P_1 X_1$$

The Lagrangian function becomes

$$\overline{U} = X_1^{\alpha}\left(T - \overline{X}_2\right)^{\beta} X_M^{\gamma} + \lambda\left(P_2 \overline{X}_2 - P_1 X_M - P_1 X_1\right)$$

Therefore

$$\frac{\partial \overline{U}}{\partial X_1} = \alpha X_1^{\alpha - 1}\left(T - \overline{X}_2\right)^{\beta} X_M^{\gamma} - \lambda P_1 = 0$$

$$\frac{\partial \overline{U}}{\partial X_M} = \gamma X_1^{\alpha}\left(T - \overline{X}_2\right)^{\beta} X_M^{\gamma - 1} - \lambda P_1 = 0$$

And

$$X_1^e = \frac{P_2\overline{X}_2\alpha}{P_1(\alpha+\gamma)}$$
$$X_M^e = \frac{P_2\overline{X}_2\gamma}{P_1(\alpha+\gamma)}$$

where, X_1^e is defined as the effective demand for consumption goods X_1; $X_{M.}$ is defined as the effective demand for $X_{M.}$

The effective demand defined according to disequilibrium theory here is not the same as the definition of Keynes. According to disequilibrium theory, a product with rationing constraint will influence demand for another product, so that market demand for the latter will deviate from the original quantity demanded in the Walrasian market. It's not hard to prove that X_1^e will be smaller than $\tilde{X}_1$ at this point. A proof by contradiction will also hold in this regard.

If the following equation holds

$$\tilde{X}_1 = \frac{\alpha P_2 T}{P_1(\alpha+\beta+\gamma)} \le \frac{\alpha P_2\overline{X}_2}{P_1(\alpha+\gamma)} = X_1^e$$

There will be

$$\overline{X}_2 \ge T(\alpha+\gamma)/(\alpha+\beta+\gamma) = \tilde{X}_2$$

This obviously violates the assumption impossible, there can only be $X_1^e \le \tilde{X}_1$. The relationship between X_1^e and X_1 disequilibrium theory by assuming that

$$\begin{aligned}
\tilde{X}_1 - X_1^e &= \frac{\alpha P_2 T}{P_1(\alpha+\beta+\gamma)} - \frac{P_2\overline{X}_2\alpha}{P_1(\alpha+\gamma)} \\
&= \frac{\alpha P_2 T(\alpha+\gamma) - P_2\overline{X}_2\alpha(\alpha+\beta+\gamma)}{P_1(\alpha+\beta+\gamma)(\alpha+\gamma)} \\
&= \frac{\alpha P_2\tilde{X}_2(\alpha+\beta+\gamma) - P_2\overline{X}_2\alpha(\alpha+\beta+\gamma)}{P_1(\alpha+\beta+\gamma)(\alpha+\gamma)} \\
&= \frac{\alpha P_2\tilde{X}_2 - P_2\overline{X}_2\alpha}{P_1(\alpha+\gamma)} = \frac{\alpha}{\alpha+\gamma}\frac{P_2}{P_1}(\tilde{X}_2 - \overline{X}_2)
\end{aligned}$$

that $\overline{X}_2 < \tilde{X}_2$. Since $X_1^e \ge \tilde{X}_1$ is has been further analyzed by.

Then,

$$X_1^e = \tilde{X}_1 + \frac{\alpha}{\alpha+\gamma}\frac{P_2}{P_1}(\overline{X}_2 - \tilde{X}_2)$$

Thus, the effective demand X_1^e equals the Walras's demand $\tilde{X}_1$ plus a term called the spillover term, which is expressed as follows

$$\frac{\alpha}{\alpha+\gamma}\frac{P_2}{P_1}(\overline{X}_2-\tilde{X}_2)$$

It can be seen from the above analysis that disequilibrium theory distinguishes the concepts of Walras's demand and the effective demand perceived by the market under the existence of rationing. This theory also further studies the internal relationship between the two concepts, and puts forward a new concept of the spillover effect. This inspires us to distinguish between these two kinds of demand when studying inflation. The first is the demand with the monetary payment ability, and the other is the demand under the rationing constraint for the purchasing ability of money. Only the latter demand will be reflected in the market and accepted by the producers through price signals. The Dual-Gap Model of Inflation studied in Chapter 8 precisely employs the concept of effective demand of disequilibrium theory as an important theoretical pillar. Inflation itself is exactly the spillover effect of excess supply over demand in the money market on excess demand over supply in the product market, which is reflected in the increase of the price level and expansion of shortage.

Under China's current economic system, the institutions affecting aggregate supply and aggregate demand mainly include the SPC (the State Planning Commission), the Ministry of Finance, the Banking system, the State Bureau of Commodity Prices, and the State Economic and Trade Commission (the functions of the State Economic and Trade Commission are roughly substituted by the State Production Commission). From a perspective of the functional divisions, the State Planning Commission is in charge of construction of infrastructure; the State Economic and Trade Commission, technical renewal and transformation; the Ministry of Finance, the receipt and expenditure of funds within the budget (the fiscal funds can be divided into two parts: one is for living, that is, the funds of the administrative sectors, and the other is for construction, namely, the provision of part of the funds for infrastructure construction); the Banking system is responsible for money supply and loan arrangements; the State Bureau of Commodity Prices, for managing changes of planned prices.

After the reform of the economic system, the function of SPC as the main body of the comprehensive balance of the national economy has been greatly weakened, resulting in a lack of unity and coordination among various sectors. In fact, the government is no longer able to comprehensively arrange an overall plan for money supply and demand, let alone know fairly well about the size of the aggregate supply and aggregate demand in advance. The economic regulation approach of the government has been transformed from the traditional direct material control to the current direct value control. The so-called macroeconomic indirect regulation system has not yet been established, and presently it still relies on the command plan to control the supply and demand of funds, or alternatively, to regulate the supply and demand of funds through rationing. As a result, the concepts of effective demand and spillover in disequilibrium theory are more consistent with the current economic situation in China.

In accordance with the prevailing economic system, this book views the SPC, the Ministry of Finance, the State Bureau of Commodity Prices, and the State Economic and Trade Commission as the planning system, corresponding to the product market; the banking system as the monetary system, corresponding to the money market. The research will focus on the impact of rationing of these two systems on inflation. On the surface, the Ministry of Finance is responsible for managing money, but it is in fact a sector responsible for survival and construction. It is therefore reasonable to correspond it with the product market. The relationship between these two systems and these two markets will be the objective foundation and primary level for the studying inflation. Then, the relationship among the SPC, the Ministry of Finance and banking system will only be discussed in some chapters as a necessary supplement.

Part II
Intrinsic Formation Mechanisms of Inflation

Chapter 4
Formation Processes of the Aggregate Demand and Aggregate Supply Function

The relationship between the initial distribution income and the final expenditure incurred after redistribution income has been explored in Chap. 2. The initial distribution income is equal to the amount of national income produced, and the final expenditure is equal to the amount of national income spent. The relation between the amount of national income produced and the expenditure can be illustrated as

$$\begin{aligned}\text{Amount of National Income Spent} = {} & \text{Amount of National Income Produced} \\ & + \text{Imports} - \text{Exports.}\end{aligned}$$

From the ex ante perspective, the amount of national income spent can be considered as part of the realized aggregate demand, that is

$$\begin{aligned}\text{Aggregate Demand} = {} & \text{Amount of National Income Spent} \\ & + \text{Unrealized Aggregate Demand}\end{aligned}$$

The unrealized aggregate demand means the amount of goods and services that an affordable economic actor is willing to buy at prevailing prices but does not take action due to some constraints, which represents the mandatory balance of monetary purchasing power referred to as shortages. Such mandatory balance of money is called forced savings. Shortages are essentially consistent with forced savings but not necessarily equal in quantity because the purchasing power of money can be achieved only by multiplying the quantity of the money supplied with its velocity.

The amount of national income spent is the total amount of goods and services an economic actor who is willing to buy and has already purchased at the prevailing prices. Integrating the above two definitions, aggregate demand can be defined as the total amount of goods and services purchased at prevailing prices based on willingness and monetary affordability.

The word "willingness" here indicates the ex ante or anticipating nature of the aggregate demand.

L. Li, *The Inflation Mechanism and Expectations*, Understanding China,
https://doi.org/10.1007/978-981-97-2570-0_4

As per the flow analysis in Chap. 2, the aggregate demand is an integral part of the total income of the economic actor who does not necessarily spend all income on purchasing. At the prevailing prices, only part of such income will be spent on goods and services he or she is willing to purchase. Part of the income goes to transfer payments, while the rest is saved, which is commonly known as voluntary savings. Therefore

$$\text{Total Income} = \text{Aggregate Demand} + \text{Voluntary Savings} \\ + \text{ Other Transfer Payments}$$

It can also be expressed as

$$\text{Total Income} = \text{Realized Aggregate Demand} + \text{Forced Savings} \\ + \text{Voluntary Savings} + \text{Other Transfer Payments}$$

Therefore,

$$\text{Expenditure of National Income} = \text{Aggregate Demand} = \text{Total Income}$$

The aggregate demand used to be ex ante, invisible and untouchable, while national income spent and total income is ex post and visible. Thus, changes in the aggregate demand can be analyzed on the basis of changes in national income spent and total income. The analysis of formation process of the aggregate demand can therefore be commenced with the formation process of the total income.

4.1 Formation of Aggregate Demand at a Micro Level

It is derived from the analysis in Chap. 2 that enterprise original revenue g is split into employee income V and profit M after deducting compensation C, namely

$$g = C + V + M$$

where, M can be further separated into two small components. One is the enterprise retaining profit $M1$, the other is the enterprise profit $M2$ submitted to the government, so

$$g = C + V + M1 + M2$$

What to be studied now is what sort of hands split g into the above four components. The logical basis for analyzing this decomposition process lies in the propositions of the rational economic man and softness of budget constraint which have been discussed in the introduction of this book.

There are three economic actors involved in splitting g, namely households, enterprises and governments. All economic actors strive for their own benefit maximization under certain constraints, which is reflected here as income maximization. Since g is constant, more gains to one mean losses to other two. Interest friction and conflict therefore exist objectively among these three actors.

Let's look at how enterprises and households view the division of V. Due to the nature of the state-owned system, the ownership of enterprises fixed assets belongs to the government. If enterprises expand their fixed assets through their own funds, it will be undoubtedly similar to paying tributes to the government. Therefore, according to the proposition of rational economic man, enterprises have a lack of enthusiasm to accumulate their own assets, so in the division, they tend to increase the proportion of V. Of course, for further development, they also strive to expand their investment. However, in the fight for investment share $M1$, they will try to squeeze $M2$ and be in more favor of V. From the above analysis, it can be inferred that the proportion of V will tend to increase.

Let's check the division of $M1$ and $M2$ by enterprises and government. Based on the two propositions aforesaid, enterprises will try to expand $M1$ while the government expands $M2$. Superficially, the government enjoys a favorable position in this interest conflict since it can formulate policies to stipulate that how much enterprises could retain and how much to be paid over. However, the proposition of profit transfer allows enterprises to erode the $M2$ stipulated by the government and convert part of it into $M1$. As commonly stated, enterprises will firstly refuse to pay part of their profits so that they can spend the government finance; then they spend funds from the bank by refusing to pay back part of their loans or interest; finally they will spend their own funds by converting part of C into V or into investment, leaving the gap to be bridged by the bank or government finance. It is because of these three processes of enterprises that cause the government to face the policy dispute of whether to pay back the tax first or repay the loan first. Therefore, it is not difficult for us to judge that the proportion of national fiscal revenue (proportionate to the national income) will trend downward.

It should be noted that the two conclusions inferred from the above proposition (the proportional increase of V and decrease of fiscal revenue in the national income) are related to the current economic system. The current economic system is characterized by both enterprises and government are bound by finance contracting. Only in this context can such a conclusion be drawn from the basic proposition above mentioned. Such a conclusion would be invalid in case the highly centralized fiscal regime was implemented such as during the period of the "Cultural Revolution".

Whether the above deduction conforms to reality remains to be verified by practice. However, practical statistics do indicate the validation of this conclusion, as shown in Tables 4.1 and 4.2.

Table 4.1 shows that from 1977 to 1987, the proportion of household income in the national income increased by 10.5% from 72.1 to 82.6%, reflecting the proactive position of the household in this conflict of interests with a constant benefit improvement. On the contrary, Table 4.2 reflects that the government benefits have been constantly encroached in this conflict.

Table 4.1 Proportion of household disposable income* in national income (%)

Year	Proportion of household Disposable income in national Income	Year	Proportion of household Disposable income in national Income
1977	72.1	1984	82.3
1978	69.9	1985	84.4
1979	73.5	1986	85.2
1980	78.2	1987	82.6
1981	80.3	1988	79.6
1982	81.8	1989	83.2
1983	81.3		

* Household disposable income consists of their disposable monetary income and physical income. The disposable monetary income can be calculated from the data provided in the table of "Sources and Distribution of Social Commodity Purchasing Power" in the *China Statistical Yearbook*. The physical income can be calculated from the data provided in the table of "Total Retail Sales of Social Commodities" and the table of "Consumption and Composition of National Income" in the *China Statistical Yearbook*. Data for all tables in this book are sourced from the *China Statistical Yearbook*. No further explanation will be given under common circumstance

Table 4.2 Proportion of fiscal revenue in national income

Year	Proportion of fiscal revenue in national income	Year	Proportion of fiscal revenue in national income
1977	33.1	1983	25.6
1978	37.2	1984	26.0
1979	31.9	1985	26.2
1980	28.3	1986	28.0
1981	25.8	1987	24.1
1982	25.4	1988	19.0

From the above analysis, it is clear that in the initial distribution of national income, the proportion of household income is constantly increasing, while the proportion of fiscal revenue is constantly decreasing. Thus, the pattern of national income distribution during this period is not reflecting the final expenditure pattern of the national income, which needs to be finalized through the process of redistribution. The final expenditure pattern of national income can only be realized with the completion of such redistribution. It should be pointed out that the final expenditure of national income only corresponds to the ex post aggregate demand and aggregete supply, not the ex post ones. The ex ante aggregate demand and aggregete supply are determined during the process of initial distribution and redistribution of the national income. The initial distribution of national income establishes a micro basis for the formation of aggregate demand. At this stage, it is basically a distribution process of national income under the system constraint (mainly by ownership and management power). Expectations also play a certain role in this process.

Anticipating an increase in inflation, households will further voice for an increase in income. As a result, inflation will boost the interest conflicts between the government, enterprise and households.

4.2 Formation of Aggregate Demand at a Macro Level

From a macro perspective, as discussed in Chap. 2, the expenditure pattern shaped by the initial distribution of national income still needs to go through the finance and credit system so as to formulate the final expenditure pattern of national income. In this section, the formation of aggregate demand at the macro level and the role of new money injection in the formation of ex ante aggregate demand will be analyzed based on the theoretical framework in Chap. 2.

First, let's look at the role of the financial system. After receiving profit taxes from enterprises, the government will return parts of it to the household through various subsidies. At the same time, the government will also generate parts of its revenue through taxing the household. Therefore, the final formation of the household income is the household disposable income, which is expressed as:

$$\text{Household Disposable Income} = \text{Household Income from the Initial Income Distribution} + \text{Household Income from Government Finance} - \text{Household Expenditure to Finance}$$

It should be noted that the indirect income obtained by households from the finance, such as the financial education subsidy, is not included in the income obtained by households from finance. Money borrowed by households from the banks for consumption is ignored here because it rarely happens,[1] especially if households spend far more on banks (savings) than what they receive from banks (interest and withdrawals on deposits and loans), so it makes more sense to do so.

Upon determining the disposable income of households, the internal fiscal income and expenditure arrangement will be examined. As known to all, fiscal expenditure cannot be adjusted to match the level of revenue which may relatively shrink because the government must invest in basic and strategic engineering projects to ensure sustainable economic development as well as the long-term interests of the economic system. These projects could not be cut down even if fiscal revenue declines. In addition, other financial expenditures, such as the educational expenditure and so on, were all rigid and therefore generate a consequence that fiscal revenue was unable to offset expenditure. The government could only rely on deficits to maintain its balance of payments. So there will be

[1] In rural areas, some households borrow money from credit cooperatives to build houses.

$$\begin{aligned}&\text{Fiscal Revenue} + \text{Deficit} = \text{Fiscal Expenditure}\\&= \text{Government Investment} + \text{Government Consumption}\\&\quad + \text{Other Spending}\end{aligned}$$

The deficit here is not only the financial overdrafts from banks, but also includes net income from other fiscal debts (borrowing income less principal and interest payments).[2]

Now let's examine the role of the banking system. The main source of bank revenue is the quantity of currency in circulation and various deposits. The expenditure of the banking system is the loans to enterprises and governments. So there are

$$\begin{aligned}\text{Bank Revenue} = {} & \text{Cash} + \text{Household Savings} + \text{Public Institution}\\&\text{and Enterprise deposits} + \text{Other Revenue}\end{aligned}$$

$$\begin{aligned}\text{Bank Expenditure} = {} & \text{Corporate Loans} + \text{Government Loans}\\&+ \text{Other Expenditures}\end{aligned}$$

It is difficult to judge whether a financial overdraft from the banks results in excessive money supply since bank revenue equals its expenditure.

Under the role of banks, the final expenditure of enterprises becomes

$$\text{Enterprise Final Expenditure} = \text{Enterprise Initial Distribution}$$

$$\begin{aligned}&\text{Income} + \text{Fiscal Income} - \text{Fiscal Expenditure} + \text{Revenuefrom}\\&\text{Banks} - \text{Expenditure to Banks} + \text{Net Income from Other Transfer}\\&\text{Payments}\end{aligned}$$

Through the role of banks, the savings of household disposable income will be converted into enterprise and government investment.

First, a closed economic system will be examined. Total Social Savings can be defined as

$$\begin{aligned}&\text{Total Social Savings S} = \text{Household Savings } \mathrm{S}_1 + \text{Enterprise Savings}\\&S_2 + \text{ Government Savings } S_3\end{aligned}$$

Here, savings is a flow variable rather than a stock variable as deposits, namely[3]

$$S_2 = \text{Enterprise Retained Profits } M1$$

[2] The deficit does not include net debt income as per prevailing regulations.

[3] The proportion of enterprise retained profit distributed to the employees is counted as income of the employees, therefore the enterprise retained profit here only refers to the accumulation of the enterprise per se.

$$S_3 = \text{Profit Tax to Government } M2 - \text{Government Consumption } G \\ - \text{Other Expenditures } GG$$

$$S_1 = \text{New Household Deposits } S_{11} + \text{New Quantity of Currency in Circulation } S_{12}$$

Therefore,[4]

$$S = S_1 + M1 + (M2 - G - GG)$$

The total social investments can be defined as

$$\text{Total Social Investments } I = \text{Household Investment } I_1 \\ + \text{Enterprise Investment } I_2 + \text{Government Investment } I_3$$

However,

$$I_2 = M1 + \text{Net Fiscal Revenue} + \text{Net Bank Revenue} \\ + \text{Net Income from Other Transfer Payments}$$

$$I_3 = (M2 - G - GG) + \text{Revenue from Deficit}$$

Household productive investment has been categorized as enterprise investment, and the household investment I_1 only includes non-productive investment such as self-built houses.

Therefore

$$I_2 \geq S_2 \quad I_3 \geq S_3 \quad I_1 \geq S_1$$

From an ex post perspective (note the assumption of closed economic system), there is

$$I = S$$

Namely

$$I_1 + I_2 + I_3 = S_1 + S_2 + S_3 = S_{11} + S_{12} + S_2 + S_3$$

Since

[4] An increase in cash in the hands of the household is deemed to be equal to the quantity of the new currency in circulation. In fact, part of the new currency in circulation is owned by enterprises and public institutions, but cash is mainly used for compensation as well as procurement of agricultural and sideline products. Such assumption is roughly established.

$$(I_1 + I_2 + I_3) - (S_{11} + S_2 + S_3) = S_{12}$$

It means that the equalization of I and S is mainly regulated by S_{12}. In fact, this is the flow expression of the following equation:

$$\text{Loans} - \text{Deposits} = \text{Quantity of Market Currency in Circulation}$$

It can be seen that the new loans correspond to the investment while new deposits to savings and new quantity of market money to S_{12}.

Again, because the ex ante aggregate demand GD is

$$GD = C + I + G$$

And the ex post aggregate supply GS is

$$GS = C + S + G$$

Therefore

$$GD + GS = I - S = 0$$

And I-S equals

$$(I_1 + I_2 + I_3) - (S_{11} + S_2 + S_3 + S_{12}) = 0$$

Therefore, S_{12} is also a regulatory variable to equalize the ex post aggregate demand and aggregate supply.

Assume that S_{12} is the new quantity of market currency in circulation to equalize ex ante aggregate demand and ex post aggregate supply, then S_{12} will rise to real S_{12} in case ex ante aggregate demand is greater than ex post aggregate supply. Thus, the excessive cash supply can be defined as

$$\Delta S_{12} = S_{12} - \overline{S}_{12}$$

Alternatively, the rate of excessive cash supply can be expressed as

$$S'_{12} = \frac{S_{12} - \overline{S}_{12}}{\overline{S}_{12}}$$

From the above analysis, it can be seen that the formation process of the aggregate demand at the macro level will be finally determined by $\overline{S}_{12}$. In case the deficit does not cause S_{12} to be greater than $\overline{S}_{12}$, then the deficit itself will not generate inflation. If the finance and the bank have carried out a comprehensive balance in advance to guaranteed $S_{12} = \overline{S}_{12}$, then only a further fiscal deficit can lead to $S_{12} > \overline{S}_{12}$, namely inflation.

It can also be inferred from the above analysis that the quantity of new cash S_{12} is actually uncontrollable. To control S_{12}, the ex ante aggregate demand must be controlled firstly. With a constant ex post aggregate supply, a fluctuation in ex ante aggregate demand will lead to a fluctuation in S_{12}.

4.3 Sources of Internal Instability in National Economy

Keynes noted that the motivation for determining investment I is not consistent with that for savings S, resulting in an inequality between anticipated investment and savings. A gap between the aggregate demand and aggregate supply will consequently appear to cause economic fluctuations. As a result, such an inequality becomes the source of internal instability in the economic system.

It is noted that a new phenomenon existed in China's economy after the economic reform: investments are determined by enterprises and the governments, while more and more savings are determined by the households. From the previous analysis, it is clear that the proportion of household income in the national income tends to increase gradually. Another consequence of this trend will be that the proportion of new household savings in the national income accumulation is becoming greater and greater, as shown in Table 4.3.

As a result, the household savings becomes an important variable affecting economic stability. Yet, the motive of household savings is not consistent with that of the government and enterprise investment. Households do not save more when investment rises, nor do they save less when investment falls. Therefore, when investment rises and household savings fail to keep up, the government will rely on additional cash injection to support investment growth. Increasing in cash injection does not

Table 4.3 Proportion* of new household savings** in national income accumulation

Year	Proportion of new household savings in national income accumulation	Year	Proportion of new household savings in national income accumulation
1977	13.6	1984	48.8
1978	17.5	1985	55.7
1979	23.4	1986	57.5
1980	30.3	1987	49.9
1981	30.4	1988	53.8
1982	36.8	1989	53.5
1983	37.0		

* New household savings includes household private investment

** The data in this table are calculated from Tables 2-20, 5-1 to 14-14 of *China Statistical Yearbook* (1990). See China Statistical Press 1990 Edition, pp. 42, 153, 614

necessarily create inflation if growth in investment can boost the aggregate supply. How to analyze the relationship between *I*, *S*, S_{12} and inflation will become the focus in the later part of this book.

Before the economic reform, the household savings was not large in the accumulation of national income, reaching only 13.6% in 1977. Therefore, investment *I* and savings *S* were basically determined by the enterprise and government themselves, so that there is a greater consistency in the decision motivation between *I* and *S*. The economy could thus be stabilized.

The growth of household savings itself may also be a destabilizing factor for the national economy. In essence, household savings are a debt owed by the state to households. When households simultaneously withdraw money (and the state is required to repay it), there will be an immediate expansion of aggregate demand, leading to inflation. The key factor to stabilize household savings is that the nominal interest rate should be higher than the anticipated inflation rate of the households. In case the households are expecting a higher inflation rate, enterprises will suffer from a higher loan interest burden though the higher interest rate may help to stabilize savings. Additionally, the anticipated inflation rate of the households is uncertain. Households may run on their deposits if interest rates are not adjusted with the changes in inflation anticipation. This was evident in the first half of 1988. Of course, the increase in household savings is a good thing in itself. It can only be a source of economic instability in case it is not managed well.

The inconsistency between investment and savings reflects the inconsistency between aggregate demand and aggregate supply. Fluctuations in aggregate demand are eventually reflected in fluctuations in the increase in cash. From the banks' point of view, the increase in cash is the result of a growing gap between loans and deposits. As long as banks rein in lending, they can rein in cash growth. Therefore, loans become an important factor to control aggregate demand, and will also become an important factor to eliminate the impact of the inconsistency between *I* and *S*. This is the core of support for the study of the aggregate demand function in the following section.

4.4 The Consumption Function

The consumption function is a component of the aggregate demand function. The concept of the consumption function comes from Keynes's *The General Theory of Employment, Interest and Money*. Since then, Western economists have conducted considerable empirical research on it. According to the basic psychological laws in Chap. 8 of *The General Theory of Employment, Interest and Money*, as income increases, consumption increases, but not as much. If *C* stands for consumption, *Y* for yield, Keynes's statement can then be expressed in mathematical notation as

$$C = f(Y), \text{ and } 0 < \frac{dC}{dY} < 1$$

Keynes further assumed that the income elasticity of consumption is smaller than 1. It means that an income increase in the lower income class is more effective at raising the aggregate demand. A further argument is that changes in the monetary value of wealth will cause short-run changes in the propensity to consume, and that the marginal propensity to consume in the short-run is smaller than that in the long-run. The latter argument is based on the fact that, in the short-run, a person's standard of living is inelastic and the gap between the real income and the expenditure required to match the accustomed standard of living will be adjusted by savings. If real income rises, savings increase and vice versa. Thus, the standard of living will remain unchanged in the short-run. In other words, consumption will be relatively stable, while savings fluctuate considerably.

The research into Keynes's argument, aforesaid by Western economists, demonstrated that over a long period, the ratio of consumption to income turned out to be a constant, rather than a gradual decline as Keynes assumed. However, Keynes's argument was supported by the studies on all annual cross-sectional data. In order to explain this contradiction, the Relative Income Hypothesis of Consumption, the Hypothesis of Lagging Consumption, and the Permanent Income Hypothesis of Consumption of Milton Friedman were proposed later. The basic idea of the Permanent Income Hypothesis of Consumption is that consumers do not take into account occasional changes in income when making consumption plans, but only consider the anticipated, "normal", or the permanent income.

In the mainstream of Western economics, the distribution of national income among household, enterprise and government as well as the hidden interest mechanism behind the distribution have not been adequately addressed. They only studied the quantitative relationship between measurable variables, such as the relationship between income and consumption, rather than the interest relationship behind such a quantitative relationship. The study of the benefit mechanism behind such income consumption relationship of Marx's economic theory is much more profound.

Marx argued that there is an inherent drive to expand production in a capitalist economy but it is constrained by the insufficient demand caused by the relative poverty of the working class. Such poverty is in turn attributed to the distribution pattern determined by capitalist ownership.

Following the ideas of Marx, the formation of the distribution pattern under the socialist ownership (assuming state ownership) has been explored in the last two sections. A conclusion has been drawn that the proportion of household income has gradually increased in the national income after the socialist economic reform.

It is easy to fallback on Keynes's idea that consumption rises more slowly than income. Specifically, while the proportion of household income is rising in the national income, the proportion of household consumption is basically stable in the national income, as shown in Table 4.4.

At present (1991), two internal mechanisms exist in China's household consumption pattern. The first is the mechanism of fiscal subsidy consumption. In China, many consumption items are low cost such as rent, education, health costs and so on. The real costs of these expenditures are not reflected accurately in China's national accounting, leading to the underestimation of the Gross National Product (GNP)

Table 4.4 The proportion of household consumption in the national income

Year	The proportion of household consumption in the national income	Year	The proportion of household consumption in the national income
1978	0.56	1984	0.60
1979	0.57	1985	0.57
1980	0.60	1986	0.57
1981	0.63	1987	0.57
1982	0.63	1988	0.57
1983	0.62	1989	0.57

in China. The statistical data employed are insufficient to reflect this reality, and therefore the consumption function constructed from these statistics alone is insufficient to reflect the changes in these consumption factors. After the economic system reform, the distribution mechanism has changed substantially but the consumption mechanism (that is, the fiscal subsidy consumption mechanism) has remained nearly constant. Therefore, the relationship between income and consumption cannot be expressed completely by the relationship established by Keynes. It can be roughly estimated that the total real cost of those consumption factors of the urban households would not be less than the total real consumption expenditure of households at present. In order to comprehensively picture out China's consumption pattern, it is necessary to re-verify the GNP to adjust the understated value. This task cannot be accomplished only by several economists.

The second is the mechanism of government's planned consumption. In China's economic life, the government tries to control the proportion of consumption and accumulation in the national income. Such control is effective in the long-run though various practical factors may interfere with it. The government can directly limit households' consumption by means of rationing or limit the expansion of the consumption sector by means of controlling the economic structure, discouraging households to buy more consumption goods though they may enjoy the purchasing power or increasing the prices of consumption goods. Consequently, such government measures have led the long-run accumulation rate to fluctuate around 30%, while the consumption rate fluctuates around 70%. The government consumption is included herewith the household consumption fluctuating around 60%. According to these two consumption mechanisms, the household consumption can be matched with the national income to formulate our consumption theory, which helps to establish a consumption function as

$$C = f(NI)$$

After the economic reforms, although the proportion of household income in national income keeps rising, the proportion of its consumption does not increase at all. The consumption capacity reflected by this consumption function is relatively stable and reliable. It can be expressed linearly as

$$C = \alpha_0 + \alpha_1 NI$$

Data of 36 consecutive years of the household consumption and national income from 1953 to 1988 (both calculated with 1952 constant prices[5]) are used to conduct a regression, the results of which are as follows

$$C = 148.15 + 0.4838NI$$
$$(8.4) \qquad (70.7)$$

$$R^2 = 0.99 \; DW = 0.73$$

From the regression results, it can be seen that the fitting effect is excellent, and the T test is also satisfactory. A low DW value indicates that the residual term is autocorrelated. Given that this is a univariate regression, a low DW value is acceptable. Further analysis shows that the random error is positively autocorrelated. The distribution of the errors along the regression line resembles a sinusoidal curve, suggesting that the government is constantly using trial and error to keep consumption within bounds as it thinks fit.

Therefore, according to the actual situation in China, it is advisable to use $C = f(NI)$ to reflect the relationship between consumption and the national income.

4.5 The Investment Function

Another important component of aggregate demand is investment. In China, the government, businesses, and households are all involved in investment. Household investment generally refers to residential building investment, which is non-productive investment and will not be discussed here. All discussed here are productive investments only. Household savings has an indirect impact on investment, but it is not a direct investment behavior. Therefore, the household investment factor will be subtracted from the investment discussion in the following section.

There are two types of government investment, namely the investment by the central government as well as by the local government. The investments of the central government are mainly in key projects related to the national economy and people's livelihood. Since the government is concerned more about the overall interests of the entire economic system, such investments are aimed at meeting the needs of the economic system rather than pursuing profits. Local governments and enterprises are generally reluctant to invest in basic industries which are lengthy with large inputs

[5] If the constant price of national income is converted by the national income deflator and that of the household consumption is converted by the consumer price index, the proportion of the household income in the national income is lower than the current value calculating at prevailing prices. For example, in 1978, the proportion of the household income in the national income was only 51%, and 52% in 1986.

but low profits. Therefore, basic industries have become the focus of the investments of the central government. With the constant decreasing proportion of central fiscal revenue in the national income, the central government has to guarantee these key investment projects without any reduction in the fiscal expenditure. The fiscal deficit correspondingly arises. This is the common statement that infrastructure squeezes fiscal revenue.

What the local governments consider are the overall interests of the local economic system. For local governments, the purpose of investment is to make a profit, and the non-profit investment projects will be a burden to the central government. Since the financial package rationing, local governments hold their own interests, so they enjoy an inherent enthusiasm for investment. However, as a unified national market that has not really been established, the local governments are easy to engage in repetitive construction projects, such as color TV, refrigerator's investment projects and so on.

Enterprises also invest for profit. It has already been pointed out that since the property rights of enterprises are owned by the state, they are not enthusiastic to invest with their retained funds, but very proactive to invest with the funds from the government.

The central government is under heavy pressure for investment, while local governments and enterprises also bear strong internal enthusiasm for investment. China therefore faces an intensive demand for investments, which is referred to as the *Hunger for Investments*.

There are two types of restrictions on investment. The first is the national income restriction, and the second is the quantitative restriction. The national income is a hard restriction. The proportion of investment in the national income should not be too large, otherwise it will weaken consumption and cause discontent among households. Hence, the central government has always employed quantitative restriction to keep investment at an acceptable level. There are two types of quantitative restriction: one is the monetary restriction, and the other, the project restriction. Monetary restriction refers to the government's control of the money supply to prevent local governments and enterprises from extracting money from the central government by any means to discourage their investments. Project restriction refers to the central government's direct regulation on all types of projects invested by enterprises and local governments. Without the approval of the central government, no local enterprise will be entitled to invest in any large- and medium-sized projects even if they are financially sound. Project restriction is a sensitive brake that no Western countries can follow. Once the central government is determined to hold down investment, it can brake much faster than the market economies, but the waste of resources that comes with such a brake is also huge.

From the above analysis, the formulation of the investment function can be deduced from these two aspects, namely, either the national income or the money supply. The national income is much more in favor of illustrating the long-run trend of investment; the money supply is more appropriate to explain the relationship between short-run investment and money. This will be discussed in more details later.

What is analyzed above is the institutional behavior of investment, which refers to the investment behavior of economic actors in pursuit of their own interests under the current economic system. In addition to such institutional factors, other factors such as population growth, technological advancement, the discovery of new resources and new products can also cause changes in investments. These are all called exogenous factors which will not be explored here. In addition to the institutional factors and exogenous factors, there are still other very important factors that cause changes in investments. These are the impacts on investment caused by changes in inputs or consumption, which can be referred to as the endogenous factors.

There is a term called "induced" investment, or the "accelerator principle" in Western economic theory. Harrod, Hicks, Hansen, and others have argued that Keynes ignored or did not pay enough attention to the "accelerator principle", which is a flaw in his theoretical system. The Hansen- Samuelson model, as it was later called, integrated Keynes's multiplier theory and the accelerator principle to analyze economic fluctuations, which remedied the flaw in Keynes's theoretical system. The main content of the accelerator principle is that investment is not only a function of income (or consumption), but the independent variable of this function is the rate of change not the absolute level of income (or consumption). The investment rate fluctuates more than the rate of change in income (or consumption), and after investment changes first, then income (or consumption) follows. That is, small changes in anticipated income or consumption can lead to substantial changes in investment. Thus, income or consumption can either "expand" investment or "shrink" it during a recession.

The accelerator principle does exist in China, but it is severely restricted in functioning. Although investment in China fluctuates more than that of consumption, owing to China's inherent investment stimulator in the economic system, investment does not automatically fall in economic downturns, but it is intentionally suppressed by the central government instead. As a result, the intrinsic link between investment and consumption or income is less sensitive than that of Western economies.

The induced investment in China is not only by consumption, but more importantly, by previous investment which carried a critical impact on the investment in later periods. A large scale investment in the previous period will lead to an expansion in later investment. There are several reasons behind this phenomenon: (1) a large number of entrapping projects exist to boost future investment. Since the central government only regulates the large- and medium-sized projects, the local governments and enterprises tend to reduce the scale of investment in reporting in order to commence the projects, and then constantly demand additional funds from the central government. (2) In order to complete the projects commenced in the previous period, additional funds will be further acquired in later period regardless of their economic benefits. Investments here become purely for the sake of the completion of the projects themselves since they are on track. (3) Production and consumption have been stimulated by investments in the previous period. A corresponding level of investment must be maintained in order to ensure the then growth momentum of such production and consumption in the current period. Therefore, in China's investment function, not only the national income or money supply but also the amount of investment in the previous period should be considered. That's our theory of induced investment, which possesses both similarity and differentiation aspects with the accelerator principle.

An investment function of our own therefore can be established at this point. It will be firstly established from the national income expressed as

$$I = f[I(-1), NI]$$

(-1) here means investment in a previous period. The linear expression of this function is

$$I = \alpha_0 + \alpha_1 I(-1) + \alpha_2 NI$$

Data from 1954 to 1988 will be used to conduct a regression on the above equation, and the results are as follows

$$I = 0.57I(-1) + 0.10NI$$
$$(4.7) \qquad (4.4)$$

$$R^2 = 0.94 \; DW = 1.07$$

The regression test results above are acceptable. The intercept term α_0 is not significant in the regression because it is the result after the omission of α_0, and the value of DW is relatively smaller.

Interestingly, if only $C = f(NI)$ is used for the regression, the R^2 value would only be 0.85, which is smaller than the value of 0.99 when $C = f(NI)$ is used for the regression, indicating that I is more fluctuating toward NI than C. After adding $I(-1)$, the value of R^2 is significantly improved, indicating that the previous investment has a significant induced role upon the next investment, and the role is relatively huge.

The investment function will then be established in terms of the money supply as

$$I = f[I(-1), M]$$

where, M stands for the quantity of money supply in the function. The linear expression of this function is

$$I = \alpha_0 + \alpha_1 I(-1) + \alpha_2 M$$

Data from 1953 to 1988 will be used to conduct a regression on the above equation, and the results are as follows

$$I = 0.815I(-1) + 0.075M$$
$$(9.2) \qquad (3.2)$$

$$R^2 = 0.93 \; DW = 1.3$$

The regression test results above are acceptable and the value of DW is improved. For a contrast, let's consider the regression results after omitting $I(-1)$,

$$\begin{aligned} I = &145.44 + 0.22M \\ &(4.8) \qquad (14.0) \end{aligned}$$

$$R^2 = 0.85 \; DW = 0.55$$

In addition to the smaller R^2 value, the value of DW also decreased significantly. However, a value of 0.85 to R^2 could also indicate that M carries a significant impact on I in the short-run.

The DW values are all low in the regression analysis of the investment function. Further analysis shows that this is attributed to the positive autocorrelation of random errors. Such a positive autocorrelation also indicates that the government attempts to restrain the investment within an acceptable range in the process of trial and error.

4.6 The Aggregate Demand Function

The previous analysis demonstrates that loans are an important factor affecting aggregate demand. Since loans are equal to the sum of money in circulation plus deposits, then loans actually represent the money supply. This will be discussed in more detail later. Loans will be viewed as the money supply in this section.

In addition to the impact of loans, size and structure of aggregate demand will also be reflected in the real interest rate, which carries significant impact on household savings though not that much on investment. Based on the previous analysis, the amount of household savings will influence the amount of additional cash injection S_{12}. However, the increase in household savings itself will not lead to any reduction in aggregate demand. It merely indicates that consumption decreases while investment increases. The total amount of aggregate demand remains constant with changes only in the structure of aggregate demand. Since the real interest rate equals the nominal interest rate subtracting the inflation rate, a change in the real interest rate will reflect a change in the inflation rate in case the nominal interest rate is fixed.

A high real interest rate already implies a low inflation rate while a low real interest rate implies a high inflation rate. Accordingly, the real interest rate not only possesses the function of indirectly reflecting the impact of prices on the aggregate demand, but also has the function of influencing the velocity of money. When real interest rate increases and the velocity of money slows down, aggregate demand represented by a certain amount of money will decrease. When the real interest rate decreases and the velocity of money increases, aggregate demand represented by a certain amount of money will increase. It is therefore appropriate to match the real interest rates with the money supply to reflect the aggregate demand. So there is

$$D = f(M, r)$$

where, D denotes aggregate demand; M is the money supply; r is the real interest rate. As M increases, D increases; As r goes up, D drops.

Refer to Sect. 8.6 of this book for a specific regression form of the aggregate demand function.

This aggregate demand function reflects aggregate demand with the ability to pay in money. Due to the rationing of the SPC, some money will not be utilized for this purchase. Thus, aggregate demand under such a rationing scheme can better reflect the relationship between supply and demand in the market. It can signal to the producers through the market system. This will be explored in more detail later.

The aggregate demand function above reflects the relationship between the ex ante aggregate demand and the money supply M as well as the real interest rate r in the long-run. However, in the short-run, fluctuations in expectations can deviate the ex ante aggregate demand from this relationship. Set the long-run ex ante aggregate demand as

$$D = f(M, r)$$

And the short-run ex ante aggregate demand will be

$$D^* = D + \varepsilon\left(P^* - P\right) + u$$

In the equation, P^* stands for the anticipating price; P is for the real price; u is for random errors; ε is a real number greater than zero.

Then

$$\text{As } P^* > P, D^* > D$$

$$\text{As } P^* < P, D^* < D$$

In other words, expectations are utilized as the key variable to explain the deviation of the short-run aggregate demand from the long-run aggregate demand. This explanation is represented in Fig. 4.1. In general, when real prices rise, aggregate demand will fall. However, an expected price rise will cause current aggregate demand to increase. The public then will make purchases before increases in the price level to avoid future losses from prices rise.

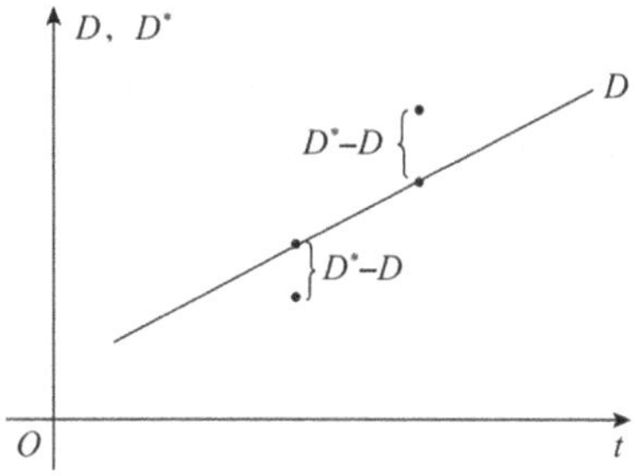

Fig. 4.1 Deviation of short-run aggregate demand from long run aggregate demand

4.7 Aggregate Demand Model I

The identity of relations between income and expenditure has been introduced in Chap. 2. If national income is viewed as the income, then NI can be categorized into three components, namely, household consumption expenditure, investment expenditure $\frac{\mathrm{d}NI}{\mathrm{d}G} = \frac{1}{1-b}$ and government consumption expenditure as follows

$$NI = C + I + G$$

Net export is ignored here because a closed-economy is under examination.

The consumption function studied previously is

$$C = a + bNI$$

where, coefficient b is called the marginal propensity to consume, which refers to the proportion of household consumption in each additional unit increased in national income (such as 1 RMB). The previous regression value shows that 0.48 yuan from every 1 yuan increase in national income will be spent on household consumption.

The following equation sets demonstrate a concise aggregate demand model.

$$\begin{cases} NI = C + I + G \\ C = a + bNI \end{cases}$$

where, I and G are exogenous variables; NI and C are endogenous variables.

Thus, a simple algebra arrangement will result in

$$NI = a + bNI + I + G$$

Then, there is

$$NI = \frac{a + I + G}{1 - b}$$

It should be noted that in the relationship between NI and I, G is not a production function. Here, NI represents income, and both I and G are expenditures. Based upon the above equation, the impact of changes in expenditure I and G on changes in income NI can be analyzed.

From the above equation, there is

$$\frac{\mathrm{d}NI}{\mathrm{d}I} = \frac{1}{1-b}$$

where, $1/(1-b)$ is called the multiplier. $1/(1-b)>1$ since $b<1$, which means that NI is changing faster than I. When $b = 0.48$, $1/1-b = 1.923$. This indicates that when the investment increases by 1 unit, the national income increases by 1.923 units.

The following equation holds based on the above formula

$$\frac{\mathrm{d}NI}{\mathrm{d}G} = \frac{1}{1-b}$$

when $b = 0.48$, it also indicates that when the government consumption expenditure increases 1 unit, the national income increases by 1.923 units.

The model above demonstrates that enhancement in both investment I and government consumption G can more quickly increase the national income, which should be comprehended from two perspectives.

When aggregate demand is greater than aggregate supply, and real aggregate supply is bigger than its potential, an increase in investment I and government consumption G may be able to further stimulate production. However, the short-run increase in real aggregate supply is constrained (such as insufficient supply in the bottleneck sectors), the multiplier effect will accordingly be suppressed. In this case, only the nominal not the real national income increases (physical outputs do not increase, but price level rises).

In case aggregate demand runs below aggregate supply, and the real aggregate supply is smaller than its potential, increases in investment I and government consumption G will be able to enhance production and boost real aggregate supply, so that the real not the nominal national income will increase.

In China's economy, aggregate demand is frequently greater than aggregate supply, so it is not appropriate to stimulate aggregate supply by encouraging investment and government consumption. This approach can only be adopted in case aggregate demand is lower than aggregate supply.

The concise aggregate demand model established above is an important cornerstone of the theoretical construction process of this book. Later studies will show that real aggregate supply fluctuates around its potential. Therefore, it becomes crucial to determine whether an increase in money supply stimulates only the nominal (that is, increase in the price level) or the real national income.

4.8 Aggregate Demand Model II

A more complex aggregate demand model can be derived from the model introduced in the previous section, provided that investment is also deemed to be an endogenous variable.

Thus,

$$I = f[I(-1), M]$$

To simplify the process, it is assumed that

$$I = d + eM$$

Namely, only investment I is viewed as the function of money supply M, then

$$\begin{aligned} NI &= C + I + G \\ C &= a + bNI \\ I &= d + eM \end{aligned}$$

Re-arranging the above equation set, it becomes

$$NI = a + bNI + d + eM + G$$

Then,

$$NI = \frac{a + d + eM + G}{1 - b}$$

The following formula is obtained from the equation above

$$\frac{\mathrm{d}NI}{\mathrm{d}M} = \frac{e}{1 - b}$$

In this formula, $e/(1 - b)$ is called the money multiplier. It means that a 1 unit increase in the money supply will generate an $e/(1 - b)$ unit increase in nominal national income. Thus,

$e + b > 1$, nominal national income increases faster than money supply;

$e + b = 1$, nominal national income increases at the same pace of money supply;

$e + b < 1$, nominal national income increases slower than money supply.

An increase in nominal national income following an increase in the money supply may include either the real or only the nominal component. It depends on whether the real aggregate supply is positioned above or below its potential.

Both aggregate demand model I and II are about viewing issues from the demand side. However, these two models themselves do not solve the problem of determining the output level, that is, whether the increase in national income is real or nominal. So, the supply side should be considered simultaneously to solve this problem. Only through analyzing both demand and supply side can a theory that determines output and prices be established, and ultimately a theoretical system of inflation can be constructed.

From the previous regression results in aggregate demand model II, it is determined that $a = 148$, $b = 0.48$, $d = 145$, $e = 0.22$. Once M and G are given, NI is accordingly determinable.

Since

$$e + b = 0.22 + 0.48 = 0.7 < 1$$

Therefore, in this model, the increase in national income is smaller than that of the money supply.

Chapter 5
The Formation Processes of the Aggregate Supply and Aggregate Supply Function

Aggregate supply is determined by two categories of factors.

The first is the production technical factor, which denotes the output level with a certain input of raw materials, labor, and corresponding fixed assets. Such input–output relationships are usually demonstrated by various production functions.

The second is the socioeconomic factor, which indicate show inputs are determined by the economic system. In the study of aggregate demand, the investment behavior has been examined with analysis upon the decision- making process of investment, especially the inherent contradiction between investment and savings, as well as its impact on the economy.

Generally speaking, the production technical factor is relatively stable without substantial change in the short-run. However, the socioeconomic factor is unstable and may change sharply in the short-run. Therefore, fluctuation of aggregate supply is more closely related to the socioeconomic factors. In this chapter, both the relationship between aggregate supply and the production technical factor as well as the socioeconomic factor will be scrutinized. An integration of the production technical factor with the socioeconomic factor will be applied in the analysis.

Production theory in Western economics begins with the study of two fundamental variables of capital K and labor L, and the relationship between the output level and these variables. Here, capital and labor are substitutable factors of production, and any combination of the two can generate a corresponding output level Q, which is expressed as

$$Q = f(K, L)$$

Production function is purely a technical relationship, which must be integrated with relevant economic theories in order to interpret any economic issues. In Western economic theory, the integration of production function with marginal productivity theory helps to explain how the price level and the utilization level of factors of

L. Li, *The Inflation Mechanism and Expectations*, Understanding China,
https://doi.org/10.1007/978-981-97-2570-0_5

production have been determined. This has played a central role in the theoretical analysis of economic growth and income distribution.

Research on China's production function can only be used to explain China's economic problems when it is integrated with China's economic theory.

$$Q = \min(D, S)$$

Disequilibrium is a common phenomenon in China's economy. Generally, aggregate demand is greater than aggregate supply in more years; it runs on the opposite only in a fewer years.[1]

Based on the short side rule of the disequilibrium theory, there is

$$Q = \min(D, S)$$

If the production function is employed to describe the aggregate supply at the macroeconomic level, then the first difficulty encountered is that there are more possibilities for Q to represent the aggregate supply S, but there are also fewer possibilities for Q to represent the aggregate demand D.

Consequently

$$Q = f(K, L)$$

It must not be employed as a production function for aggregate supply, since the real observed values may not completely be aggregate supply S; it may also be values of aggregate demand D. The required function should be $S = f(K, L)$, where S is not measurable. However, this problem can be solved with the aforementioned disequilibrium approach, as discussed in Sect. 8.6 of this book.

5.1 Analysis of Supply Behavior at a Micro Level

The reality of China's economy is that enterprises seldom go bankrupt and employees seldom get sacked. Therefore, stock variables K and L grow steadily with only slight changes in the short-run. However, since some young graduates are temporarily laid-off, the annual increased employees ΔL will be more sensitive to economic growth than that of L. When economy expands, ΔL becomes correspondingly larger and vice versa. Similarly, the annual increase in fixed assets ΔK will be more sensitive to economic growth than that of K. ΔK also becomes larger with economic expansions and vice versa. Therefore, when comparing K and L, the increased ΔL and ΔK are more fluctuating.

Therefore, a basic economic behavior in Chinese enterprises is that when a certain level of output is determined by any demand condition exogenously, enterprise is not

[1] This will be proven in Sect. 8.6.

going to choose the combination of K and L to minimize the total cost because such a combination cannot be determined by the enterprise under the prevailing economic system. However, enterprise is in fact authorized to choose ΔK and ΔL as well as ΔQ. Thus, enterprise will prioritize the incremental analysis rather than a stock analysis in determining its minimum total cost. So, there is

$$\min \Delta TC = r\Delta K + \omega\Delta L$$

$$s.t.\ \Delta Q = f(\Delta K, \Delta L)$$

where, r denotes the price of newly added fixed asset ΔK; ω is the price of newly added labor force ΔL; st is the constraint condition; ΔTC is the increased total cost.

The Lagrangian Function used to describe this problem is

$$Y = r\Delta K + \omega\Delta L - \lambda\{\Delta Q - f(\Delta K - \Delta L)\}$$

The first order condition for finding the extremum is

$$\frac{\partial Y}{\partial \Delta K} = r + \lambda f\Delta K = 0$$

$$\frac{\partial Y}{\partial \Delta L} = \omega + \lambda f\Delta L = 0$$

It can also be recorded as

$$\frac{\partial f(\Delta K + \Delta L)}{\partial \Delta K} = f_{\Delta K}$$

$$\frac{\partial f(\Delta K + \Delta L)}{\partial \Delta L} = f_{\Delta L}$$

Therefore

$$\frac{f_{\Delta L}}{f_{\Delta K}} = \frac{\omega}{r} \text{ Since}$$

$$\mathrm{d}(\Delta Q) = f_{\Delta K} \cdot \mathrm{d}(\Delta K) + f_{\Delta L} \cdot \mathrm{d}(\Delta L)$$

$f_{\Delta K}$ can be approximated as the contribution rate of ΔK to ΔQ and $f_{\Delta L}$ as the contribution rate of ΔL to ΔQ. If ΔQ is given, the enterprise will equalize the ratio of these two contributions to the ratio of their corresponding prices (note that prices are sticky here) to determine its minimum cost.Of course, a highly abstract analysis is conducted here. In fact, many other factors are considered by a enterprise in determining its lowest cost. Moreover, both new capital and new labor force will be engaging in production with the existing capital and labor force, and they should not be separated. However, the enterprise will still carry out an analysis on gains and losses of the new assets and new labor force in advance.Here, the lowest cost achieved after determining the level of output will be in turn reflecting the maximum profit generated at that level of output.As for the short-term plan of a business, only after determining ΔK and ΔL can ΔQ be considered "the higher, the better" because the average cost of production can be reduced in this way. Enterprise will not regard ΔQ as the higher the better if ΔK and ΔL are still undeterminable. That is to say, from the perspective of short-run economic benefits, when finalizing Q, ΔK and ΔL or considering its scale of output expansion, enterprise only pursues an appropriate scale rather than "the bigger, the better". The primary prerequisite for such an appropriate scale is the anticipated demand of the business. When anticipated demand is low, large production scales will not be the objective. The hardship in economic stimulation in 1990 demonstrated that "the bigger, the better" was not the choice of appropriate output scale for a business. This has also been illustrated in the analysis here. Of course, a enterprise does possess endogenous enthusiasm to increase its output scale in the long-run. This has been also pointed out in the previous analysis.The proposition of price stickiness has been employed in the previous analysis, that is, in response to a certain change in demand, a enterprise does not adjust the price but the output in the short-run. This is a typical quantitative adjustment. In addition, the proposition of rational man has also been used in the analysis, that is, under the constraint of output, a enterprise's pursuit of minimum cost is in equivalent to its pursuit of the maximum profit.It is a core proposition in our theory of supply that in the short-run enterprise adjusts output level rather than prices to adapt to changes in demand. This proposition will play a critical role in the analysis of China's inflation problem.In a perfectly competitive market economy, price is imposed externally to a enterprise that only needs to adjust its own output level. But for the entire market economic system, price is viewed as a function of the gap between supply and demand, which fluctuates with supply and demand conditions. Therefore, price is endogenous in a market economy. Under China's prevailing economic system, part of the price is endogenous and part exogenous, which is reflected in its stickiness. Although price is externally imposed and enterprise adjusts only its own output, the focus point for enterprise to adjust such output is different from that of enterprise in a market economy. The former adjusts output according to the price stickiness, while the latter follows price elasticity. The output adjustment of the former seldom follows the market fluctuations, while the latter is completely determined by the market forces.

5.2 Impacts of Economies of Scale and Technical Progress on Aggregate Supply

Under certain technical conditions, output level will be consistent with a given input mix. As input increases, output increases accordingly. In the case of constant-returns to scale, input and output is directly proportionated; as economies of scale incurred, output increases more than input; diseconomies of scale indicates that output decreases as more inputs are involved. These three relationships can be represented in Fig. 5.1.

If the Cobb–Douglas production function is utilized as the production function of aggregate supply, it will be

$$S = AK^{\alpha}L^{\beta}$$

Then, the value of $\alpha+\beta$ corresponds to the following:

$$\alpha + \beta < 1, \text{ diseconomies of scale;}$$

$$\alpha + \beta = 1, \text{ constant-returns to scale;}$$

$$\alpha + \beta > 1, \text{ economies of scale.}$$

In addition to economies of scale, the relationship between input and output will also be influenced by technical progress. More outputs can be produced from the same input mix under technical progress, which usually refers to the neutral technical progress defined by Hicks. Such neutral technical progress can maintain a constant marginal rate of substitution between capital and labor, or a constant slope of the isoquant.

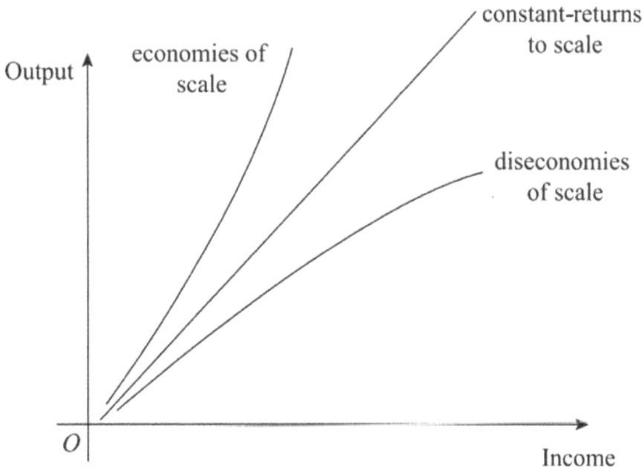

Fig. 5.1 Three types of economies of scale

Solow adopted the following approach to analyze the influence of technical progress on output level. Assume that

$$Q_t = A(t)F(K_t, L_t)$$

The following holds when taking the derivative of both sides with respect to a time dimension, there will be

$$\dot{Q} = \dot{A}F(K_t, L_t) + A\frac{\partial F}{\partial K}\dot{K} + A\frac{\partial F}{\partial L}\dot{L}$$

Divide both sides of this equation by Q to get the relative rate of change in output

$$\frac{\dot{Q}}{Q} = \frac{\dot{A}F(K_t, L_t)}{Q} + A\frac{\partial F}{\partial K}\cdot\frac{\dot{K}}{Q} + A\frac{\partial F}{\partial L}\cdot\frac{\dot{L}}{Q}$$

Now add an assumption from microeconomics theory that input prices equal their marginal product under perfect competition, there will be

$$\frac{\partial Q}{\partial K} = A\frac{\partial F}{\partial K} = \frac{r}{P}$$

$$\frac{\partial Q}{\partial L} = A\frac{\partial F}{\partial L} = \frac{\omega}{P}$$

Solow utilized $\omega_K = rK/(PQ)$ and $\omega_L = \omega L/(PQ)$ to represent the proportion of capital and labor respectively. Then $\dot{Q}/Q$ can be expressed as

$$\frac{\dot{Q}}{Q} = \frac{\dot{A}}{A} + \omega_K\frac{\dot{K}}{K} + \omega_L\frac{\dot{L}}{L}$$

$$\frac{\dot{A}}{A} = \frac{\dot{Q}}{Q} - \omega_K\frac{\dot{K}}{K} - \omega_L\frac{\dot{L}}{L}$$

Thus, since $\dot{Q}/Q$, $\dot{K}/K$ and $\dot{L}/L$ are the corresponding growth rates of each variable, as long as ω_K and ω_L are given, $\dot{A}/A$, the growth rate of technical progress can be computed.

On the basis of the conclusion from theoretical analysis under perfect competition, the proportion of wages and profits in the national income is ω_L and ω_K respectively (assuming constant-returns to scale exists). However, in China's economy, there is no internal mechanism for that, it therefore becomes problematic to determine the accurate values of ω_L and ω_K. According to the previous analysis, after the reform of the economic system, the proportion of household income in the national income has increased annually as a result of competition among various interest factors. Such a tendency is not attributed to an increase in the labor force due to capital and labor substitution effect, but because the benefit mechanism tends to be more in favor of household income distribution after the economic reform.

Technical progress in China's economy has been estimated by the above-mentioned approaches. Given $\omega_K = 0.6$, $\omega_L = 0.4$, the results from the World Bank demonstrate that such neutral technical progress carries very tiny impact on China's economic growth. Some Chinese scholars are suspicious of the World Bank's assumption, arguing that an increase in labor force contributes more to the economic growth than capital does. They therefore set $\omega_K = 0.4$, $\omega_L = 0.6$, and the results indicate that neutral technical progress contributes significantly to China's economy growth.

The differences between the two estimates of technical progress in China's economy originate from their opposite assumptions. In addition, the fundamental data adopted in the calculations are also different since there are inadequate indicators such as the overall social original value and net value of fixed assets in China's statistical data source. Since they have to be included in the computation of technical progress, these data have to be roughly estimated. Consequently, the results will naturally differ with different estimation methods.

The original and net value of fixed assets as well as the number of labor force of the industrial enterprises owned by the whole people with an independent accounting system can be found in the national financial statistical data in China. On the basis of these data, the neutral technical progress in those enterprises has been measured with two sets of assumptions, they are $\omega_K = 0.6$, $\omega_L = 0.4$ and $\omega_K = 0.4$, $\omega_L = 0.6$. The two hypothetical estimations can thus be contrasted on the same data set. The results are shown in Table 5.1.

A price column is added to Table 5.1 in order to contrast with the inflated price level in the growth rate of the present value.

According to the results, the neutral technical progress is obvious in the industrial enterprises owned by the whole people with an independent accounting system under

Table 5.1 Contribution of technical progress in economic growth rates

Year	$w_K = 0.6$ $w_L = 0.4$	$w_K = 0.4$ $w_L = 0.6$	Growth rate of net output (at current prices)	National income deflator
1978	2.3	4.1		1.4
1979	4.0	5.1	9.6	4.0
1980	2.7	3.4	8.5	3.5
1981	−6.6	−6.0	−0.01	1.8
1982	−1.0	0.0	4.5	0.0
1983	2.8	4.3	8.6	1.1
1984	9.4	10.85	14.7	5.3
1985	8.4	10.77	19.6	10.0
1986	−3.8	−1.8	5.9	3.9
1987	6.2	8.4	16.2	7.0

Table 5.2 The proportion of contribution of neutral technical progress to net output growth rates

Year	$w_K = 0.6$ $w_L = 0.4$	$w_K = 0.4$ $w_L = 0.6$
1979	42	53
1980	32	40
1981	–	–
1982	–	–
1983	33	50
1984	64	74
1985	43	55
1986	–	–
1987	38	52
Average	42	54

either hypothesis (except for some years in adjustment, such as 1981 and 1986, when economic downturns incurred following the implementation of contractionary macroeconomic policy).

There is a pitfall in this calculation: value of the fixed assets has been somewhat imputed. The value of the fixed asset is expressed as

$$\begin{aligned}\text{Value of Fixed Assets} &= \text{Original Value of Fixed Assets} \\ &\quad + \text{Net Value of Fixed Assets}/2\end{aligned}$$

The original and net values of the fixed assets here are calculated on current prices. For consistency, the net value data will base on current prices. In order to eliminate the impact of price level to some extent, equation $(\dot{A}/A)/(\dot{Q}/Q)$ will be employed, which denotes the proportion of contribution of neutral technical progress to the net output growth, as shown in Table 5.2.

It can be seen from Table 5.2 that among the industrial enterprises owned by the whole people with an independent accounting system, the contribution rate of technical progress to the growth of net output value is between 42 and 54%.

The calculations also indicate that the impact of economic fluctuations is reflected in $\dot{A}/A$ because it is calculated by using the residual method. To use average value is to eliminate the influence of economic fluctuations. Since the three years with negative values are not counted in this average calculation, the results are believed to be overestimated. Since the years without average values account for only one third of the time period, if the technical progress in these three years is assumed to be 0, then the average value will drop from 42 to 28, and 54 to 36 respectively. The result shows that the technical progress is still prominent.

It should be pointed out that the technical progress of the industrial enterprises owned by the whole people is higher than that of the entire society since advanced technology and equipment are mostly adopted by those enterprise organizations, which meanwhile enjoy more qualified employees than that in the entire society.

As a result, contributions of technical progress of the entire society to economic growth will be smaller than the above estimations. Especially in the rural areas, a big number of modes of agricultural production remain quite primitive, which substantially diminish the degree of the technical progress of the entire society.

The concept of neutral technical progress helps illustrate the sources of economic growth. In addition to the investment in physical and human capital, the science and technology embodied in them are also crucial to economic growth. The transformation from the so-called intensive economy to extensive economy does emphasize the degree of technical progress. In other words, economic growth comes not only from investment in natural resource but also from investment in intellectual resources.

5.3 Determination of Input Factors

A enterprise mainly considers two factors in determining its input factors. One is the anticipated demand level, and the other is the level of corporate loans. A highly anticipated demand level and a huge loan offer will stimulate enterprise to invest more. A low anticipated demand level will on the contrary discourage investment. Such enterprise behavior has been more obvious in recent years. Particularly in 1990, the low anticipated demand level caused deficient enterprise investment despite the easing of the lending policy.

Of course, high anticipated demand level but a low loan offer will discourage enterprise investment. In the case that supply growth lags behind demand growth, enterprise may raise product prices to earn higher profits. However, in general, prices will not change over time to cope with demand changes, or prices are not changed too frequently with demand in the short- run. Enterprise accommodates changes in demand by adjusting its output level.

Output level adjustment can be implemented in both the short and long- run. The long-run approach means an expansion of production scale, that is, to increase fixed assets and labor force; the short-run approach, however, does not involve in expansion of production scale, but in accelerating pace of production, overtime to increase the output level on the basis of original fixed assets and labor force. The behavior of enterprise to expand production scale has been analyzed in Sect. 5.1 of this chapter. The short-run approach of output adjustment will be constrained by the technical ability of the fixed assets and physical fatigue limits of labor. Therefore, accelerating the pace of production cannot be sustained indefinitely. On top of that, short-run output adjustment will also be restricted by bottleneck sectors, such as power, fuel, transportation, raw materials, and so on, which will adversely affect the production pace.

Internally, there exists a huge potentiality for short-run output adjustment in Chinese enterprises because of the "big pot" employment policy, which indulges idle labor and low working rhythm. Thus, an increase in working rhythm would be in equivalence to an increase in the labor force. Moreover, in the long-term sectors, more fixed assets are staying idle so that the breaking down of equipment becomes quite a common phenomenon. Such potential productivity could be fully cultivated if enhancements in these bottleneck sectors are quickened.

It can thus be stated that the potentiality of enterprise internal output adjustment is a physical foundation for China's economic fluctuations.

According to Keynesian economic theory, the idleness of fixed assets within enterprises in Western economies originates from insufficient effective demand. Such problems can be solved as long as effective demand is stimulated. In China, the idleness of fixed assets exists when demand surpasses supply. Therefore, stimulating the demand only is not very helpful to solve this problem. China's idle fixed assets are a result of its economic structure, which must be restructured so that this problem can be solved. Furthermore, such economic restructuring will be mainly dependent upon the diversion of new production factors towards the bottleneck sectors. The accomplishment of this task depends on the national macroeconomic planning policies. Enterprises themselves are unable to deal with this problem alone due to their capital flow restrictions.

5.4 The Short-Run Aggregate Supply Function

In the short-run, output is not adjusted by expanding the production scale, but by accelerating the pace of production, which is of huge latent potential in China. So what are the key variables determining the pace of production in China? It is believed that the key variable is the level of credit available to businesses. From a macro level perspective, China experiences more frequently a situation where aggregate demand surpasses aggregate supply, which imposes an external pressure on enterprises to expand output level. However, such an attempt will be restricted by loan levels since banks are not always able to meet loan demands from businesses. In general, expansion of the loan scale is equivalent to the expansion of aggregate demand. As a result, enterprises can only adjust their output level by following the degree of the tightness of bank loans.

Given a constant amount of a fixed asset K and labor L, different amounts of loans achieved by the enterprises will determine the pace of production, and thus the level of output. So the short-run supply function is

$$S = f(M)$$

where M denotes the amount of loan or quantity of the money supply, as M increases, S goes up in the short-run. However, the pace of production cannot rise indefinitely because there is a ceiling beyond which even more loans cannot enhance supply in the short-run. In the last section of this chapter, several types of factors that constrain increase in aggregate supply will be examined, which is undefined here.Interest rates have not yet become a critical factor in adjusting output levels in China. Owing to the soft budget constraints, the interest rate is inelastic to businesses. That is to say, a rise in the interest rate will not substantially discourage loan demands from

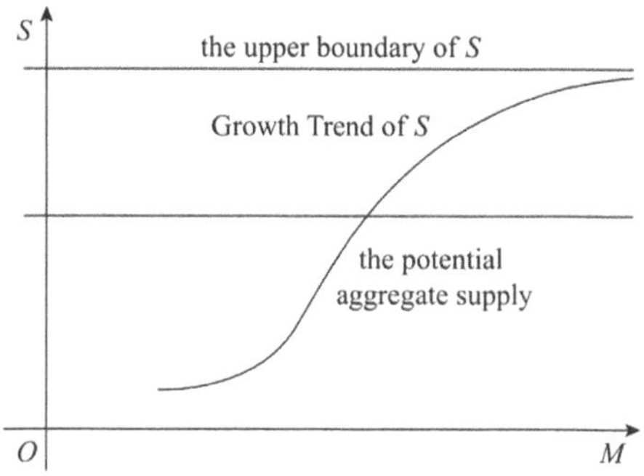

Fig. 5.2 The short-run aggregate supply curve

businesses. That is why the interest rate variable is not integrated into the short-run supply function. This is completely deviated from Western economies where the interest rate carries a relatively heavy impact on supply.According to the above analysis, the short-run aggregate supply function is not linear. Assuming that K and L are constant, the increase in S will gradually slowdown and eventually cease as M increases. At this point, S reaches its growth upper boundary, which is determined by limits of the pace of production and constraints of bottleneck sectors as shown in Fig. 5.2.

As shown in Fig. 5.2, when S runs below potential aggregate supply, M carries a greater effect on S and it rises faster owing to the greater potential for accelerating the pace of production. When S lies above potential aggregate supply, the impact of M on S is also weakened because of the diminished potential for accelerating the pace of production. Accordingly, S becomes sluggish and tends to its upper boundary with an increase in M.

Similar to the previous aggregate demand function, short-run aggregate supply is also related to the money illusion of the producers. Assuming that the planned production S^* (or anticipated supply) of the producer in a given period is related to the planned money acquisition M^* (or anticipated money achievable, which is the real quantity of money deemed by the businesses) of the producer. The planned production of the producer can be expressed as

$$S^* = f\left(M^*\right)$$

If a producer is enslaved to a money illusion, that is, when the nominal money received M is greater than M^* (in fact, M is equal to or even less than M^* due to the rise in prices P), the producer will regard the difference between M and M^* as an additional money gain. The supply will thus be further expanded, and accordingly, there is

$$S = S^* + \eta\left(M - M^*\right)$$

where, η is the proportional coefficient.

If the planned production S^* is equal to the potential aggregate supply, the above equation will represent the mechanism between the expansion of the money supply and real aggregate supply exceeding its potential level. In the long-run, the enterprise planned output should be based on its potential level, therefore, it is reasonable to assume that S^* is equal to the potential aggregate supply. This formula also shows that in the long-run, S will verge to S^* when the money illusion of producers disappears through learning. This demonstrates that a long-run inflationary policy will be unable to stimulate the real aggregate supply.

5.5 The Long-Run Aggregate Supply Function

The determinants of the long-run aggregate supply function are different from those of the short-run aggregate supply function. In the short-run aggregate supply function, lending is the determining factor, and the short- run output is further subject to the money illusion. On the contrary, money has no effect on output in the long-run aggregate supply function because the money illusion will be eliminated by the economic actors through learning in the long-run. Therefore, in the long-run, it is the technical conditions that determine the output level, that is, the output level relies upon K and L. Thus, the long-run aggregate supply function can be expressed as

$$S = f(K, L)$$

Obviously, this function can also be viewed as the potential aggregate supply function, which represents the normal supply capacity determined by technology in the economic system.

The following will be an analysis of the relationship between the short- run aggregate supply function and the long-run aggregate supply function.

Assuming that the short-run aggregate supply function is

$$S_S = f(M)$$

The long-run aggregate supply function is

$$S_L = f(K, L)$$

In any particular year, the size of the short-run aggregate supply function will be restrained by its long-run aggregate supply function. The short-run aggregate supply can only exceed the long-run aggregate supply to a certain extent, or there is a limit for the short-run aggregate supply to surpass the long-run aggregate supply. Once this limit is reached, no matter how many loans are achieved, the short-run aggregate supply can no longer be expanded.

Fig. 5.3 The short-run aggregate supply fluctuates around the long run aggregate supply

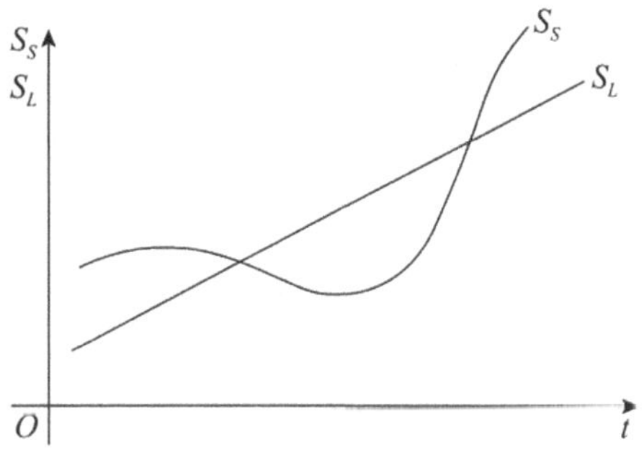

The short-run aggregate supply always fluctuates around the long-run aggregate supply in the long-run. In some years, the short-run aggregate supply may run above the long-run aggregate supply, and the opposite may hold in other years, as shown in Fig. 5.3.

Main reasons for the short-run aggregate supply to deviate from the long-run aggregate supply include the following: (1) if aggregate demand constantly surpasses aggregate supply, aggregate demand will drive the short- run aggregate supply to exceed its potential or the long-run aggregate supply level in a certain period of time; (2) insufficient aggregate demand will drag down the short-run aggregate supply to a level lower than its potential or the long-run aggregate supply level; (3) expectations play an important role in driving the short-run aggregate supply to deviate from the long-run aggregate supply. The stickiness of expectations will impose a certain level of stickiness on the short-run aggregate supply, and invalidate the immediate effectiveness of the regulation policies on supply of the government.

Contrasting with Fig. 5.2, if the short-run aggregate supply curve is a curve with an upper boundary, then the long-run aggregate supply will be a linear line perpendicular to S_L (the potential aggregate supply curve in Fig. 5.2) in the same coordinate system. This suggests that, in the long-run, the money supply M is neutral to supply, or it is invalid to supply itself, as shown in Fig. 5.4.

The shape of the aggregate supply curve indicates obvious policy significance: in the short-run, the aggregate supply curve is upward sloping, indicating the short-run effectiveness of demand management policy, and supply can be stimulated by raising the money supply. The vertical aggregate supply curve indicates that the demand management policy is ineffective in the long-run. The real supply remains

Fig. 5.4 The long-run aggregate supply curve perpendicular to the output axis

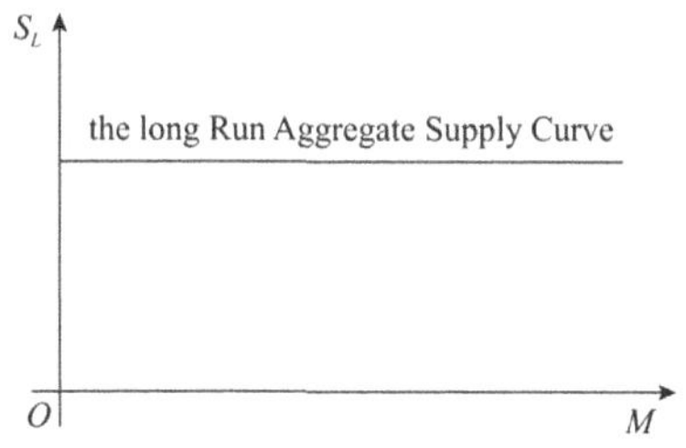

unchanged, no matter how the money supply increases, which will merely boost the nominal supply so that inflation becomes intensified. This property of the aggregate supply curve lays a theoretical foundation for subsequent policy analysis.

5.6 Constraints on Aggregate Supply

The growth of aggregate supply in China has been constrained by the following four factors:

1. Resource or bottleneck sector constraints. For a long time, products offered by the primary industrial sectors such as electricity, raw materials, fuels, transportation as well as the agricultural sectors have been unable to match with the demands of other sectors in the national economy. Consequently, growth in aggregate supply is severely repressed by these bottleneck sectors.
2. Government policy constraints. When it believes that the economy is overheating and inflation is rising, government will contract the economy through restricting investment and growth in aggregate supply, especially in the long-term sectors. This can be regarded as constraints on supply growth by insufficient demand under the contractionary policy. The Chinese economic growth pattern in 1990 well illustrated this point.
3. The increasing proportion of consumption in the national income also restricts the growth of aggregate supply. The more national income is spent on consumption, the less is on accumulation. As a result, the long-run increase in aggregate supply is driven by national income accumulations.

The determination of accumulation and consumption is influenced by many factors and is far beyond government's control. From the distribution point of view, a greater growth rate of household income over the national income will be conducive to the growth of consumption. However, from the perspective of the sector structure, in the case that the growth rate of production of consumer goods is unable to meet with that of household income, such household income will not be translated into real consumption. Thus, interest rate regulation and rationing (such as housing allocation) of the government have deemed to be a means to regulate consumption.

In terms of time dimension, the ratio between consumption and accumulation is a dynamic optimization issue. Although a near term rise in accumulation may adversely influence the near term consumption, it is conducive to enhancing consumption in the long-run. There is no such a mechanism in the Chinese economic system for consumption to boost the optimal growth curve. How the government can achieve such a goal remains an issue for research. The difficulty of such an issue is not in relying in mathematical means but in optimal goal determination and policy control because such a dynamic optimization issue can be resolved through mathematical dynamic programming and the Pontryagin's maximum principle. Optimal goal determination is not a problem of economic theory in essence; it is framed by the government's political goals.

Fig. 5.5 Diminishing marginal returns

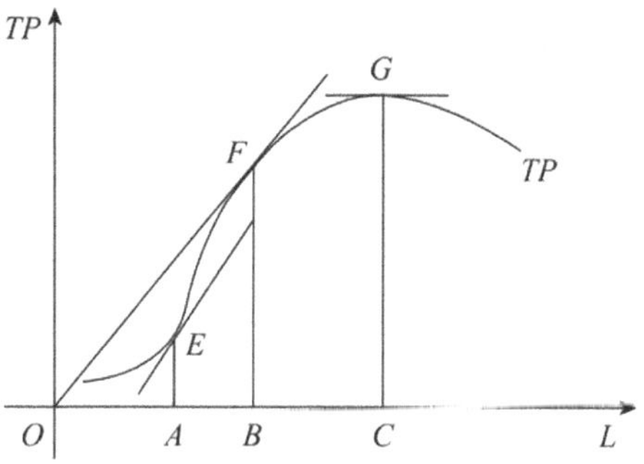

4. Diminishing marginal returns. Specifically, this can be expressed as when other inputs remain constant, the total output (or production) of a product will increase with an increase of a given input. However, such output will eventually become less and less after reaching a certain level. In this case, the total output increases while its incremental quantity diminishes.

Usually the total product (*TP*) curve rises at an increasing rate, and then it reaches its maximum point at a diminishing rate, beyond which it declines, as shown in Fig. 5.5.

In Fig. 5.5, the slope $\Delta TP/\Delta L$ of the *TP* curve is the marginal product. Three tangency points can be seen in Fig. 5.5. Point *E* has the highest slope and represents the maximum marginal product (*MP*). The slope at point *G* is 0, so *MP* equals 0. The slope at point *F* is *FB/OB*, but *FB/OB* also represents the average output from *OB* units of input *L*. This point is also the maximum point of the average product since *OF* is the steepest tangent line to *TP* drawn from the origin.

According to microeconomic theory, the point at which a enterprise can generate its maximum profit is:

$$\text{Marginal Cost} = \text{Product Price}$$

In China, if output value is the main target for assessment, then the highest production constraint of the enterprise will locate at point *G*. In short, no enterprise will continue to produce anything beyond point *G*.

Part III
Operational Mechanisms of Inflation

Chapter 6
The General Inflation Gap and Its Formation Mechanism

The general inflation gap is formed when aggregate demand exceeds aggregate supply. It can be categorized in two components i.e. the rise in the price level and shortages. This chapter only analyzes the formation mechanism of this gap and the relationship between prices and shortages will be explored in next chapter.

6.1 Relationship Among Aggregate Supply, Aggregate Demand and General Inflation Gap

The relationship between aggregate demand and aggregate supply can be scrutinized through the aggregate demand and aggregate supply function. The relationship between the aggregate demand function and the short-run aggregate supply function will be studied primarily. These two functions are expressed as follows

$$D = f(r, M); S = f(M)$$

For the convenience of analysis, the real interest rate r is assumed to be constant. In this case, the aggregate demand function and the short-run aggregate supply function can be denoted as

$$D = D(M); S = S(M)$$

Both D and S are now the functions of money supply M. According to the previous analysis, D increases as M rises. D is assumed to be the linear function of M, but not of S. S rises more rapidly when it runs below the potential aggregate supply while it rises more slowly when it becomes greater than the potential aggregate supply, and S approaches to its upper bound as M rises. The increase of D and S is demonstrated in Fig. 6.1.

L. Li, *The Inflation Mechanism and Expectations*, Understanding China,
https://doi.org/10.1007/978-981-97-2570-0_6

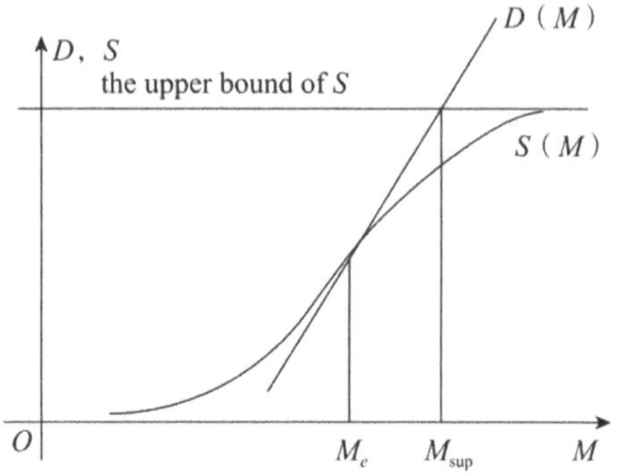

Fig. 6.1 The general inflation gap

In Fig. 6.1, M_e is the quantity of money supply when aggregate demand equals aggregate supply. When M is less than M_e, aggregate supply is greater than aggregate demand; when M runs over M_e, aggregate demand is greater than aggregate supply. Therefore,

$$\text{When } M > M_e, D(M) - S(M) > 0$$

$$\text{When } M = M_e, D(M) - S(M) = 0$$

$$\text{When } M < M_e, D(M) - S(M) < 0$$

$$\text{Let } DS(M) = D(M) - S(M)$$

$DS(M)$is obviously the surplus aggregate demand. When it is positive, $DS\ (M)$ becomes the general gap of inflation.

It can be seen from the above analysis that the reason why $DS(M)$ is greater than zero is that $D\ (M)$ increases as M rises, but $S(M)$ diminishes and falls within its upper bound. Therefore, $D\ (M)$ will be greater than $S(M)$ when M becomes greater than a certain value (such as M_e).

Two basic points are depicted in Fig. 6.1, M_e and M_{sup}. M_e stands for the quantity of the money supply equalizing aggregate demand to aggregate supply, which is generally viewed as the appropriate quantity of money supply. When the real money supply exceeds M_e, inflation occurs while a recession is triggered in case the real money supply is lower than M_e. M_{sup} represents the quantity of the money supply driving aggregate demand to reach the upper bound of aggregate supply. In the case of $M_e < M < M_{\text{sup}}$, although aggregate demand runs over aggregate supply, $DS(M)$ is still not too huge, which can be regarded as a moderate inflation. When $M > M_{\text{sup}}$, aggregate supply diminishes while aggregate demand increases progressively, and inflation tends to be worsen.

It should be noted that both aggregate demand and aggregate supply here are ex ante, so is *DS*(*M*). This indicates that the inflationary pressures have already been in place even before the actual purchase and production. At this point, *DS*(*M*) is merely a potential pressure. It will be turned into a real inflation when purchase starts. Whether *DS*(*M*) can be translated into the real general inflation gap depends on if the real aggregate supply is equal to the ex ante aggregate supply. In case the real aggregate supply equals the ex ante aggregate supply, *DS*(*M*) will be all translated into the real inflation gap. If the real aggregate supply is greater than the ex ante aggregate supply, part of *DS*(*M*) will be translated into the real inflation. If the real aggregate supply runs below the ex ante aggregate supply, *DS*(*M*) will be smaller than the real inflation.

The real aggregate supply is not necessarily equal to the ex ante aggregate supply. It depends not only on *K*, *L* and *M* but also on other factors such as climate, political situation, and so forth. However, the real aggregate supply should fluctuate around the ex ante aggregate supply, so it can be functioned as

$$\overline{S} = S(M) + U$$

where, *S* represents the real aggregate supply; *U* is the random error term; *S*(*M*) is the ex ante aggregate supply. Thus, the relationship among the real aggregate supply, ex-ante aggregate demand and real inflation will be

$$D = D(M)\ \overline{S} = S(M) + U\ DS = D - S$$

The above correlations are depicted in Fig. 6.2.

Another inflation gap can be defined as the gap between aggregate demand and the potential aggregate supply. Because the potential aggregate supply is expressed as the average production capacity, theoretically, it is considered tight in the utilization of the production technology and equipment or the economy is considered overheating when aggregate supply runs above its potential level. The gap between aggregate demand and the potential aggregate supply is viewed as the potential inflation.

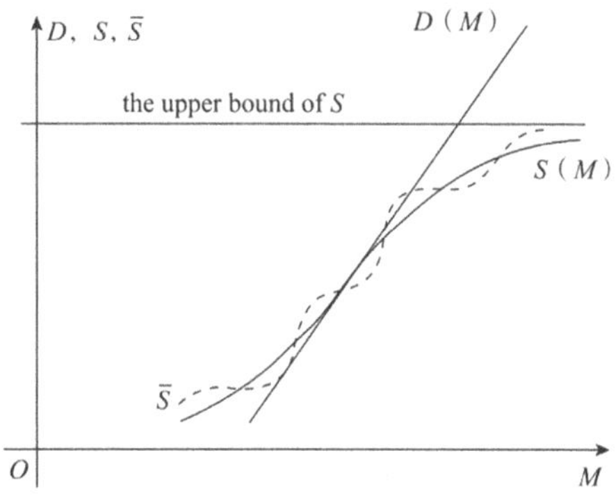

Fig. 6.2 The general gap of real inflation

Although the potential inflation has not yet incurred, it can also reflect inflationary pressures. Since the average production capacity is reflected in the potential aggregate supply, such an inflation gap can also be regarded as the average inflation gap, which is to a certain extent more stable than the real inflation and the ex ante inflation gap. This is because the potential aggregate supply function is not influenced by the money supply, and only changes in the aggregate demand are taken into account here. Therefore, it is easier to interpret the impact of the changes in aggregate demand on inflation through the potential inflation gap.

When inflation is sustained for a period of time, the public's money illusion will disappear and aggregate supply will return to its potential level. Therefore, the excessive money supply will only result in inflation. This phenomenon can be described by the following formula

$$D = D(M) = a + bM$$

$$S = S(M) = S^* + \eta(M - M^*)$$

The inflation gap is

$$DS = D(M) - S(M) = a + bM - S^* - \eta(M - M^*)$$

It can be determined that DS is smaller when a money illusion exists. When it disappears, DS becomes

$$DS = D(M) - S(M) = a + bM - S^*$$

In this case, DS becomes relatively larger. Thus, an excessive money supply will continuously stimulate aggregate demand. Aggregate supply will not be pushed up when the money illusion disappears, and the inflation gap will accordingly be expanded.

The above shows the fundamental theory for describing inflation. The specific formation mechanism of the general inflation gap will be further analyzed below.

6.2 The Demand-Pull Inflation

Inflation used to be associated with an excessive money supply, which reflects the aggregate demand inflation. Consequently, inflation is usually shown as aggregate demand greater than aggregate supply regardless of its mode. That is to say, aggregate demand being greater than aggregate supply is merely a phenomenon of inflation, which is merely an inflation being reflected through an excessive money supply. However, the occurrence mechanism of different inflation is changed even under the same phenomenon.

The demand-pull inflation is firstly reflected in its initial formation stage. At this stage, both aggregate demand and aggregate supply are stimulated by the money supply, which hence carries an inconspicuous impact upon the price level with the existence of a money illusion. Meanwhile, the government is easily induced to further increase the money supply since it witnesses the rapid expansion in production, the increase of nominal income of households, and the prosperity of both purchases and sales. Such a period may last for some time until the households' money illusion gradually vanishes, which enhances the influence of money upon the price level to accelerate inflation. As aggregate supply reaches or approaches near to its upper limit of growth, such aggregate demand-pull inflation starts to jump into its typical stage. At this time, any increase in aggregate demand will be directly reflected as an increase in inflation. In Chap. 4, both the aggregate demand model I and II have been employed to illustrate the impact of expenditure on the nominal national income. They can well reflect the inflation mechanism then. At the initial stage, the demand-pull inflation enhances aggregate supply and causes the increase in the price level to fall behind the money supply, which generates an illusion that more money supply is deemed to be a lubricant for economic growth. Such an illusion becomes a crucial inducement of inflation because it can easily induce the government to follow the path of inflation under the pressures of internal demand expansion in the economic system.

The terminology of aggregate demand inflation is commonly used in China's economic circles, which reflects the basic nature of demand- pull inflation. Aggregate demand inflation can be further reflected in both consumption demand inflation and investment demand inflation. There used to be two fundamentally opposite views on inflation from 1984 to 1988 (5 years). One view held that consumption demand inflation and investment demand inflation can occur simultaneously. The other believed that the consumption demand remained unchanged and inflation was applied only to the investment demand. That is to say, the initial diagnosis was applicable to the determination of the demand-pull inflation, since there was no consensus on whether it was mono or dual inflation. Of course, the prescription for treating inflation would not be identical with these two different diagnoses.

The main theoretical basis for the belief that consumption demand inflation did not exist is that, during these five years, the accumulation rate of national income tended to increase, averaging higher than 30% and closer to 35%. Most economic scholars believed that the appropriate accumulation rate should be between 25% and 30%. Investment is considered to be too high and consumption too low in case the accumulation rate is above an upper boundary of 30%. From this point of view, it was not a problem of inflation in consumption demand but rather a corresponding contraction from 1984 to 1988. It is logical to draw such a conclusion in light of the traditional theoretical framework.

Those who believed in consumption demand inflation held that the term itself did not mean the real consumption amount but the household disposable income. An indicator reflecting the proportion of household disposable income to the national income has been designed and measured, the results of which are shown in Table 4.1 of Chap. 4. This result shows that the growth rate of household disposable income is faster than that of the national income. It is thus believed that it is more convincing to use the proportion of household disposable income to national income (of course, the proportion of household disposable income to the Gross National Product can also be used here) to illustrate the increase of the household disposable income. However, the increase in household disposable income does not mean an expansion in consumption demand. The reasons are as follows:

Consumption demand itself is a function, influenced by interest rates, prices, and disposable income according to our previous analysis. With a rise in the interest rate and the price level, the consumption demand may not be boosted that much or may even fall, despite an increase in disposable income. In short, consumption demand is not the same as the household disposable income. Moreover, whether there is consumption demand inflation should not be discussed in terms of consumption demand per se: it should be contrasted with supply for consumption. Consumption demand inflation exists only when demand exceeds supply for consumption. Therefore, it is necessary to calculate its size first in order to determine whether there is a consumption demand inflation. Nonetheless, it is difficult to calculate this directly since consumption demand is ex ante. Fortunately, as China's consumer goods market has been generally liberalized and bargaining opportunities also applied to the few un-liberalized consumer goods, the fluctuation in the price level can therefore roughly reflect this ex ante consumption demand. With the rapid increase in the price level of consumer goods, it can be concluded that consumption demand inflation did exist in recent years.

In Western countries, the excess of aggregate demand over aggregate supply is generally believed to be the consequence of excessive investment over savings (in a closed economy), and consumption demand inflation is then not considered. Therefore, some Western economists also deny the viewpoint of consumption demand inflation in analyzing China's inflation. They believe that even if wages were touching a high level, it would be a cost- push inflation, not a demand-pull one. So there would be nothing concerned with consumption demand inflation. This would make sense if China were a market economy. However, China's economy is different from a pure market economy because a planned plus market regulated economic system is adopted.

As can be seen from the analysis in the earlier chapters, the Chinese economic system inherently enhances household disposable income, while government favors investment in non-consumption goods sectors in the redistribution stage of national income. Therefore, from the perspective of industrial structure, when initial distribution is dominated by more proportion of consumption, the light industry is emphasized. However, if redistribution is dominated by more proportion of production, the heavy industry becomes dominant. Discordance of these two kinds of objective requirements has induced the consumption demand to exceed the consumption supply. On top of this, China's capital flow is restricted by these sectors and largely depends on government planning arrangements. As a result, once the supply of consumer goods cannot meet its demand, there will be little room for improvement in supply in the short-run. This can be regarded as the internal mechanism of consumption demand inflation in China.

It is the characteristic of Chinese economic theory to further categorize consumption demand inflation and investment demand inflation in the demand-pull inflation scenario, which is a theoretical outcome nurtured by Chinese economic practice. No such conclusion can be drawn if Western economic theory is blindly copied.

Investment demand inflation will not be discussed here since it has become the consensus of most people. It should be pointed out that some people believe it an overestimation that the accumulation rate of national income is close to 35%. They maintain that, in recent years, due to the underestimation of depreciation and other factors, this investment amount has been exaggerated. If these factors are deducted, the accumulation rate should not be that large. Excessive compression of investment will bring undesirable consequences. Whether the accumulation rate is overestimated or not is a matter for discussion in the national income accounting, which will be ignored here due to data limitations. However, this issue is really noteworthy.

6.3 The Cost-Push Inflation

Inflation occurs not just from demand-pull but also from cost-push. The study of demand-pull inflation is mainly from the aspect of demand while the supply side is prioritized for the study of cost-push inflation. However, both demand-pull and cost-push are triggers of inflation in reality and they are mutually causative and difficult to distinguish clearly. In theory, however, it is necessary to distinguish between these two concepts because they represent two different formation mechanisms for inflation.

Three causes are believed to be embedded in the cost-push inflation.

The first cause is the rise in endogenous costs, such as the proportion of wages in product costs. In China's current economic system, employees in different enterprises tend to compare their incomes with one another. When employees in firms with high economic performance enjoy a pay raise, workers in firms with low economic performance will follow suit to demand a pay raise, which enhances the proportion of wages in the production costs. As costs increase, so does the price level. In case a product is not sold out due to its poor quality and high price, the enterprise will also transfer the burden to the government through submitting less profit, refusing to repay loans, taxes, and so forth. Therefore, from the perspective of the economic system, there is an internal impetus mechanism of the wage cost due to such comparisons. It is difficult to calculate the proportion of wages in the product cost objectively (wages include income such as bonuses, which are hard to measure), but based upon the proportion of household disposable income in the national income, we are still able to roughly estimate if the proportion of wage in total cost has tended to escalate. For example, based on the data from 1978 to 1987, the proportion of compensation C in the total social product $C + V + M$ can be found. It is worth noting that M stands for the surplus products, which is obtained by deducting compensation and wages from the total social product. Without hinting at the generality of the problem, let the household disposable income be V' and the national income be $V + M$. It is known that in 1978, the following equation holds:

$$\frac{C}{C+V+M} = 56\%$$

By re-arranging this equation, there is

$$V+M = 0.44(C+V+M)$$

Due to $\frac{V'}{V+M} = 69.9\%$ (refer to Table 4.1)
Then

$$V' = 0.699 \times 0.44(C+V+M)$$

Because

$$C = 0.56(C+V+M)$$

Then

$$C+V' = 0.56(C+V+M) + 0.699 \times 0.44(C+V+M)$$

Therefore

$$\frac{V'}{C+V'} = \frac{0.699 \times 0.44(C+V+M)}{0.56(C+V+M) + 0.699 \times 0.44(C+V+M)} = \frac{0.699 \times 0.44}{0.56 + 0.699 \times 0.44}$$

It is not difficult to prove that the approximate value will be high when $V'/C+V'$ is used to roughly substitute $V/C+V$. If $V'/C+V'$ is relatively stable, then this kind of substitution is feasible. Accordingly, the proportion of wages in the total cost in any individual year from 1977 to 1989 can be computed, as shown in Table 6.1.

Table 6.1 The proportion of wage in the total cost (%)

Year	The proportion of wage in total cost	Year	The proportion of wage in total cost
1977	36.2	1984	38.2
1978	35.4	1985	38.2
1979	36.4	1986	37.4
1980	37.3	1987	35.9
1981	38.1	1988	34.0
1982	37.8	1989	33.7
1983	37.5		

It is shown in Table 6.1 that the proportion of wages to the total cost was basically stable from 1977 to 1989, fluctuating around 35%, and trended downward gradually after 1985.

On one hand, wages and other incomes are constantly rising on the basis of ownership analysis. On the other hand, real data suggest that the proportion of wages to the total costs is roughly stable. This phenomenon can be interpreted from the following two aspects.

Firstly, enterprise can transfer wage costs to the government, which is reflected in the withholding of profits, taxes, and so forth. Therefore, the increase in wages leading to a reduction in government profits will prevent the wages from being amortized to the overall costs. Accordingly, such kind of wage raise is only reflected in the loss of government revenue, not in the cost of production, which is regarded as an erosion of wages towards profits. With a decrease in the national fiscal revenue, the government will be forced to engage in deficit finance in order to maintain a certain level of fiscal expenditure. Such deficits will ultimately be remedied by the bank through the money supply, thus turning the cost-push inflation into a demand- pull one. This transformation mechanism of inflation is closely related to the proposition of the enterprise mechanism of profit transfer.

Secondly, the rise in the proportion of enterprise wages to total costs will cause the product price to rise. As the overall price level increases, so does the price of the enterprise compensation C. The increase of C offsets the increase in the proportion of wage cost to the total cost caused by the increase of wage V. Therefore, in more recent years, the rising trend of wages to the total costs is clearly mirrored. For example, in 1981, the proportion of wages to the total costs was 0.381, which was 2.6% higher than that in 1978. In 1981, the total retailing price index reached 102.4 and the national income deflator was 101.8. Given the implementation of a dual tightening policy in 1981, the increase in the price level could be viewed as a cost-push, which was different from the inflation nature in 1984.

The above measurements indicate that though rise in the proportion of wages to the total costs pushes up inflation, it is not the primary factor because its effect is weakened by the first reason aforesaid. This is different from Western market economy. In Western countries, rising wages usually result in higher costs, leading to a cost-push inflation. In China, however, the rising wages would cause a reduction in national fiscal revenue to induce the bank to expand the money supply, thus triggering a demand-pull inflation. Such a phenomena was strongly illustrated by the fall in the proportion of China's national fiscal revenue to the national income from 33.1% in 1977 to 19% in 1988. Therefore, the growth rate of the proportion of household disposable income to the national income roughly coincides with the decline rate of the proportion of the government fiscal revenue to the national income.

The second cause is the rise in exogenous cost reflecting in the prices of imported equipment and materials. This is considered categorized as an imported inflation. However, such a cost rise has not yet constituted the main driving force of inflation since China is a huge country implementing a managed exchange rate system.

The third cause is the increase in various product prices triggered by demand-pull inflation. Such a price rise will in turn push up the production cost, which consequently further drives up the price level. It is hard to measure such a causal relationship, and it becomes a common phenomena when inflation rises to a certain level. This is defined as the Hybrid Inflation, which will be particularly studied in the next section. It is with the existence of the hybrid inflation that the wage costs are stabilized. This is attributed to the constant ratio of $V/C+V$ when the price of C increases at the same proportion as that of income V.

6.4 The Expected Inflation

As long as inflation continues for a period of time, the demand-pull and cost-push inflation will mutually propel each other, generating a hybrid inflation. With such inflation, the expectations of households and enterprises will keep pace with, or even exceed, real inflation. In order to fight against such inflation, enterprises will raise their product prices in advance, and households strive for a higher nominal monetary income as per anticipated inflation rate. Even the government has to increase its money supply in advance to cope with the increase in money demand triggered by prices rise. At this point, inflation itself will propel more inflation per se as to make it a more vicious cycle.

In China, changes in the price level are not determined by the market forces of supply and demand but by the government sectors due to the long time implementation of government price control policies. Under such circumstances, the expectations of households and enterprises for changes in the price level are stable. This means that it is meaningless to study inflation expectations from a theoretical point of view. However, this situation changed after 1984. With the gradual relief of price controls, and especially with the gradual rise in price levels, inflation expectations of households and enterprises have been gradually shaped. The inflation expectations of Chinese households and enterprises can be separated into three stages based upon the prevailing data.

In the first stage, the inflation expectations of households and enterprises are lower than the real situation. It is reflected in the fact that the gap between the growth rate of the money supply and GNP does not fully translate into the growth of the price level, but leads to a reduction in the velocity of money. In 1984, for example, $M1$, $M2$, $M3$ (all are defined in Sect. 7.3 of Chap. 7) and GNP grew by 49.5, 34.5, 27, and 14.5% respectively. The difference between the growth rate of $M3$ and GNP was 12.5%, but the corresponding GNP deflator (a reflection of the overall price level) was only 4.9%, which was 4.9% higher than that of the previous year. Obviously, of the 12.5% of the money growth exceeding the GDP growth, 4.9% was translated into the price level and 7.6% into the reduction of the velocity of money. Of the many factors causing a reduction in the money velocity, the inflation expectations of households and enterprises was therefore viewed as the most critical.

In 1984, the growth rate of money supply jumped to a new level since China began to implement price reforms. Prior to 1984, the price level had been relatively stable and the public was generally dominated by a money illusion. Consequently, an excessive money supply did not shock the price level nor worsen the situation of shortage. On the contrary, since then, Chinese people began to gradually abandon all kinds of coupons, such as cloth coupons, which were maintained until 1987. In that year, the growth rate of $M3$ was 21.6% with a GDP growth rate of 10.6%, while the GDP deflator was only 5.6%. Of the 11% of $M3$ growth rate outpacing GDP, only 5.6% was translated into the rise in the price level, while the remaining 5.4% was turned into a reduction of the velocity of money.

In the second stage, the inflation expectations of households and enterprises are synchronized or higher than real inflation. This is reflected in the fact that the gap between the growth rate of the money supply exceeding the GNP was almost translated into the increase of the price level, or even higher than the gap. This situation was reflected in 1988, during which $M3$ grew by 19.4%, GNP by 11.2% and the GNP deflator by 12%. The gap between $M3$ and the GDP growth rate was 8.2%, while prices rose by 12% simultaneously, which was greater than this gap. This reflected the fact that the inflation expectations of households and enterprises were higher than the real inflation rate. They therefore sold their money as quickly as possible in order to procure physical commodities. They also ran on bank deposits when interest rates fell below the increase rate of the price level.

In the third stage, the inflation expectations of households and enterprises become negative: the price level they anticipate runs below the real prices. In this case, the gap between growth rate of the money supply and GDP is not translated into higher prices, or very little of it. In 1990, $M3$ grew at a rate of about 19% (estimated), while prices grew at a rate of 2.1% (expressed in the Retail Price Index). The GDP growth rate was 6%, and the gap between $M3$ growth rate and GDP growth rate was 13%.

As can be seen from the above analysis, when inflation expectations dominate households and businesses, the relationship between the money supply and prices will change with the variation of expectations. This has been pointed out in the analysis of aggregate demand. Expected price changes will affect the size of aggregate demand: the higher the expected prices in the short-run are, the larger the changes of aggregate demand are. The fluctuations in the relationship between money and prices could not be explained without considering the role of expectations, because such fluctuations cannot be interpreted by traditional economic theory.

Meanwhile, it can be seen from the above analysis that the sudden increase in the inflation expectations of households and enterprises in 1988 was closely related to the excessive money supply from 1984 to 1987. Such an excessive money supply in consecutive years amplifies inflation expectations. Moreover, the vigorous publication of price reforms in 1988 by the government implanted the perception of price surges in the public, which led to a rapid rise in public inflation expectations, resulting in a run on bank deposits and a rush to buy physical commodities.

6.5 The Structural Inflation

The adjustment of economic structure is a slow process, so is its determinant, the supply structure. Changes of aggregate demand and the aggregate demand structure are comparatively quicker. As a result, there will exist not only a gap between aggregate demand and aggregate supply in the short-run, but also a mismatch between the aggregate demand structure and the aggregate supply structure, leading to a structural inflation.

Before the reform of the economic system, China's economic structure was basically determined by the government. The contradiction of the economic structure was mainly reflected as "an emphasis on heavy industry and ignorance of light industry", resulting in the disharmony between heavy industry and light industry. After the reform of the economic system, China's economic structure is determined by both the powers of government and business, and the contradiction of economic structure is mainly reflected in the incompatibility between basic industry and the processing industry.

Because basic industry cannot keep pace with the development of processing industry, the fixed assets of the processing industry sector appear to be relatively in surplus. In order to maximize profits, firms in the processing industry can apply for bank loans on the basis of the amount of flow capital needed for the normal operation of their fixed assets. Although local banks are not administratively under the leadership of local governments, local banks also try their best to meet such loan requirements for the sake of local interests.[1] Once firms' demand for money in the processing industry is satisfied, the contradiction of insufficient supply of basic industry sectors is immediately exposed, which results in rise of the price level of products in the basic industry.

In addition to the contradiction between processing industry and basic industry, a similar contradiction between agriculture and industry in China is very prominent. China's population has reached more than 1.1 billion in 1989 but the natural conditions for agriculture are not ideal, and the land resources available for agriculture are decreasing as time goes by. Resource limitation also makes China's agricultural development relatively rigid. The contradiction between backward agriculture and industrial development still exists but is not that prominent with low level industrialization. However, as industry develops, the demand for agricultural products is constantly rising, and the contradiction between supply and demand of agricultural products is exposed, resulting in the rise of price levels for the agricultural products. Nonetheless, such price rise momentum was rigidly suppressed by the government's financial subsidy to agricultural products. On the contrary, price controls for subsidiary agricultural products were gradually relieved, and thus it enhanced

[1] Local bank loans breakthrough the central bank loan plan, leading to the so-called "reversed transmission mechanism" of inflation. It shows that inflation can be created at a local level, and ultimately, the central government has to accept inflation as a*fait accompli*. China's theoretical circles is quite consistent in this regard. Refer to literature [31, 57]. No particular analysis in this aspect will be done in this book.

obvious price rises for these products in recent years. On one hand, as the agricultural raw materials prices rose with the agricultural product prices, the prices of industrial products had to rise correspondingly. On the other hand, employees sought to increase wages to offset the negative impacts of rising agricultural prices on their lives (food stuffs occupy a relatively large proportion in the Chinese household consumption, so households are very elastic to agricultural product prices), firms would accordingly raise the prices of their products.[2]

Inflation caused by structural factors is reflected not only in undersupply but also in oversupply. In fact, some products in the processing industry in China have been oversupplied. From a longitudinal time dimension, the main feature of China's economy is that demand exceeds supply, but this does not negate the coexistence of shortage and surplus. Relatively speaking, shortage appears to be more prominent than surplus. And a surplus of some products also carries impacts upon China's economy. Here focus merely on the relationship between surplus and inflation without touching these issues since it has been explored a few years ago by Chinese economists. In a market economy, a surplus will cause price level to fall, so inflation cannot be triggered by a surplus. Nonetheless, this may potentially happen in China.

China's current statistical system stipulates that all products produced in a statistical period should be deemed to be the production outputs of that statistical period, no matter whether they are sold or not. So the surplus (or unmarketable) products overstocked in warehouses have been calculated at full value and finally included in the national income. The aggregate demand and aggregate supply planned by the government are based upon such nominal national income data. As a result, some of the demands cannot find corresponding products in the marketplace, which exacerbates the contradiction between supply and demand and so triggers the inflation.

Therefore, in China's economy, it is necessary not only to measure a shortage, but also to measure a surplus. It is meaningful to carry out theoretical research on this aspect. At present, there have been some overseas research papers on these issues, but they are not yet mature.[3] Research on this area is still recommended in China.

From the above analysis, structural factors, like the institutional factors mentioned, are also the internal factors causing inflation in China. It can then be concluded that the influence of structural and institutional factors on inflation is the internal mechanism of the formation of inflation in China.

---

[2] Refer to Ref. [57].

[3] Refer to Ref. [22] in I. This paper has attracted the attention of economic theorists by measuring both shortage and surplus. According to the opinion of the author of this book, there exist two shortcomings in the methodology of this paper: the first is that the value of one of the variables is determined by subjective factors; the second is that there is a huge standard error in the calculation results. The author of this book used this method to estimate China's shortage and surplus when working in Stanford University, but eventually abandoned it because the standard error of the coefficients was too large. The assessments of this paper by foreign counterparts can be found in the relevant journals in recent years. But this methodology is worth noting. It is very practical to China's economy in case the limitations are removed. Attention should be paid on the international review of this paper as well as any possible update of the methodology.

Chapter 7
The Money Demand and Supply

7.1 Introduction

Inflation is a problem related with both the product market and money market. In previous chapters, through the phenomenon of money, inflation has been directly analyzed from the gap between aggregate supply and aggregate demand. Namely, the problem in the product market has been primarily analyzed.[1] In this chapter, the problem of money market will be further explored.

The formation of China's money market lags far behind the product market. The three methods employed by Western countries to regulate the money market—the required reserve ratio (RRR), the open market operations, the discount rate and there financing rate—carry very limited effects under the current banking system in China. At present, the People's Bank of China (The central bank of China) mainly controls the money market through quantitative regulation, which directly controls the loan scale through monetary rationing, special funds, and other measures. Furthermore, the fiscal expenditure plans formulated by both SPC and the Ministry of Finance can directly affect the determination of a loan's scale. The traditional Comprehensive Balance Theory has provided a comprehensive analysis of the relationship between these three loan scales, which forms a foundation for the study of the money markets in this chapter.

There are two levels of the theory of money in Marx's economic theory system. The first level is the theory of metallic money, and the second the theory of paper money. Metallic money is a special type of commodity that functions as a general equivalent of other products. Metallic money is still a commodity and the value of itself will still be determined by the socially necessary labor hours. In a metallic money economy, the supply and demand of metallic money will automatically reach equilibrium in the market since the metallic money itself is not the determinant of product prices. Banknotes are merely the symbol of the metallic money functioning

[1] Refer to references [35, 45, 54, 56].

L. Li, *The Inflation Mechanism and Expectations*, Understanding China,
https://doi.org/10.1007/978-981-97-2570-0_7

as a medium of exchange without any intrinsic value. However, its influence on the price level can be expressed in the following equation

$$MV = PQ$$

where, M stands for the quantity of money; V is the velocity of circulation; P is the price level and Q is the market exchange quantity. With constant values of V and Q, the greater the M, the higher will be the P.

Money and its functions are in harmony with Marx's economic theoretical system.

In modern Western economic theory, the theory of money is not in harmony with the utility theory microeconomics; or the say, money is not in harmony with microeconomics which is structured upon the utility theory. Up until now, Western economists have not yet found a satisfactory approach to incorporate money into the system of general equilibrium theory. However, Western economics has made great progress in the study of the theory of money from the perspective of macroeconomic theory, which has a strong coordination with the theory of money. This is well demonstrated in the *IS- LM* model.

The study of the theory of money is relatively lagging behind China's overall economic theory. It remains to be explored on how to effectively and concertedly incorporate monetary factors into China's macroeconomic theory. In China, for instance, there has not yet been a comprehensive macroeconomic theoretical framework to integrate the study of the relationship between the growth of money supply and economic growth. The relevant research in this regard is focusing on only particular issues, so the ability of persuasiveness and explanation is constrained. Nonetheless, some scholars have integrated an in-depth analysis of the theory of money in the research of inflation theory, resulting in publication of monographs and high quality of research papers.

In this chapter, efforts will be exerted to explore the influence of the demand and supply for money on the economic system. The issue will be examined from both the long-run and the short-run perspectives. It will show that, in the short-run, money is not neutral because of factors of expectation stickiness or money illusion and that the direction of output of the functions of money is closely related to the state of supply itself.

7.2 The Demand Function for Money

Keynes believed that money demand originates from three motives, namely, the transaction motive, the preventionary motive and the speculative motive. These three motives determine an individual's demand for money, or his/her flexibility preference. Keynes's demand for money is expressed as

$$M^d = kPY + L(r)$$

There are two components in the demand for money. The first is to meet the needs of the transaction and preventionary motive, and the second is to satisfy the needs of the speculative motive. The first component is a function of the price P and the income Y, where k is the coefficient. The second component is a function of the real interest rate r.

The demand for money of Chinese households and enterprises primarily originates from the transaction motive. Transactions need money as an intermediary, and no transactions can be carried out without money. Therefore, households and enterprises must hold a certain amount of money in hand to meet their transaction needs. For households, the money needed for transactions refers to cash and transfer of payments. For businesses, it refers to cash and the portion of deposits held in banks after settling such transfers.

Chinese households also possess the motivations for money savings. The reasons for these households' motivations of money saving are complicated, which can be roughly separated into the following categories: (1) saving for purchasing durable consumer goods, housing, or future education for children; (2) savings for emergencies such as illness, disasters, and so forth; (3) savings for interest; (4) savings because no suitable products are available. The money savings of Chinese households can be regarded as a function of income and real interest rates. They are expressed in the form of long-term and short-term deposits of the households.

Enterprises and governments also hold bank deposits, which are not for the sake of incentive but as an institutional requirement since banks are required to manage the unspent money on behalf of the enterprises and governments. Therefore, such deposits can only be regarded as a need for the enterprise transaction motivation.

Thus, the demand function for money represented by $M2$ (cash plus deposits of enterprises and institutions) can be expressed as

$$M2^d = kPY$$

where, P represents the price; k is the coefficient; Y is the product trading volume in the market. Usually Y is substituted by the national income or GDP. Based on the available statistical data, the total quantity of market transactions can also be counted as a subtraction of the physical transactions from the national income or GDP.

The demand function for money represented by $M3$ ($M2$ plus other deposits) is denoted as

$$M3^d = kPY + L(r, HR)$$

where, L represents the demand function for the savings of households; R is the real interest rate; HR is the disposable income of households.

Therefore, China's demand for money can be defined as the sum of money required to meet the transaction needs and the savings demand of households.

For the convenience of theoretical analysis, the demand function for money represented by $M3$ can be simplified. Assuming that the national income is the quantity of the transaction, and because the disposable income itself is a function of the national income, only the national income variable and the real interest rate variable are retained (changes in prices are reflected in changes of the real interest rate). Therefore, the demand function for money represented by $M3$ can be simply written as

$$M3^d = f(r, NI)$$

Its linear form is

$$M3^d = a_0 + a_1 r + a_2 NI$$

where, a_0, a_1, a_2 are all coefficients of the function, NI stands for the national income.

Its exponential form is

$$M3^d = A \cdot r^{a_1} \cdot NI^{a_2}$$

where, a_1 represents the elasticity of interest rate r to the demand for money; a_2 represents the elasticity of national income to the money demand; and A is the coefficient.

The concise economic connotation of the demand function for money is that the demand for money is the function of national income and real interest rates. When national income increases, the demand for money increases; when real interest rates rise, demand for money decreases. While higher real interest rates encourage households to save more, it also leads to a reduction in the quantity of money used for transactions and quickens the money velocity during these transactions (i.e. higher real interest rate reduces the quantity of cash in hand). Therefore, in general, the demand for money decreases with the rise of the real interest rates.

It should be noted that the demand for money, like the demand for other goods, cannot be measured directly. The demand for goods is constrained by money, while the demand for money is constrained by the supply. When the national income and interest rates are given, the demand for money will also be fixed. Consequently, the demand for money is not the quantity demanded of the loan application of the producer. In China, the loan application of the producer is just a desire, which is the same as the consumer's desire for commodities. Desire and demand are different.

In discussing the demand for money, we need distinguish between nominal money, measured in current purchasing power units, and real money, measured in constant purchasing power units. Nominal money is directly proportional to the price level while real demand for money is independent of the price level and varies only with the changes in real incomes and interest rates. If M refers to nominal money, then the above formula should be expressed as

$$\frac{M}{P} = f(r, NI)$$

The impact of nominal money on the economy is closely tied to expectations. When the expected inflation rate is lower than thereal one, people do not realize that the increase of money in their hands is only the increase of nominal money, not real money. Such a money illusion hinders the impact of nominal money on prices. It represents an illusion of increased demand for money. Otherwise, why don't prices go up when money supply increases? In addition to the increase of national income, the other reason can only be the increase in the demand for money. Such an explanation is quite convincing in case expectations are not considered. If we take expectations into account, there is only a temporary increase in demand for money, which will fallback once the money illusion disappears. This phenomenon can be expressed as

$$M^d = M^* + \delta(P - P^*)$$

where, M^* is the quantity of money needed in the long-run; M^d is the quantity of money needed in the short-run; P^* is expected prices; P is real prices; δ is a real number greater than 0. When $P^* < P, M^* < M^d$. When $P^* = P, M^d = M^*$.

7.3 The Velocity of Money

The velocity of money is an important factor affecting the demand for money, and it is also the most difficult element to be commanded in the theory of demand for money. When the velocity of money increases, the demand for money decreases accordingly, and vice versa.

When we analyze the demand for money, a crucial theoretical premise is whether the velocity of money is stable. If the velocity of money is unstable, how does it change? Different conclusions can be drawn based on different theoretical premises. Therefore, the measurement of the velocity of money is of great significance to our theoretical analysis.

There are many factors that affect the velocity of money in an economic system, and it is difficult to make a comprehensive analysis. Only a theoretical abstraction by ignoring some unimportant details with a focus on the important variables will be done here.

From the long-run perspective, the factors affecting the velocity of money contain two major types: one is the institutional factor, the other is the income factor.

In a traditional planned economy, the proportion of exchange of physical products is relatively huge, which reduces the demand for money and enhances the velocity of money. In an economy with semi-barter and semi- monetary transactions, money is merely used for essential purposes, such as the purchase of consumer goods, and so forth. In those economic systems, money functions primarily as an intermediary of transactions and circulates very quickly. When the proportion of a rural commodity economy gradually expands, the inflow of money into the rural areas increases as time goes by. However, due to the slow paces of economic activities in rural areas, the velocity of money slows correspondingly. As a result, when the economy is transiting from a traditional planned economy to a planned commodity economy, the velocity of money gears down in step. This is an inevitable phenomenon in the process of economic monetization.

Let's look at the relationship between income and the velocity of money. Before the economic reform, the income of Chinese households was very low, and they are only satisfying the basic needs of survival without much ability to save. After the reform, the growth rate of the household income is faster than that of the national income, and the part of the income shared for savings also increases, as shown in Table 7.1.

The majority of household deposits will be put back into circulation by banks. At the same time, the increase in household cash (which is also part of the household savings) is regarded by banks as a source of income, which becomes an expense of the banks. However, the increase of cash in the hands of households will reduce the velocity of money. On top of that, the required reserve of the banks also increases with the increase in households' deposits, which further retains some reserves in the banks, and thus reduces the velocity of money.

Similarily, the velocity of money is also decreasing as enterprise deposits increase in the banks.

Therefore, at present, with the increase of national income in China, the velocity of money tends to be slowing down, which will lead the growth of the money supply to be faster than that of national income.

The velocity of money can be measured by the equation of exchange.

$$MV = PQ$$

where, M stands for money; V is the velocity of money circulation; P is the price; and Q is the exchange volume. Here, M is represented by $M3$, P by the GNP deflator, and Q by the monetized portion of GNP (i.e., GNP minus the physical product transaction portion). It is therefore not difficult to compute the value of V for each year by the equation

Table 7.1 The Proportion of Household Accumulation in Household Disposable Income

Year	The proportion of household accumulation in household disposable income	Year	The proportion of household accumulation in household disposable income
1977	6.09	1983	13.52
1978	9.12	1984	16.76
1979	11.02	1985	23.3
1980	12.21	1986	23.35
1981	10.71	1987	20.96
1982	12.96		

$$V = \frac{PQ}{M}$$

Refer to Table 7.2 for the results.

It's not hard to see that V is actually decreasing every year. Regression with the above V value to time T, then

$$V = 112.51 - 0.056T$$

$$(16.58) \ldots (-16.37)$$
$$R^2 = 0.98\,DW = 1.358$$

The regression equation shows that the annual V value decreases by 0.056 on average.

According to the practices in Western developed countries, when the national income grows to a certain period, the velocity of money is not slowing down, but moving more quickly. Since there is currently a gap between China and Western economies, it is expected that there is still a time period for China's velocity of money to decline.

In the short-run, the main factor affecting the velocity of money is inflation expectations. When households and enterprises expect a high rate of inflation, they sell money and panic buy physical products in an attempt to reduce losses caused by inflation, thus speeding up the velocity of money. This phenomenon can be expressed in the following equation

$$V = V^* + \delta(P^* - P) + u$$

where, V^* refers to the appropriate velocity of money in the long- run, which is determined by institutional factors and income levels. V is the velocity of money in the short-run. The degree to which it deviates from V^* is determined by the degree to which the expected price level deviates from the real price level. u is the random error, a real number greater than 0.

When $P^* > P$, there will be $V > V^*$, so the purchasing power of money represented by MV increases. In case Q remains unchanged, the consequence will be an increase in P. It can be seen that greater expectations can lead to higher inflation.

When $P^* < P$, there will be $V < V^*$, so the purchasing power of money represented by MV decreases. When Q is constant, it can only lead to a decrease in P. When the expectations stick to a lower level, the increase in money supply M will

Table 7.2 The velocity of money (%)

Year	1981	1982	1983	1984	1985	1986	1987
V	1.58	1.49	1.43	1.38	1.31	1.27	1.24

be absorbed by a lower P^* . This is the trap effect of expectations, which will be explained in detail in Section 5 of this chapter.

7.4 The Determinants of the Money Supply

Let's start with a broader definition of the money supply. The money supply is equal to the total expenditures of the national banks, where

$$\begin{aligned}\text{Total Expenditure of National Banks } (M) = {} & \text{Various Loans } (D) \\ & + \text{Gold and Foreign Exchange } (GF) \\ & + \text{Assetsin International Financial Institutions } (IM) \\ & + \text{Financial Loans } (FM) + \text{Other Expenditures } (EZ)\end{aligned}$$

The quantity of the money supply in this broader definition will be the total amount of funds on the balance sheet of the loanable funds of the national banks. Since the use of funds equals the source of funds, there is also an equivalence between quantity of the money supply and total revenue of the national banks.

$$\begin{aligned}\text{Total Revenue of National Banks } (M) = {} & \text{Various Deposits } (Z) \\ & + \text{Liabilities to International Financial Institutions } (IZ) \\ & + \text{Currency in Circulation } (M1) + \text{Banks Money } (BM) \\ & + \text{Current Year Revenue } (BR) + \text{Others } (ER)\end{aligned}$$

The following are the three common definitions of the money supply $M1 = \text{Money}$ in Circulation

$$M2 = M1 + \text{Deposits of Enterprises and Institutions } (EM)$$

$$M3 = M2 + \text{ Other Deposits (HM)} = M1 + V\text{arious Deposits (Z)}$$

All the above definitions are from the perspective of the funding sources for the national banks.

The money supply of the national banks starts with lending of loans. If only three items including loans, deposits, and currency in circulation are considered without counting other revenue and expenditure items in the national bank loan funds (assuming their revenue and expenditure are exactly equal), there will be

$$\text{Loans} - \text{Deposits} = \text{Money in Circulation}$$

From the government's point of view, the control of the money supply is to actually control the quantity of loans. And the quantity of loans is a stock variable, which can be controlled through regulating the money supply. That is why the money supply is firstly defined in terms of bank expenditures. According to the preceding equations, there is

$$\text{Loan} = \text{Currency in Circulation} + \text{Deposits} = M3$$

Obviously, $M3$ is essentially a type of loan. Thus, the analysis of changes of $M3$ can also be seen from the perspective of loans.

The following is an analysis on how bank loans come into being.

Let's start with the functions of China's State Planning Commission (SPC). One of its important functions, whether traditional or new, is investment. The investment plan set by SPC needs to consider the balance of both the physical products and capital. If the physical product balance is a hard balance, then the capital balance will be a soft one, which is flexible to a certain extent. The fiscal expenditure plan set by the Ministry of Finance, on one hand, should take into account the amount of financial receipts to make both ends meet. On the other hand, the investment plan of the SPC must be considered to guarantee the construction of key projects. When financial spending exceeds revenue, the Ministry of Finance has to acquire loans from banks.

In determining its monetary revenue and expenditure, banks should consider both the investment plan of the SPC and the fiscal plan of the Ministry of Finance, without altering the pattern of the two. While trying to meet the above two requirements, banks also need to satisfy the liquidity loan regulations from the businesses. Determination of the total amount of liquidity loans becomes the main gate for banks to control the money supply. When loans exceed deposits, banks will have to issue new cash to bridge the shortfall. Cash is merely a token that banks hold to break-even with the gap.

As for the government, in order to control the scale of new loans, that is, to control the money supply, the first step is to control the investment plan of the SPC and the second, the fiscal expenditure plan, and finally to regulate the liquidity loan plan of the banks.

Based on China's current economic system, there is no incentive for enterprises to invest by their internal capital accumulation but rather by attracting government funds. Such a enterprise investment impulse can hardly be restrained by the government through fine-tuning measures such as raising loan interest rates but by rigidly cutting off the investment plans (including discontinuing projects already underconstruction) so as to restrain investment and other types of loans derived from this investment and consequently regulate the money supply.

Above, the formation process of the money supply has been explained from the controllable perspective of regulating the money supply or the power distribution perspective of money supply. The following will be the analysis upon the intrinsic relationship between the money supply and the economic system.

The short-run money supply can be viewed as

$$M_t^s = \text{Total Loans in Previous Year} + \text{Total New Loans}$$

Or

$$M_t^s = M_{t-1}^s + \Delta M_t^s$$

where, the total amount of new loans can be viewed as an exogenous variable determined by the government.

The equilibrium point of the short-run money supply and its demand is the intersection of the short-run money demand and supply function as follows

$$\begin{cases} M_t^s = M_{t-1}^s + \Delta M_t^s \\ M_t^d = a_0 + a_1 r + a_2 NI \end{cases}$$

In the above simultaneous equations, given the NI and r, the required quantity of the money supply can be calculated. Conversely, if $M_t{}^s$ and r are fixed, then the expected NI or the total supply can be determined. However, the crux of the problem now is that $M_t{}^s$ is given, but $M_t{}^d$ is unknown. The above formula can only be regressed under the assumption that $M_t{}^s = M_t{}^d$ so as to confirm the three parameters a_0, a_1 and a_2. The way to solve this problem is to organically link the money supply and demand function with the previous aggregate supply and aggregate demand function to form a holistic body. Specifically, in the analysis of the aggregate supply and aggregate demand models, it has been assumed that

$$D_t = D(M_t^s) \quad S_t = S(M_t^s)$$

Both D_t and S_t will be determined (this analysis is on the assumption of the constant values of r, K and L) once M_t^s is given. In turn,M_t^s is the reverse function of D_t and S_t, that is

$$M_t^s = S^{-1}(NI)$$

NI is set here as the aggregate supply. In other words, as long as NI is ensured, the appropriate money supply M_t^s can be determined accordingly. Generally speaking, when there exists a money illusion, the supply of products will increase with the increase in the money supply, which consequently augments the demand for money. In this case, the money supply will not exceed the money demand. However, when the money illusion disappears, or when the supply has reached its upper boundary, an increase in the money supply will not stimulate the supply of goods. Since the demand for money does not increase, the money supply exceeds the money demand.

The appropriate money supply or equilibrium point of money supply and demand M_e (see Fig. 6.1 in Sect. 1 of Chap. 6) is determined by the intersection of $D_t = D(M_t^s)$ and $S_t = S(M_t^s)$. At this point, the product market and the money market reach equilibrium simultaneously. Therefore, the equilibrium point of the money market can be sought from the product market. This greatly reduces the technical difficultyin handling the problem, which is now transformed to the question of whether to determine firstly NI and then M_t^s or vice versa.

As per plan arrangement of the Chinese government over the years, it is started from determining the growth rate of *NI* (i.e., from determining the growth rate of national income). That is to firstly set the growth rate of national income, and then arrange the money supply to ensure that growth rate. This is reasonable from the views of the traditional planned economy. A detailed implementation will be commenced from the balance of materials to set the growth rate, and then to arrange the balance of capital. This is because a material balance is the foundation, which is a rigid balance, while the capital balance is soft and adjustable. Moreover, the capital balance should ensure the need of the material balance. This can be called the "Speed Determinism".

The above process will be reversed in case a guiding plan is to be implemented. The government will decide the quantity of the money supply before determining the rate of economic growth. This can be called "Monetary Determinism". In this process, the government can only rely on financial balance to guide the material balance, because the government can no longer directly intervene in the material production process. Here, the direct determination of the quantity of the money supply by the government is still a means of quantitative adjustment and an immediate approach. However, when the capital market is really established, the supply and demand of money will be determined by indirect factors such as the interest rate. As a result, the government will be able to adjust the indirect factors like the rate of interest to determine the money supply and demand, thus setting the economic growth rate, which is the initial step towards the indirect regulation measure.

Of course, the output level and the price level can also be regulated in terms of the adjustment of M_t^s and *NI*. This issue will be further discussed in Chap. 9 of this book. The contents concerning the relationship between product market and money market of this chapter constitute the theoretical foundation of Chap. 9.

7.5 The Equation of Exchange

The common form of the Equation of Exchange is

$$MV = PQ$$

In the equation, M is the quantity of money; $V$is the velocity of money; P is the price; and Q is the volume of exchange. This is an identical equation.

Another commonly used form is

$$M = kPQ$$

In this equation, $k = 1/V$. It is also an identical equation.

The so-called classical monetary school makes some assumptions on the basis of this identical equation. For example, based on $MV = PQ$, they assume that if V and Q remained unchanged in the short-run, then the increase of M will definitely push up P, or the growth rate of M is the same as the growth rate of P. It can be proven as follows

Firstly, take the logarithm on both sides of $MV = PQ$, it becomes $\ln M + \ln V = \ln P + \ln Q$.

Then take derivatives on both sides of the above formula

$$\frac{M'}{M} + \frac{V'}{V} = \frac{P'}{P} + \frac{Q'}{Q}$$

Since $V$and Q are assumed to be constants, there is

$$\frac{M'}{M} = \frac{P'}{P}$$

The approximation is

$$\frac{\Delta M}{M} = \frac{\Delta P}{P}$$

Therefore, the growth rate of $M$is equal to the growth rate of P.

If Q is assumed to be variable in the short-run, but V remains constant, there is

$$\frac{\Delta P}{P} = \frac{\Delta M}{M} - \frac{\Delta Q}{Q}$$

That is, the difference between the growth rate of M and Q is the growth rate of P.

$M = kPQ$ is often called the equation of Cambridge. The assumption of this identical equation is that the quantity of money, or cash balance normally held by the economic unit, holds a fixed or stable relationship with the national income. Therefore, it is called the money holding rate. The conclusion is exactly the same as the previous one on the basis of this assumption.

Western modern monetary theory originated from Keynes. In the Keynesian monetary theory, the price level does not move in proportion to the quantity of money. Neither V nor k is constant, and the demand for money is extremely sensitive to the changes of the interest rate. In case the rate of interest falls to a point where no further reduction is possible, the demand for money will increase indefinitely. Since nobody is willing to hold government or other types of bonds, money becomes the only choice. This is known as the "liquidity trap". With a low interest rate, the increased money supply will be absorbed by the liquidity trap without affecting the price level. The existence of the liquidity trap is attributed to the uncertainty in public expectations of future economic development. Because it is hard to predict the future accurately, money is considered to be relatively safer than other assets. Thus, holding money is a necessity not only for the transaction motive but also for the asset motive.

Keynes thus divided the demand for money into two components: the transaction demand determined by the quantity of transactions (or the national income) and the asset demand determined by the rate of interest.

On the basis of the Keynesian monetary theory, further studies of the Keynesian economists found that although the transaction demand for money changes in the same direction as the transaction volume, its growth rate is lower than that of the latter. The so-called square root law is an attempt to explain this phenomenon, which states that money, even as a purely trading instrument, is sensitive to the rate of interest or opportunity costs and exhibits economies of scale to the quantity of exchange. However, the conclusion from the mathematical formula of the square root law is no longer commonly employed by Western economists presently.

Milton Friedman's monetary theory, on one hand, adopted Keynes's core idea of money as an asset, on the other hand, it affirms the basic conclusion of the classical quantity theory of money, that is, the change of the quantity of money reflects the change of the price level. Although Friedman denied that V was a constant and viewed it as a function, the function was stable and measurable. Friedman also believed that the demand for money was less affected by the rate of interest. The money demand function proposed by Friedman is more complex not only than the classical equation of exchange $MV = PQ$, but also than the Keynesian monetary theory, which will not be introduced in detail here.

Presently, when Chinese economists cite the equation of exchange, they basically adopt the identical equation $MV = PQ$ to explain the problems of money and price levels in China's economy. There are at least two consensus reached by the majority of Chinese economists: (1) V presents a downward trend; (2) Q is exogenous. The effect of a change in M on a change in P has been discussed on the basis of a known value of V (or an estimate is given) under the condition of a given Q.

Given the current problems facing the China's economy, it is necessary to conduct in-depth explorations on the following questions.

1. Is money merely a medium of exchange, or is it still an asset? The money mentioned here is not referred to as Marx's metallic money, but to the RMB.
2. What causes value of V to decline?
3. The relationship between M and Q. As a comprehensive monetary theory, not only the relationship between M and P but also the relationship between M and Q must be discussed. Is the growth of Q driving the growth of M or vice versa?

Only by unequivocally answering the above questions can an in-depth analysis on the inflation problem be continued. That is why the analysis of inflation in this book starts not from the well-known equation of exchange $MV = PQ$, but from the aggregate supply and aggregate demand functions since the above questions can be answered on the basis of these functions. Only when the above three questions are answered can the analysis of the relationship between M and P and M and Q in depth be carried on. The equation of exchange $MV = PQ$ alone can answer little of theoretical questions. It can therefore be concluded that a theoretical pillar, with only the identical equation $MV = PQ$, will be unable to sustain the theoretical tower for analyzing inflation.

The answers to the above three questions then have been gradually given in the previous theoretical analysis.

1. Money is not only a medium of exchange but also an asset. From the perspective of Chinese households, money is not only with the function of exchange, but also a token of wealth. That is why people tend to run on their bank deposits with an attempt to convert monetary wealth into physical wealth whenever money depreciates. That is also why people tend to deposit money in the banks whenever value of money is stable. For enterprises and public institutions, money also stands for a kind of wealth, which gives birth to their competing for loans and investment.

It is just because of the belief that money not only possesses the function of exchange but is also a token of wealth that demand for money can be divided into two components, namely, the demand for transaction and the demand for wealth. Generally speaking, for enterprises and public institutions, money, as wealth, should be spent without the motive to save. Bank deposits from enterprises and public institutions are consequences of the provisions of the current economic system. In viewing money as wealth, households have the incentive to save. It remains to be studied as for how much of their total wealth are households willing to either keep as physical wealth (i.e. consumption) or save in the banks as monetary wealth.

As long as the government is able to control the economy and inflation does not evolve in an opposite direction,households will be confident of the conversion of paper money into physical products at any time, so that their paper money is regarded as a token of wealth. Nonetheless, paper money is not metallic money after all. In case inflation evolves in an opposite direction, or the government is unable to control the economy, households will no longer view paper money as a token of wealth, and thus they run on bank deposits and resort to panic buying to reserve physical products.[2]

2. Both reasons, namely the institutional reason and the income reason, leading to the decline of V have been analyzed. The institutional reason is roughly a common consensus while the income reason needs to be further explored. That is to say, the opportunity cost of holding money is not high enough to generate a motive power for the scale of thrift. The low opportunity cost also depends on two aspects: (1) Money can only be deposited in banks. The proportion of stocks and bonds is still very low, and households enjoy little choice for investment, which leads to a decrease in the opportunity cost. (2) The real interest rate is low. The real interest rate has hovered around zero for a long time, and it is

[2] Generally speaking, as long as the real interest rate is greater than zero,paper money also possesses the function of a "reservoir" to a certain extent, but it is not as huge as the "reservoir" function of the storage of metallic money. The "reservoir" function of paper money disappears only if the real interest rate is below zero. When the real interest rate is slightly below zero, some of the paper money is still converted into deposits, as determined by the opportunity cost of holding money. There is still not a thorough understanding of such opportunity costs. In the short-run, the opportunity cost is influenced by the inflation expectations of the households against their propensity to save in the long-run.

not too costly for households to hold cash in hand. Furthermore, owing to the convenience for exchange and uncertainty about future expectations, households tend to hold more cash in hand as income increases. In other words, the fallen V has caused the money supply to grow faster than national income.

3. Analysis should not only be applied to the relationship between M and P but also between M and Q. In discussing the aggregate supply and aggregate demand models, it has been pointed out that Q increases with M in the short- run. When Q reaches its upper boundary, an increase in M will cause inflation to rise. The analysis can be summarized as follows:

   (1) Demand increases with M but it will not reach the upper boundary
   (2) When running below its potential, aggregate supply increases with M, and increase of M completely works on Q but not on P.
   (3) When running above its potential, aggregate supply increases with M but at a slower rate. At this point, an increase of M works less and less on Q, but more and more on P.
   (4) When reaching its upper boundary, aggregate supply will not increase with M, and an increase of M completely works on P.

Based on the above theoretical analysis, $MV = PQ$ can be used to analyze the inflation problem. This is actually a simplified analysis of the above theory.

In case the speed determinism is taken, then upon determining Q, assuming P remains unchanged and $V$is estimated, the corresponding money supply can be calculated. It should be particularly pointed out here that the value of P is related to whether aggregate supply is positioning above or below its potential level. P can only be viewed as constant in case aggregate supply runs below its potential level. If aggregate supply runs above its potential, P may not be constant unless the price level is rigidly froze. Under such circumstance, it becomes meaningless to determine M by Q.

In case the monetary determinism is adopted, upon determining M, V then can be estimated so as to compute MV, which is aggregate demand, from where Q can be calculated. Here, special attention should be paid to the potential changes of Q. If Q reaches its upper boundary, all changes of M will work on P; if Q is below potential aggregate supply, all changes of M will work on Q; if Q is between the upper boundary and potential aggregate supply, then changes of M will partially work on P and partially on Q. Division of the roles of M depends on the position of Q between the potential aggregate supply and its upper boundary.

In the short-run, it is difficult to estimate the change of V accurately due to the uncertainty in expectations. However in the long-run, the downward trend of V can be determined in case expectations are no longer functioning. Thus, a long-run analysis on the basis of $MV = PQ$ will make sense, but its conclusion is not very reliable from analysis in the short-run.

With the existence of expectations, the effect of M on both Q and P becomes much more complicated. In 1990,M grew by about 19%, Q by about 6% while P with a lower rate of 2.1%. The reason lies in the low inflation expectations of households who tend to hold monetary wealth, which leads to a market sluggishness.

Correspondingly, enterprises run in high inventories, overstocking a large amount of working capital, which is reflected in a substantial decline in the value of V. There was a reverse situation in 1988, which was analyzed previously and will not be repeated here. Thus, with the existence of expectations, $MV = PQ$ plays a very limited role and is inadvisable to use it as a crucial tool to analyze inflation.

Of course, from the study of the traditional empirical data of cash ratios to inventories, to the analysis of the identical equation $MV = PQ$, and then to the quest for the change of V, great progress has been achieved in China's economic theory. This can be regarded as a turning point of the transition from the traditional economic theory to empirical economic theory. However, it has not yet been satisfactory because new situations and problems need to be discussed and solved, and the old problems require new theories to deal with. It is therefore becoming a task for us to seek a theoretical framework with more in-depth and broader insights.

7.6 The Transmission Mechanism of Money

If only starting from $MV = PQ$, there would be no problem of the monetary transmission mechanism. Since M has nothing to do with Q, what needs to be studied is the relationship then between M and P. In other words, the excessive money supply will be absorbed by a rising price level. Here, we can't see the effect of money on Q. To study the monetary transmission mechanism is to study what effect the money supply may carry on Q, which is the foundation for studying the effect of M on Q. As a result, the effect of M on P is not immediate here but through the effect of M on Q with many twists and turns.

In Western countries, the rate of interest is the key research object of the monetary transmission mechanism theory. Although the rate of interest also plays a role in China, it is far less than that of Western countries. Therefore, the study of China's monetary transmission mechanism must start from the real situation of the China's economic operating mechanism.

In the traditional planned economy, it is the SPC that sets investment plans, which is followed by the banks through issuing money. As a result, money carries less impact on the economy. However, after the economic reforms, the traditional planned product economy has transitioned to the planned commodity economy, the role of money has thus been greatly reinforced. Hence, money can affect aggregate supply through the following transmission pathways.

1. The wealth portfolio effect. The wealth portfolio effect is an important conduction way for the quantity of money to affect the supply. As a token of wealth, or due to its convertibility into wealth, money possesses dual functions. The first is its purchasing power for goods and services. The second is its ability to generate interest. Due to the low opportunity cost of holding money in China, its interest effect is not significant on the economic system, but it carries greater effect on the economy when used as an asset with general purchasing power. Households

separate income into two parts: one is monetary wealth, the other is physical wealth. It can be seen from the previous analysis that with the increase of income, the proportion of monetary wealth in income gradually increased from 6.09% in 1977 to 20.96% in 1987 (refer to Table 7.1). And the rising monetary wealth of the households (i.e. the rising remanent purchasing power) is itself a potential pressure on the economy (economists call the remanent purchasing power a '*caged tiger*'). The increase in the money supply generally enhances the nominal income of the households, which leads to an increase in the monetary wealth when the money illusion exists.

One direct effect of the increase in monetary wealth is that the accumulation rate increases and consumption decreases. Usually, a high level of accumulation generates huge supply. If households are anticipating a higher inflation rate, the money supply will increase, thus pushing up the nominal income of households, who at this time will convert more monetary income into physical wealth. Accordingly, this will cause supply to run below demand (supply will be stimulated in case aggregate supply has not yet reached its upper boundary), and it will directly push up prices. Therefore, under the expectation effect, different portfolios of monetary wealth and physical wealth formulated by households from their monetary income will influence the economy.

Driven by higher inflation expectations, enterprises will also hoard goods, turning monetary wealth into physical wealth. This is the same as the wealth portfolio effect of households.

2. The rationing effect. In China, when demand for money exceeds the money supply, there is a constraint for banks to restrain increase in demand by raising the rate of interest. Rationing therefore becomes the only alternative. Owing to its higher profit levels and shorter loan payback periods, the processing industry sector enjoyed the priority of such rationing and their loan demand is much easier to be satisfied. On the contrary, it becomes more difficult for those enterprises with low profits and long loan payback periods to obtain loans.
3. The expectation effect. Under different expectations, the increase of the money supply will affect wealth portfolios; conversely, an increase or decrease in the money supply also affects expectations. When households feel that growth of their nominal income is lagging behind the inflation rate, their inflation expectations will get higher and higher. This change in expectations will bring about a series of profound changes in the economic system. An expectation trap will be born with low inflation expectations of households. At this point, much of the increase in the money supply is absorbed by the expectation trap, which neither pushes up price levels nor enhances supply. The sluggish market in 1990 can be regarded as a typical case of the expectation trap. In 1990, the many rounds of money injections by the government to stimulate the economy failed because most of the injected money was absorbed by the expectation trap and accumulated into stock capital. These money injections carried no effect upon the supply and price levels. Without an expectation trap, an increase in the money supply will cause

supply to increase if aggregate supply runs below its potential level. This also demonstrates how large expectations can affect economic activities.

4. The phase effect. The previous analysis shows that the impact of the increase of the money supply on the increase of aggregate supply can be divided into three phases. When aggregate supply runs below its potential, the increase of the money supply completely affects aggregate supply; when aggregate supply is in between its potential and the upper boundary, money supply effects partially on the price level and partially on aggregate supply; when the aggregate supply reaches the upper boundary, the money supply will completely affect the price level.

According to the classical quantity theory of money, if Q is constant, M will completely effect P.

According to Keynes, before reaching full employment levels, M will completely effect P when P is constant.

Friedman brought in the factor of expectation to broaden the field of analysis, however, the final conclusion was that M would still entirely have an effect on P.

The stage effect of monetary transmission introduced includes both the conclusion of the classical quantity theory of money and that of Keynes. However, our conclusion is not a simple combination of these two conclusions, but is reached from a gradual analysis completely based on the actual situation of China's economy. The comparison with Western economic theories is made only upon finalization of the analytical results.

7.7 The Theory of Interest

The theory of interest involves two aspects, one is the interest, the other is the rate of interest. The theory of interest focuses on the nature and source of interest and is a qualitative analysis theory. The theory of the rate of interest focuses on the study of the changes of the rate of interest as well as its determinants. It is a quantitative analysis theory.

In Marxist economic theory, interest is a component of the surplus value, or the transformation form of the surplus value. Thus, the generation of interest is determined in the field of production, and the rate of interest in the field of circulation. The rate of interest is determined by the money supply and demand in the market, and its upper boundary is the average profit rate. When the rate of interest is higher than the average rate of profit, no one would like to borrow capital so the demand for capital declines. At the same time, if the rate of interest is higher than the average rate of profit, people would tend to increase their money savings, and the loanable funds will thus be enhanced. Both the increase and decrease in the capital will cause the rate of interest to drop.

Keynes believed that the rate of interest was determined by the money supply and demand conditions. Keynes held that interest was the cost of using money or the reward forgiving up liquidity.

In the socialist economy, interest is still viewed as an output in the field of production. It is the transformation form of value generated by the surplus of labor. However, the rate of interest is believed to be exogenously determined by the national banks depending on the supply and demand of money and other factors. The rate of interest set by the national banks is called the nominal interest rate, and the difference between the nominal interest rate and the expected inflation rate is called the real interest rate. The concept of real interest rates is usually adapted in practice. China's economic theorists generally divide the rate of interest into the deposit interest rate and the loan interest rate, with their research focus being on the deposit interest rate side.

In China, the rate of interest is not only a tool to regulate investment, but also an instrument to regulate savings. As per the above analysis, enterprises lack the motivation to accumulate by themselves, but they are enthusiastic to strive for national investment because they are able to transfer investment costs to the government. Therefore, although the increase of bank loan interest rates augments the investment cost of enterprises and negatively affects the quantity of enterprise investment to a certain extent, it is not adequate to solve the problem of investment hunger in China. Only when the enterprise contracting mechanism truly takes full responsibility for its own profits and losses can the loan interest rate be employed to regulate investment.

It should be noted that when enterprises are generally in extremely difficult conditions, they are not proactive enough in obtaining loans. For example, in 1990, the enthusiasm of enterprise for loans was low. This was not just a problem of investment costs caused by interest rates but also a matter of overstocking products. Also production expansion would only worsen the situation. Under such circumstances, even if enterprises might be able to transfer some of the burden to the government, the problems caused by expanding investment would have to be solved by the enterprises themselves. This caused negative impacts on incentive for investment.

The impact of deposit interest rates on household savings is more obvious in China. Chinese households regard money as a kind of wealth, which bears an opportunity cost in itself. Such opportunity cost determines whether money should be deposited in a bank or be converted into physical wealth. Since deposit interest rates reflect the opportunity cost of money, households tend to save more when the real interest rate rises. An increase in household savings means a corresponding increase in investment so higher deposit interest rates indirectly stimulate investment. However, a high deposit interest rate will enhance the loan interest rate, which will increase the enterprise investment cost. In contrast, the indirect stimulating effect of the increase of deposit interest rates is greater than the depressing effect of the increase of loan interest rate on investment. Because of this, China's adjustment of interest rates in recent years has focused upon the adjustment of the deposit interest rate, the increase of which is followed by an increase of the loan interest rate.

In 1990, the deposit interest rate was cut in an attempt to stimulate household consumption to address market sluggishness, but no desired effect was achieved. It was attributed to the low inflation expectations of the households. The households still expected high real interest rates even though the nominal interest rate had been lowered, thus the saving enthusiasm was enhanced. It demonstrates that the nominal interest rate carries little impact on households' savings, and the real impact is on the change of the anticipated real interest rate on the households. Of course, the structural issues are also fatal causes for the market sluggishness. Therefore, adjustment of interest rates alone will not be adequate to solve such market problems.

There are diverse motives for household savings, which certainly does not mean that households do not comprehend the concept of the opportunity costs of money. In lacking of such a concept, there would not have been the run on deposits and panic buying behaviors seen in 1988.

In general, with the establishment of the commodity market system, households' awareness of money opportunity costs will be strengthened. Consequently, adjustment of the deposit interest rate will impact household savings. With the gradual establishment of the financial market in the future, adjustment of loan interest rates will also carry an impact on investment. Nonetheless, only when the issue of dependency of enterprise upon the government is finally solved will it be possible to establish the genuine financial markets that regulate investment by adjusting loan interest rates.

Currently, the main means of macroeconomic adjustment in China is still the adjustment of the quantity of money (adjusting the money supply) and index rationing adjustment (such as a commodity under special government control, direct regulation of numbers of investment in different regions, departments, and businesses, and regulation of increases in price levels). The so-called mandatory plan relies on these two means of adjustment with adjustment of interest rate as a supplement. Although the role of interest rate adjustment is relatively stronger than before, it is still impossible to rely on it to solve the balance problem of aggregate supply and aggregate demand. Currently, even more emphasis has been placed upon the proportion of market regulation, the problem of macro-regulation cannot be completely solved through only this approach. These two means of quantitative regulation should not be abandoned prior to the establishment of new macro-control measures. In comparison, the monetary quantitative adjustment means should be more reliable. Index rationing adjustment should not be implemented too frequently as it takes effect more quickly, and may cause large losses.

At present, the theory of rate of interest has not yet been studied in China, which is due to the completely exogenous nature of the rate of interest itself. Only when interest rates become an endogenous variable in the economic system can such research be more theoretically and practically significant. For the time being, even some fundamental questions have not been explored, such as how to choose a set of interest rate indicators. Further, there is still no consensus in economic theory circles on how to define these sundry indicators to generate a general interest rate indicator. The common and simple approach is to designate a one-year interest rate indicator to represent the general deposit interest rate indicator. Such an approach is problematic because a large number of deposits have been converted to the three-year value-preserved savings when the banks implement this business. Moreover, the suitability or optimality of deposit interest rates is also worth discussing. More potential research areas include the suitability of the respective structure of deposit interest rates and loan interest rates as well as the suitability of coordination between the two.

Chapter 8
The Dual-Gap Model of Inflation

Inflation takes two forms in China. One is the increase in the price level, which is reflected in the increase of the national income deflator and the social general retail price index. The other is the existence of a shortage, which drives money into forced savings. It is not appropriate to use equilibrium theory only to analyze inflation in China, because it is unable to reflect on the shortage problem. Thus, the disequilibrium approach has been applied in this book. For instance, when discussing aggregate demand in Chap. 4, the stimulating effect of institutional factors on aggregate demand expansion is explored, which demonstrates the mutual relationship and operational mechanism of the institutional structure, benefit structure, and distribution structure in the disequilibrium theory. The discussion of aggregate supply in Chap. 5 indicates the stimulating effect of the expansion of aggregate demand on aggregate supply and how aggregate supply stagnates under the constraint of a resource bottleneck, which expresses the behavior mechanism of aggregate supply in the disequilibrium theory. In Chap. 6, the disequilibrium state upon the encountering of aggregate demand and aggregate supply in the market can be observed when the general inflation gap is studied. Further, Chap. 7 focuses on the discussion of the disequilibrium mechanisms in the money market. In this chapter, the formation mechanism of the gap of the price level and the shortage gap and their relationship will be further explored to construct the theory of the dual-gap model of inflation.

The research paradigm of disequilibrium theory can be divided into two categories. One is the market disequilibrium, which investigates the behavior mechanism of aggregate supply and aggregate demand on the basis of equilibrium theory and the constraint of price rigidity. The other is the institutional disequilibrium, which focuses on institutional factors to analyze the benefit mechanism and constraint conditions so as to derive the behavioral mechanism of aggregate demand and aggregate supply under a planned economic system. This book focuses on the latter type of disequilibrium analysis. In this chapter, particular attention will be placed upon the factor of the rationing constraint when we analyzing the formation mechanism of the shortage gap. In addition to price rigidity, the rationing constraint is also a crucial

L. Li, *The Inflation Mechanism and Expectations*, Understanding China,
https://doi.org/10.1007/978-981-97-2570-0_8

factor leading to shortages in China's economy. It is clear that the majority of product prices have been liberalized, so rationing constraint is deemed to be the main factor in forced savings. In the money market, price rigidity (that is, interest rate rigidity) and rationing constraint work together since the interest rate mechanism is not yet decisive.

8.1 The Basic Framework of the Dual-Gap Model of Inflation

For convenience of analysis, it is assumed that both aggregate demand and aggregate supply have been determined in the economic system as shown in Fig. 8.1.

In Fig. 8.1, DD represents aggregate demand and S_1S_1 is aggregate supply. From Fig. 8.1, aggregate demand D is greater than aggregate supply S_1, so the gap is DS_1. If the price level is completely rigid, that is, the price level does not change with DS_1, then DS_1 represents the shortage gap. At this point, the general inflation gap is exactly equal to the shortage gap. If the price level is completely elastic, that is, the price level changes infinitely, the nominal value of aggregate supply S_1 will change, which causes aggregate supply S_1 to shift to the nominal value of aggregate supply S_2 , and the difference between S_2 and S_1 will becomes S_2S_1, which represents the price rise gap. Again, the general inflation gap is perfectly equal to the price rise gap.

In China, both cases are extreme. The reality is somewhere in between these two as shown in Fig. 8.2.

In Fig. 8.2, aggregate demand D is greater than aggregate supply S_1, and the general inflation gap is DS_1. But prices are partially rigid, that is, they are neither completely fixed (perfectly rigid) nor completely liberalized (perfectly elastic). Thus, aggregate supply S_1 moves to its nominal value S_2, where the price rise gap becomes S_2S_1 and the shortage gap is DS_2. The general inflation gap DS_1 is equal to the sum of price rise gap S_2S_1 and the shortage gap DS_2, that is

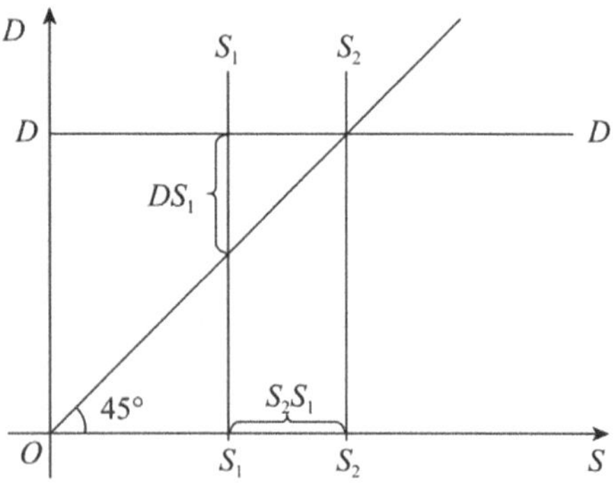

Fig. 8.1 The shortage gap or the price rise gap under extreme situations

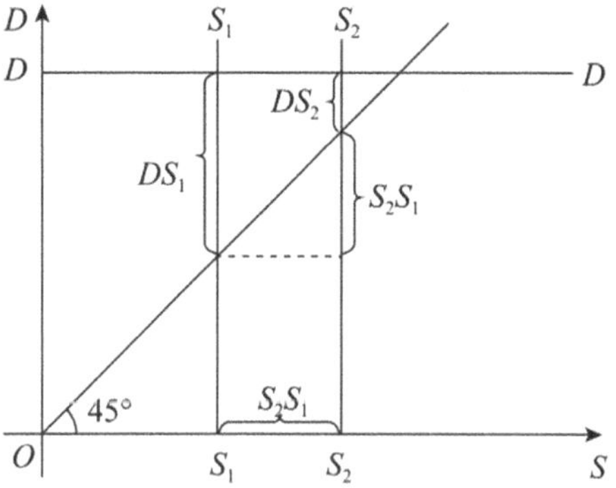

Fig. 8.2 The co-existence of the shortage gap and the price rise gap

$$DS_1 = S_2S_1 + DS_2$$

It is obvious that under the condition that aggregate demand exceeds aggregate supply, if aggregate supply S_1 is given, aggregate demand D changes (becomes larger or smaller), and the general inflation gap DS_1 also changes (becomes larger or smaller), S_2S_1 and DS_2 will also change correspondingly. Conversely, when D is given, DS_1, S_2S_1 and DS_2 will change following the change in S_1. In both cases, the relationship in the above equation remains valid. It indicates that no matter how much D and S_1 change, as long as $D>S_1$, the equation above is valid.

It should be noted that when S_1 is greater than D, DS_1 represents not the general inflation gap but the surplus, as shown in Fig. 8.3. In China's current economic system, this is always followed by a surplus whenever the government implements a tightening of economic policy, such as the market sluggish in 1990. The overall market sluggishness in 1990 not only indicated that the central government was still powerful in regulating the economy, but also showed that after a period of institutional reform, an internal self-restraint mechanism had been gradually established in businesses. Though relatively weak, such a self-restraint mechanism has aroused enterprises to respond to market prices, market demand, and to the rate of interest of loans. This new factor is worthy of special attention from economists. DS_1 in Fig. 8.3 represents the gap when aggregate supply exceeds aggregate demand.

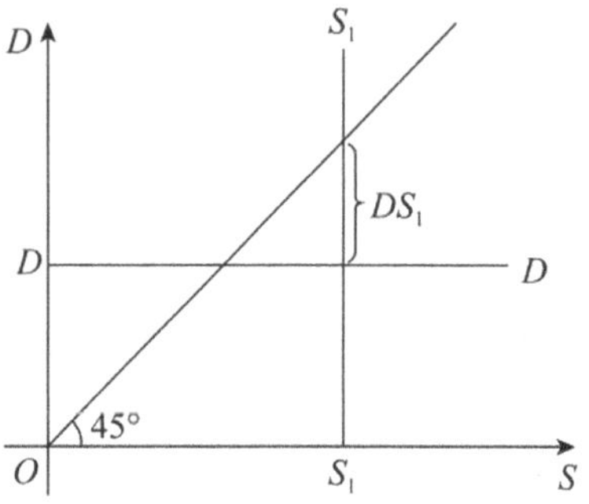

Fig. 8.3 The surplus gap

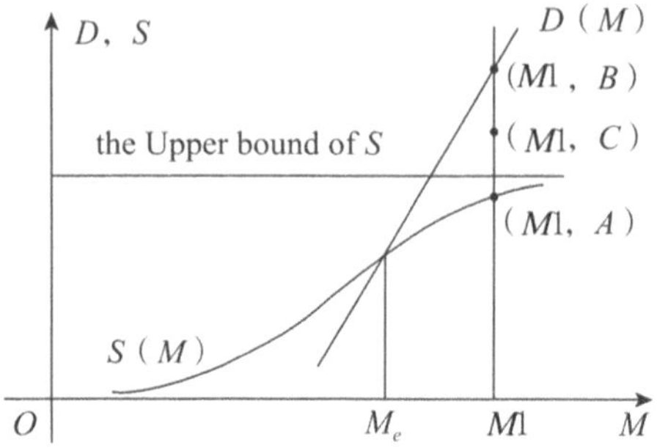

Fig. 8.4 The shortage gap and the price rise gap under a complex case

Now let's look at a more complex case, where aggregate demand is $D(M)$ and aggregate supply is $S(M)$, as shown in Fig. 8.4.

In Fig. 8.4, when the money supply is set as $M1$, S $(M1)$ equals A; $D(M1)$ equals B; the general inflation gap equals $D(M1)$-$S(M1)$, which is B-A. If prices are partially rigid, then aggregate supply will shift to point (M, C), where the nominal value of aggregate supply $S(M1)$ equals C. Therefore, the price rise gap becomes CA, and the shortage gap is BC, where

$$B - A = CA + BC$$

It can be seen that there is still a general inflation gap equal to the sum of the price rise gap and the shortage gap.

Given the general inflation gap, there exists a wax and wane relationship between the price rise gap and the shortage gap. The shortage shrinks as price levels increase. The basic relationship between the two is the framework for analyzing the dual-gap problem. The following will be a step-by-step analysis of what variables (or factors) divide the general inflation gap into these two sub-gaps, or what factors determine these two sub-gaps.

8.2 Distinguishing the Two Shortage Gaps

Two main factors lead to the shortage gap: one is price rigidity, and the other is the rationing constraint. The rationing constraint means that the government sets quotas of what and how many products producers, households and social organizations are permitted to purchase. Thus, even though the prices of these goods are fully liberalized, people are unable to spend their money due to the rationing constraint of these products, resulting in forced savings that triggers the shortage.

Rationing constraint still plays a very crucial role in the macroeconomic regulation and control system currently in China. In addition to the rationing constraint for social organizations regarding purchasing of products, a rationing index will also be assigned to the bank loans, which is determined at different levels, and no

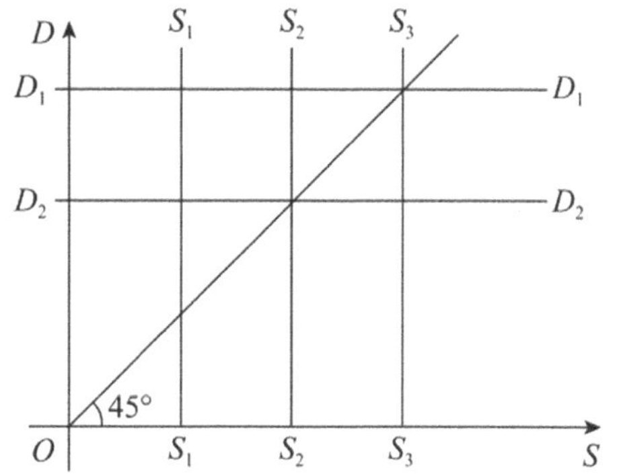

Fig. 8.5 The shortage gap caused by rationing

excessive loan will be allowed to surpass the index level. The lending principle set by the banking system in China in 1991 remained unchanged. Another example is investment. Investment quotas are determined at different levels, and no level will be allowed to break through the stipulated amount of investment.

There is an intrinsic relationship between a shortage caused by the rationing index and a gap caused by the price rise and a shortage caused by price rigidity. Until the price level is completely liberalized, part of the purchasing power cannot be realized due to the index rationing constraint. The pressure of this purchasing power is therefore not perceived in the market. At this point, the price determined by supply and demand forces in market can be taken as the quasi-equilibrium price. Once the rationing index is eliminated, this part of the purchasing power is transformed into the purchasing power perceivable in the market, so the original quasi-equilibrium price is destroyed, and the new quasi-equilibrium price will be higher than the original quasi-equilibrium price. The price rise gap here will be the shortage caused by rationing. This relationship is shown in Fig. 8.5.

In Fig. 8.5, D1 denotes the effective aggregate demand for goods and services. Due to the index rationing constraint and part of the money cannot be converted into purchasing power, the real perceived aggregate demand in the market is D_2. If aggregate supply becomes S_1, and prices are assumed to be completely liberalized, aggregate supply S_1 will shift to its nominal value S_2. From D_2, no shortage gap exists, there will only be the price rise gap S_2S_1. However, aggregate demand D_1D_2 will be turned into forced savings due to the index rationing constraint, and a shortage gap is hence formed. If the index rationing constraint is eliminated, the perceived aggregate demand in the market will be D_1, thus shifting aggregate supply S_1 to its nominal value S_3. As indicated in Fig. 8.5, there is

$$S_3S_1 = S_2S_1 + S_3S_2 = S_2S_1 + D_1D_2$$

Then

$$S_3S_2 = D_1D_2$$

Fig. 8.6 The co-existence of two kinds of shortage gaps

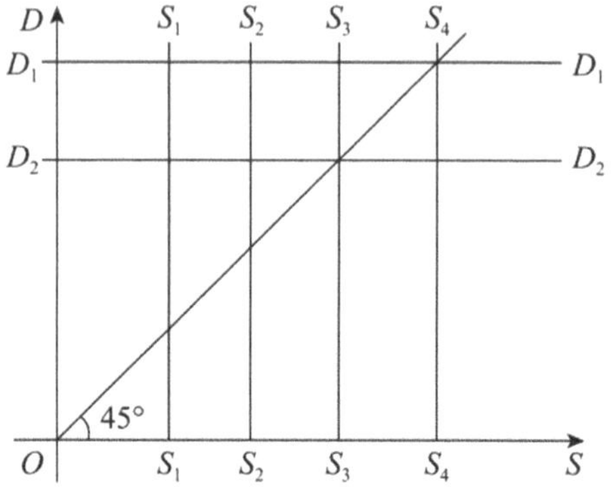

This shows that the general inflation gap S_3S_1 is equal to the price rise gap S_2S_1 plus the shortage gap D_1D_2 caused by the index rationing constraint. If the index rationing is eliminated, the general inflation gap will be the price rise gap S_3S_1. Figure 8.5 fully illustrates the relationships among S_3S_1, S_3S_2, S_2S_1, and D_1D_2.

In the case that the price level is not completely liberalized, price rigidity still exists and the rationing index still functions. Then the shortage gap can be broken down into two parts: one is caused by the price rigidity and the other by the index rationing, as shown in Fig. 8.6.

As can be seen from Fig. 8.6, the general inflation gap is S_4S_1, the price rise gap is S_2S_1, the shortage gap caused by price rigidity is S_3S_2, and the shortage gap caused by index rationing constraint is D_1D_2, which coincides with S_4S_3. Thus, the shortage gap becomes S_4S_2, which is the sum of both the shortage gaps S_3S_2 and S_4S_2.

8.3 Formation Mechanism of Shortage Gaps Caused by Rationing

After the reform of the economic system, China gradually reduced its mandatory plans for specific products. For example, after 1985, the mandatory plans for agricultural production were basically abolished, and the output of major agricultural products was regulated by guiding plans and market forces respectively. In industrial production, the number of products under the administration of the State Planning Commission (SPC) was 120, accounting for 40% of the total industrial output in 1978. In 1987, the number was reduced to 60, accounting for about 17% of the total industrial output. The number of required industrial products under the administration of various sectors decreased from over 1,900 in 1984 to about 380 in 1988. Though the gradual downsizing of mandatory state plans has played a positive role in enhancing the vitality of businesses, it has generated new problems to macroeconomic regulation.

The previous analysis points out that enterprises are not enthusiastic to invest by using internal accumulations, but proactively rely on state accumulations. Thus, the decisive factor for enterprise investment relies on the loans they win. The market demand, also affects enterprise investment, but is considered merely a secondary factor. Only when market demand declines substantially does it become a major factor affecting investment. The previous analysis has also pointed out that the pattern formed by initial allocation and the pattern formed by redistribution, will force banks to raise the money supply. Enterprises will have to invest once money is in their hands. As a result, on one hand, the investment demand will increase with the additional money supply; on the other hand, the supply for investment is limited, which will push up the prices of investment goods. Under the traditional planned economy system, dual measures were adopted to maintain the equilibrium between supply and demand of investment goods: an increase in the prices of investment must be curbed; a rationing constraint will be applied to the investment goods to regulate their quantity for different local governments and businesses.

After the reform of the economic system, China has gradually abandoned the constraint on rationing of various investment goods and simultaneously deregulated their prices. This creates a new issue of how to control investment demand. The current instrument is to implement a hierarchical allocation method for total investment: the State Planning Commission(SPC) determines the general plan, and then stipulates quota for different levels, whose investment amount should not surpass the quantitative limits specified in the quota. This is a shift from the original rationing constraint on particular investment goods to the general investment amount for each level. Under this system, although price controls on investment goods have been loosened, the increase in prices of the investment goods will be framed by the total rationing plan. If the total rationing plan is too tight, an actual oversupply may then be generated to drive down prices of the investment goods. Under this situation, although enterprises had money for investment, the money was not spent due to the rationing constraint and eventually turned into forced savings, forming a gap caused by this rationing.

The simultaneous employment of price liberalization and total rationing has become a practice formed during the course of the economic system reform, which needs to be summarized and analyzed theoretically. On one hand, it turns the price level into the critical variable of adjusting aggregate demand with aggregate supply, which possesses the function of leading to optimal allocation of resources; on the other hand, it transforms excessive money into forced savings. At present, it is still impossible to effectively control the money supply, so the instrument of a rationing constraint becomes a means to control aggregate demand. Although this instrument also results in shortages, these shortages do not appear in the market, so it will not generate queues in the marketplace. This is not the same as the shortage caused by price rigidity that manifests itself directly in shops without inventories. Such a situation will not be created by the shortages caused by the rationing constraint.

The instrument of total rationing is mainly aimed at businesses, local governments, and sectors with soft budget constraints to solve problems caused by an excessive money supply. For households, as there is no problem with soft budget constraints, a gradual reduction of rationing constraints has been adopted during the course of reform.

The shortage gap caused by the rationing constraints equals the difference between original aggregate demand and real aggregate demand after we apply these rationing constraints.

8.4 The Formation Mechanism of Shortage Gap Caused by Price Rigidity

Perfect price rigidity and perfect price elasticity are two extreme examples, which are rarely encountered in real economic life (regardless of being in the East or the West). In China, currently the price level is partially rigid, or sticky, which can bridge part of the gap between aggregate demand and aggregate supply, and the remaining gap that cannot be covered up is called the shortage gap. The shortage gap caused by the rationing constraint has been studied in the previous section. This section will focus on the shortage gap caused by price rigidity.

The first concept involved is the expectations of the economic actors for the shortage gap, especially for the ones caused by price rigidity, which is shortened as the expectations of shortage. Just like other types of expectations, the expectations of shortage also influence the behavior of various economic actors.

In the case that the economic actor has known that the price level is partially rigid, he also understands that, if under the current price level, his demand for a particular product cannot be satisfied, and he then will anticipate the future shortage of this product. Believing the future shortage tends to expand, he will spend his surplus money on another product, even if the utility of the other product is not comparable with the one he intended to buy originally. This is called forced substitution. In fact, the spillover[1] effect is usually used to describe this process in disequilibrium theory. During this process, consumers are not pursuing utility maximization under the income constraint, but they are pursuing utility sub-maximization under the income constraint. This is also a rational choice for consumers.

The outcome of forced substitution will be narrowed down due to the shortage gap caused by price rigidity. Meanwhile, low efficiency of the economy is reflected in the utility loss of consumers. Thus, the equilibrium between supply and demand reached on the basis of forced substitution is not a Pareto Optimality.[2]

Producers also face the problem of forced substitution when procuring investment goods. If one anticipates an expansion in the shortage, a producer will turn to other investment goods, too. Thus, his pursuit of profit maximization under the cost

[1] Spillover effect is a core content of multi-market disequilibrium analysis and also a major difficultyin the design of the disequilibrium model as it complicates the models estimates. Refer to Ref. I [13] to study this issue. This problem is also discussed in Sect. 3.8 of this book.

[2] Pareto optimality refers to the maximization of consumer utility, producer profit and resource allocation when the economic system is in equilibrium.

constraint will turn to the pursuit of profit sub- maximization. The shortage gap will then be bridged by forced substitution at the expense of profits to the producer.

In the case that utility maximization of the consumer is not adversely affected when he switched to buy other goods, and profit maximization of the producer is not harmed when he purchased other investment goods, then such kind of behaviors should not be viewed as forced substitution.

If a consumer or producer becomes optimistic about the expectations of a shortage, and one believes that the shortage will not expand, or not too much, which will not harm his future purchases, one will suspend the intended purchases, reserving them for the future.

When the economic situation is favorable, and the economic actors are optimistic about the expectations of shortage, they will then hold more money to buy products in the future. Adversely, with a poor economic situation, they are pessimistic about the expectations of shortage, and more forced substitution will follow.

It should be noted that, for producers, the opportunity cost of holding money for future purchases is relatively high, so they tend to engage in forced substitution.

Therefore, in the case of partial price rigidity, the disequilibrium state formed between supply and demand will result in utility loss or profit reduction, which destroys the optimal situation of resource allocation. Abolishing partial price rigidity should be one of the price reform targets in China.

In a market economy, when the quantity demanded for a good exceeds the quantity supplied, the price of that goodwill increase. This will cause demand to decrease and cause supply to increase, reaching the market equilibrium of the product. This is shown in Fig. 8.7.

In Fig. 8.7, if price is P_1, the quantity demanded is D_1. and the quantity supplied is S_1, there will then be a gap between the quantity supplied and the quantity demanded D_1S_1. This gap will cause the price to increase to P, where the quantity supplied and the quantity demanded reach the equilibrium. Hence, the quantity demanded drops to H, and the quantity supplied increases to H. If the price is rigid, the quantity demanded will not decrease, and the quantity supplied will not increase, either. Therefore, the gap between the quantity supplied and the quantity demanded D_1S_1 will exist for a long time. This is reflected in the shortage of products in stores. Once the products are put on the shelves, they are quickly snapped up and sometimes even long queues

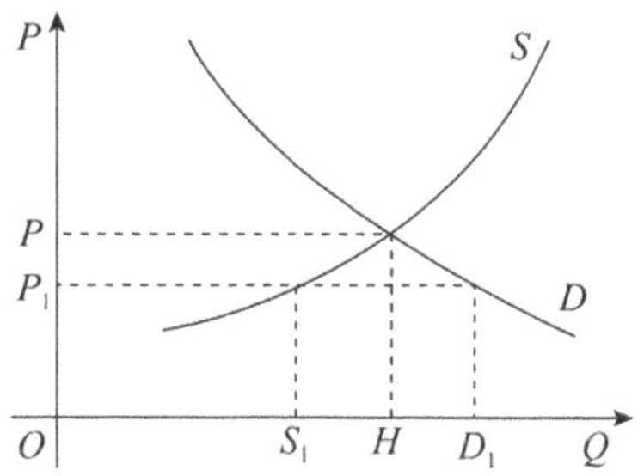

Fig. 8.7 The shortage gap caused by price rigidity

are seen. Or, this may be reflected in waiting for products to arrive a longtime after the order.

8.5 The Formation Mechanism of the Price Gap

If the price is perfectly elastic, the mechanism shown in Fig. 8.7 demonstrate show the price gap is formulated. However, since it is sticky, or it is a mark-up on the basis of the production cost, the price will in the long-run fluctuate around the level of the production cost plus the average profit. Such a price[3] is defined as the price of production by Marx, reflecting the outcome of profit equalization between enterprises and industrial sectors.

At its initial stage, an increase of the price level caused by inflation is demand-pull, since demand exceeds supply; the gap between supply and demand is bridged up by the increased price. If demand continues to surpass supply, then the higher product costs driven by an increase in the price level will in turn push up prices. The cost-push increase in the price level cannot fill the gap between supply and demand.

In China, the price level is partially rigid, so in the initial stage of inflation, it can alleviate demand from pulling up prices. However, the price rigidity will be very fragile once demand continues to surpass supply, resulting in a cost-push increase in the price level. Consequently, enterprises will voice loudly to increase prices or adopt disguised measures to increase the price level to transfer the burden of the rise in production costs.

Currently, most of the product prices in China are no longer set by the government. It has become a decentralized decision-making process. Nonetheless, the market system in China is still immature and the price level does not always respond immediately to the fluctuations of supply and demand. Even in modern Western countries, only in places such as the stock and auction market can the auctioneer immediately set the transaction price according to the quotations offered by sellers and buyers. Under other circumstances, prices will not immediately respond to fluctuations of supply and demand.

The bottom line for a enterprise to set up its product price is still in production costs. To determine the appropriate markup price, enterprise will not completely follow the supply and demand situation in the prevailing market but also anticipate the future trends of economic development, as well as the quantity supplied and quantity demanded in the future market. Once the markup is determined, the ex-factory price set by the enterprise will not be changed at any time in the short-run unless it is under special circumstances, and such a markup price is somewhat sticky. As for some large-scale businesses, there is obvious stickiness in the prices of their products. This also mirrors the credibility of these businesses.

[3] In Western economics, the average profit is the cost of capital, which is counted as a cost factor.

However, things will be different once inflation turns worse. In this case, enterprises would further markup the proportion of price rise caused by inflation expectations on the original price, which will appear to change more quickly without sticking to any certain price level. Nonetheless, the core price will generally remain stable in case such an expectation markup is ignored.

8.6 Measurement of the Dual-Gap Inflation

The price rise gap can be measured by statistical data. The basic statistical index used to calculate the rate of price level increases in China is the general social retail price index, which mainly reflects the changes of consumer prices (a little part of which reflects the changes of prices of means of production). In addition, the national income deflator or the GDP deflator is also commonly employed to measure price level changes for general products.

The national income deflator is the ratio of the total national income calculated at current prices to the total national income calculated at constant prices. Based on China's statistical data, not only the national income deflator but also the national income deflators of the five major material production sectors can be computed. This is helpful for analyzing the sectoral composition of the price level.

The shortage gap is much more difficult to measure than the price rise gap. According to the above theoretical analysis, the following methods can then be adopted to measure the shortage gap.[4] First, aggregate supply and aggregate demand functions are given as follows

$$D = a_0 + a_1 r + a_2 M + U_1$$

$$S = b_0 + b_1 K + b_2 L + U_2$$

where, D denotes aggregate demand; r is the real interest rate; M is the broad money (cash plus all deposits); U_1 is the random error; S is aggregate supply; K is the value of the fixed capital; L is the number of labor force; U_2 is the random error.

Since D and S cannot be directly observed, the short-side law of the disequilibrium theory will follow then

$$Q = \min\,(D, S)$$

where, Q is the total amount of market exchange on actual observations, which is expressed by the amount of national income produced.

[4] The calculation results here are the outcomes of my collaborative research with Professor Laurence J. Lau as I was a visiting scholar at Stanford University.

According to the *M–N* estimation method in the disequilibrium theory,[5] the undetermined parameters of the above two equations can be determined, and then *D* and *S* can be calculated. To assume that

$$DS = D - S$$

where, *DS* is the excessive aggregate demand, that is, the gap between aggregate demand and aggregate supply, which is the general inflation gap defined previously. However, there exists both the price rise gap and the shortage gap in this general inflation gap. How to separate the shortage gap from there becomes a question.

The commonly adopted method is that the constant price of a certain period will be applied to *M*, *K* and *Q* while money *M* does not follow the constant price but its constant purchasing power can be converted according to the national income deflator. On the basis of this, the aggregate supply function and the aggregate demand function can be estimated by using the *M-N* method, the value of *D* and *S* obtained will be both calculated according to the constant price of the base period to exclude the impact of the price factor, thus the resulting *DS* value will only be the shortage gap.

This method has been applied to measure aggregate demand, aggregate supply, and the shortage gap in China for a period of 24 years from 1965 to 1988. Due to the lack of the complete data of the total fixed assets of the whole society, after determining that of 1952, the amount of the total fixed assets of the whole society for all subsequent years were computed on the basis of the respective accumulation rate and the depreciation rate of the national income of each year. The base period was set in 1952, rather than 1965, because when the serial value of fixed assets was computed, it was found that there were more errors in the previous years and the values became more accurate in the latter years. The calculation of the value of fixed assets commenced in 1952, and the data became more confident for the accuracy of the results in 1965. The results of the parameters calculated are shown in Tables 8.1, and Table 8.2 shows the results of aggregate demand and aggregate supply as well as the excess aggregate demand.

Values in parentheses are two standard deviations, σ 1 and σ 2 are the variance of the random error $u1$ and $u2$, respectively.

The figures in the table are all calculated at constant prices (RMB) in 1952. DS=DEM-SUP in the table, and DEM is aggregate demand;

$$\text{DSS} = (\text{DS}/\text{SUP}) \times 100\%, \ \text{SUP is aggregate supply.}$$

The aggregate supply function being counted is the potential aggregate supply function, which is more convenient for a theoretical analysis.

According to the calculation results, aggregate supply exceeded aggregate demand in about 1/3 of the years, and in about 2/3 of the years, aggregate demand surpassed

[5] Specific estimation methods are described in Refs. [5, 13, 21]. The estimation method introduced in Ref. [13] is more easier to understand.

Table 8.1 Estimates of the parameters

	Estimations by ordinary least squares		Estimations by disequilibrium	
a0	1.3	(0.139)	1.5	(0.130)
a1	0.89	(0.045)	0.85	(0.069)
a2	−0.065	(0.024)	−0.044	(0.045)
σ1	0.21	–	0.105	(0.037)
b0	−0.47	(0.630)	−1.29	(0.520)
b1	0.57	(0.076)	0.49	(0.066)
b2	0.24	(0.228)	0.56	(0.190)
σ2	0.17	–	0.096	(0.029)

Table 8.2 Values of aggregate demand, aggregate supply, and the gap between aggregate supply and aggregate demand

Unit: 100 billion yuan

Year	DEM	SUP	DS	DSS (%)
1965	1.617982	1.072821	0.545161	50.8157
1966	1.798861	1.186264	0.612597	51.6409
1967	1.801322	1.265394	0.535928	42.3526
1968	1.871620	1.336440	0.535180	40.0452
1969	1.857007	1.430093	0.426914	29.8522
1970	1.954226	1.557972	0.396254	25.4339
1971	2.016727	1.688741	0.327985	19.4219
1972	2.058571	1.778056	0.280514	15.7765
1973	2.169015	1.927888	0.241126	12.5073
1974	2.195933	2.070678	0.125254	6.0490
1975	2.259939	2.230664	0.029274	1.3124
1976	2.286999	2.371638	−0.084639	−3.5688
1977	2.410778	2.539580	−0.128803	−5.0718
1978	2.406369	2.745024	−0.338655	−12.3371
1979	2.581101	2.998948	−0.417847	−13.9331
1980	2.935457	3.263258	−0.327802	−10.0452
1981	3.037349	3.526582	−0.489232	−13.8727
1982	3.264805	3.760185	−0.495379	−13.1743
1983	3.575955	3.995263	−0.419308	−10.4951
1984	4.207605	4.299072	−0.091467	−2.1276
1985	4.692343	4.665565	0.026779	0.5740
1986	5.177917	5.152446	0.025470	0.4943
1987	5.722526	5.622292	0.100234	1.7828
1988	6.249609	6.127944	0.121664	1.9854

aggregate supply. In the early stages of the "Cultural Revolution", the shortage gap accounted for a larger proportion of aggregate supply, and then it decreased year by year. The key reason was the implementation of the policy of freezing wages and prices during that time. Prices increased significantly in 1988, but the shortage gap was not that large, indicating that most inflation had been absorbed by the increase in price levels. This showed that the majority of prices in China had been liberalized. The conclusion from our measurements may not be perfectly consistent with the theory of shortage of Janos Kornai. Indeed, when reviewing the economic reform in more than a decade, including the sluggish markets of 1981 and 1982 (it was then called the buyer's market) and sluggish markets in late 1989 and 1990, it confirmed that it is possible for aggregate supply to exceed aggregate demand in a centrally planned economy. It seems that although Janos Kornai's theory of shortage plays a positive role in the construction of China's economic theory, there is a limitation to use this theory to explain the real economic situation in China. It can hardly be used to explain the economic situations in other socialist economies according to the measurement results of Portes.

Chapter 9
The General Model of Inflation Theory

The general model of inflation theory includes three aspects: (1) the commodity market model; (2) the money market model; (3) the rule of regulation (or the policy rule). The supply and demand in the commodity market and money market, as well as the unified equilibrium between these two markets, have been discussed respectively in the previous chapters. In this chapter, the regulation of the commodity market and the money market will be integrated through the policy rule to formulate a unified theoretical and regulatory system so as to construct the general model of inflation theory.

It should be pointed out that the establishment of a multi-market model by disequilibrium analysis method is still a subject under exploration, which is immature either in theory or in methodology. The research results in this book are only preliminary, and more research, especially the econometric research of the model, remains to be further explored in the future.[1]

The regulatory system occupies an important position in the general model of inflation theory. The regulatory system includes the regulation object, the regulation subject, the regulation signal, the regulation rule, the regulation target, the behavior of the regulation object, and so forth. The task of the general model is to analyze the interaction between the regulation object and the regulation behavior so as to analyze the operational process of inflation. The generation, development, and degeneration of inflation are not only related to the internal mechanism of the economic system but also associated with the regulation behavior. Since real inflation is the consequence of the interaction between the internal mechanism and regulation behavior, the inflation theory should include the analysis not only on the internal mechanism which generates inflation in the economic system, but also on the regulation behavior. On top of that, as a general model, it should include not only the behavior mode of the regulation object (represented by the demand and supply function) but also the

---

[1] Readers interested in multi-market disequilibrium are advised to refer to Refs. [5, 13, 16]. The literature systematically introduces the establishment of the multi- market disequilibrium model, the existing problems, and the upgrading directions.

L. Li, *The Inflation Mechanism and Expectations*, Understanding China,
https://doi.org/10.1007/978-981-97-2570-0_9

behavior mode of the regulation rule (represented by the quantitative relationship between the regulation targets, regulation signals and regulation behavior).

9.1 Expressions of the General Model

In this section, the general model of inflation theory will be introduced step by step.

The commodity market will be adjusted by the planning system with a target function as

$$J_1 = \min\left(Q_t^* - Q_t\right)^2$$

That is, the planning system should keep the real output Q_t as close to the planned output Q_t^* as possible. If the real output is too high or too low, the planned output or the economic system will be adjusted by the planning system to push the real output closer to the planned output.

The aggregate demand function and the aggregate supply function of the commodity market is as follows

$$D_t = D\left[r_t, M_t^s\left(Q_t^* - Q_t\right)/Q_t\right]$$

$$S_t = S\left[M_t^s, \left(Q_t^* - Q_t\right)/Q_t\right]$$

The proximity of the real output to the planned output will be viewed as an exogenous variable of both the aggregate demand function and the aggregate supply function. In essence, aggregate demand D_t and aggregate supply S_t are regulated by the planning system through the planned output Q_t^*.[2] In this case, Mt^s stands for the money supply, and r_t is the real rate of interest.

From the short side law of the disequilibrium theory, the real output is equal to the smaller side of aggregate demand and aggregate supply. Hence, $Q_t = \min(D_t, S_t)$.

The money market is regulated by the banking system with a target function as follows

$$J_2 = \min\left(M_t^s - M_t^d\right)^2$$

where, M_t^s is the quantity of money supply in period t; M_t^d is the demand for money in period t. This means that the banking system needs to keep the money supply as close as possible to the demand for money.The aggregate supply and aggregate demand functions for money are as follows

[2] The variable in the aggregate supply and aggregate demand function reflects the impact of various quotas in the planning system upon the aggregate supply and aggregate demand. Since it is hard to express the specific variables of the quota,the equation will be used here. Please refer to the detailed explanation later in this chapter.

$$M_t^d = M^d(r_t, S_t)$$
$$M_t^s = M_{t-1}^s + \Delta M_t^s$$

where, r_t is the real rate of interest; S_t is aggregate supply; ΔM_t^s represents the additional money supply from the banking system. The quantity of money in the money market is equal to the money supply, which is not determined by the short side law. Since the problem of uniform equilibrium between the commodity market and money market has been solved in Chaps. 6 and 7, the concise money supply and money demand function can be adopted here.

The controlling target function of the government is

$$J = \min(D_t - S_t)^2$$

That is, the government will make an effort to narrow the gap between aggregate supply and aggregate demand as small as possible. Since aggregate demand and aggregate supply are not observable, the gap can only be estimated by the government through the following controlling signals (or controlling indicators):

Firstly, the price signal, represented by

$$\Delta P1_t = \lambda(D_t - S_t)$$

The greater aggregate demand is than the aggregate supply, the greater the increase in the price level is. Here, λ represents the proportion of the price gap in the general gap, and $\Delta P1_t$ represents the price gap.

Secondly, the shortage signal, represented by

$$\Delta P2_t = (1 - \lambda)(D_t - S_t)$$

where, $\Delta P2_t$ represents the shortage gap. It should be noted that though $\Delta P2_t$ is not a statistical indicator for the government, its existence and change can still be perceived or namely, its size and change can still be estimated by the government. Here, $(1 - \lambda)$ represents the proportion of the shortage gap in the general gap, and $\Delta P2_t$ represents the shortage gap.Thirdly, the speed signal, expressed as

$$\omega_t = \frac{\overline{Q_t} - Q_t}{Q_t}$$

where, $\overline{Q}_t$ is the output upper boundary recognized by the government. The closer the real output Q_t is to $\overline{Q}_t$, the more the government perceives overheating of the economy.

9.2 The Regulation Rules and Economic Expectations

A rational government used to follow rules in its economic regulations. Throughout the 40 years of China's economic development, the only irrational behavior of the government's economic regulation occurred from 1959 to 1960. Nonetheless, the government did learn lessons from those practices of these two years to avoid similar incredible events in the future. In the rest of the years, the economic regulation behavior of the government was roughly based on the principle of slowing down in overheating and stimulating in recession. Although different criteria for growth were followed in different periods, the government no longer believed that a higher growth rate was better. Of course, this does not mean that there were no regulatory lapses in the rest of the four decades.

The basic rule of government regulation is that if prices rise too high, and the government considers aggregate demand to be greater than aggregate supply, the planning and banking systems will be required to tighten their policies. At this point, the planning system will contract the planned output Q_t^*, and the banking system will reduce the supply of new money ΔM_t^s. Similarly, if the government considers the growth rate is too high, or the shortage gap is too large, it will require the planning system and banking system to tighten the economy for narrowing the gap between aggregate demand and aggregate supply.

Conversely, if the government believes the growth rate is too low, it will require the planning system and the banking system to deregulate. Accordingly, the planning system will increase the planned output Q_t^*, while the banking system will increase the supply of new money ΔM_t^s.

In different periods, the government follows different judgment criteria on the price level and economic growth rate, leading to various levels of loose or tight regulation in different periods. This actually reflects the discretionary decision of the government upon whether to achieve a higher growth rate and thus tolerate higher inflation, or a lower growth rate and thus maintain low inflation or no inflation. The discretionary policies of the government used to focus on different aspect in different periods. For instance, from 1984 to 1988, the government regulated the economy on the basis of maintaining a high growth rate and thus tolerating a high level of inflation. From 1989 to the present, the government has made it a priority to drive down inflation at the expense of economic growth.

The question concerned at present is whether the relationship between the rate of economic growth and the rate of inflation can be expressed mathematically. To put it more simply, the following equation can be used to estimate such relationship by adopting a regression analysis based on historical data

$$P = \alpha_0 + \alpha_1 SNI + \alpha_2 SM$$

where, P presents the growth rate of the price level; SNI is the growth rate of the national income; SM is the growth rate of the money supply; $\alpha_{0,}\alpha_1$, and α_2 are the parameters to be estimated.

If this equation is a proper estimator, there will then be a certain quantitative boundary for the government to follow in a discretionary decision.

According to the theoretical analysis in this book, the relationship between the economic growth rate and inflation will be uncertain in the short-run when economic expectations are involved. With low inflation expectations, higher growth can coexist with lower inflation, as what happened from 1984 to 1987.When inflation expectations are high, the growth rate of the price level will be significantly higher than the economic growth rate, as the case in 1988. Due to the lack of in-depth theoretical analysis and sufficient understanding, the economic expectations become quite uncertain, and it is difficult to include expectation as an independent variable in the model. Consequently, it becomes problematic to determine the quantitative relationship between the price level and the economic growth rate, which can only be solved with the development of the theory of expectations. Therefore, the discretionary decision of the government is still likened "to crossing the river by feeling the stones". Only after determining the upper limit of tolerable inflation can the economy be gradually adjusted to maintain the corresponding growth rate. It can be stated that the emergence of economic expectations has led to more hardships in economic regulation. If the economy is regulated according to traditional theory or experience, it is likely to gain outcomes that go contrary to wishes. For instance, both the high inflation in 1988 and low inflation in 1990 were all beyond people's expectations.

The relationship between inflation and economic growth is shown in Fig. 9.1 assuming that no economic expectations exist.

Then, with the emergence of inflation expectations, the relationship between economic growth and inflation has changed as shown in Figure 9.2.

In Fig. 9.2, *AA* represents the relationship between inflation and economic growth without economic expectations. *BB* represents the new position of *AA* after rotating around points (P_1, g_1) with economic expectations. *BB* denotes a new relationship between inflation and economic growth. It approximately reflects the acceleration or deceleration function of the economic expectation upon inflation. However, *BB* is not necessarily a straight line, which may be a curve as shown in Fig. 9.3.

In short, there have been obvious limitations in describing the *BB* line due to insufficient research on expectations, which makes it more difficult for the established

Fig. 9.1 The relationship between inflation and economic growth without expectations

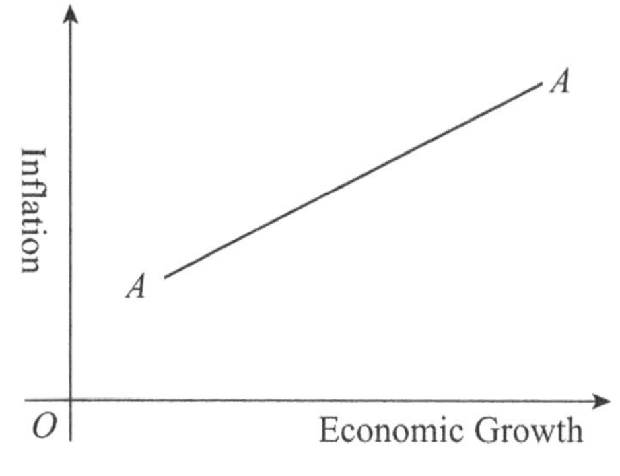

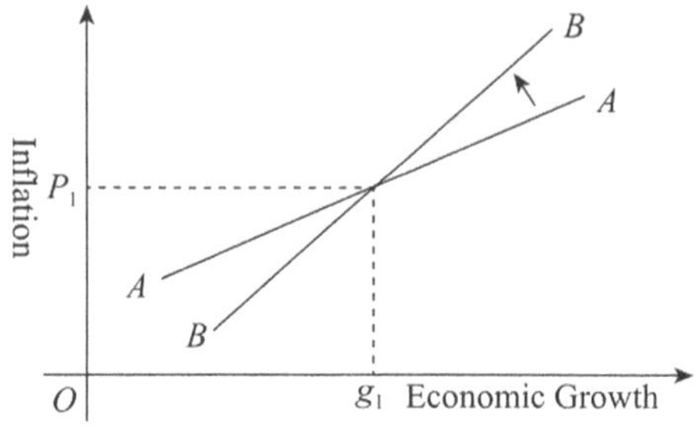

Fig. 9.2 The relationship between inflation and economic growth with expectations

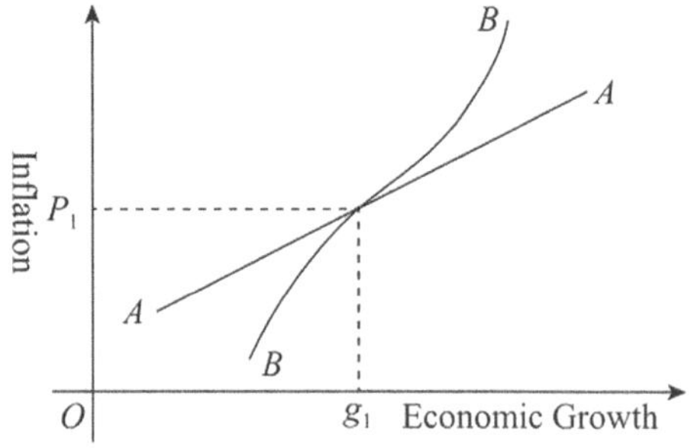

Fig. 9.3 The curvilinear relationship between inflation and economic growth without expectations

economic model to simulate and analyze short-run economic behavior. Currently, though the Chinese economists are paying more and more attention to econometric models, the impact of uncertainty and expectations on the economic system must not be ignored. If factors of uncertainty and expectations cannot be effectively incorporated into the model at present, it becomes extremely necessary to consider their impacts during the model analysis.

9.3 The Planned Regulations

The economy is regulated by the planning system on the basis of the signals from two aspects. The first is government commands. The government requires the planning system to contract the planned output Q_t^* when the economic growth rate is believed to be too high. On the contrary, the government commands the planning system to raise the planned output Q_t^* when the growth rate seems too low. The second is the planning system itself. The planning system will adjust the planned output according to factors such as inflation, economic growth rate, and so forth, so as to narrow the gap between the planned output Q_t^* and the real output level.

The main means of the planning system to regulate the economy is to adjust the planned output Q_t^*. Then how can the planning system ensure that the real output Q_t is close to the planned output Q_t^*? This can be achieved from the perspective of aggregate demand and aggregate supply.

In terms of aggregate demand, the planning system can control the investment demand in aggregate demand by means of rationing, and meanwhile also restrain the growth of government consumption and household consumption to a certain extent. At present, the main means by which the planning system restrains aggregate demand is rationing, which can directly eliminate the purchasing power of part of the money, terminate projects under construction, and postpone projects ready to be commenced.

In terms of aggregate supply, the planning system can also implement approaches such as closing down, suspending operations, amalgamating with others, or switching to the manufacturing of other products to shutdown some businesses or constrain the supply of raw materials to decelerate the production speed.

After adopting tightening measures, both aggregate demand D_t and aggregate supply S_t will fall. In general, D_t decreases more rapidly than S_t. The real output level will thus be determined by D_t, and Q_t can be reduced by dropping down D_t so as to push Q_t closer towards Q_t^*.

After Q_t^* is contracted in the planning system, the general inflation gap (D_t-S_t) will be effectively reduced through the reduction of D_t and S_t, especially if D_t is reduced more quickly than S_t. The price level will fall when the general inflation gap narrows down. It has also been pointed out earlier that the price level is only one component of the general inflation gap, so when the general inflation gap shrinks, the shortage gap will also be contracted. But it should be noticed here that the rationing measures will coerce a proportion of money to be forced savings. Consequently, it becomes a common phenomena that when the economy is tightened, a fallin the price level will substantially aggrandize the bank deposits. It can then be concluded that when prices fall, the increase of household deposits is due to the increase of voluntary savings, while the increase of deposits of enterprises and institutions is mainly alue to the increase of forced savings.

What measure will the planning system adopt in order to ensure the attempt of pushing up Q_t^*? On one hand, the planned output of the planning system per se is a stimulus signal to businesses. When observing an increase in the planned output, enterprises will perceive that the government may deregulate the economy to increase demand, they will therefore actively expand production. As pointed out in the previous analysis, under the current economic system, enterprises have inherent incentive to expand. Consequently, production will return to be normal regardless of any excessive stimulus measures. On the other hand, the planning system will reduce rationing restrictions and resume projects that had been abandoned. In addition, the planning system will also launch some new construction projects, which will enhance economic growth through their increased investment. The multiplier effect of investment is evident when aggregate supply is running below its potential level.

The planning system mentioned above includes the SPC (the State Planning Commission), Ministry of Finance, and the planning organs of various government sectors. It is a broad concept mainly relative to the regulation of commodity markets. In fact, the banking system also needs to plan, but it is relative to the money market, so it should be discussed differently. In the planning system, the role of financial department is quite special because it manages the money. Namely, the planning system manages projects, and the financial department manages the money. The difference of money management between the financial department and the banking system is that the financial department and the planning system are closely linked although they are at the same administrative level. Meanwhile, the banking system is relatively independent in managing money because it is a bit isolated from the SPC. The relationship between these three sectors is reflected in the doggerel that "planning leaves a rift, finance decides a deficit, and banking prints bills". In fact,excessive money supply would be attributed to these three sectors, not the rift left by the planning system alone. As for the effect of fiscal revenue and expenditure arrangements upon inflation, adequate research has been conducted by domestic expertise,[3] and there is no need to further explore here.

9.4 The Monetary Regulations

The banking system regulates money mainly in accordance with signals from three aspects. The first is the instructions from the government. When the government requires control over aggregate demand, banks will tighten money through controlling the money supply. When the government instructions are to stimulate aggregate supply, banks will ease money through increasing the money supply. The second is the impact of the planning system, which determines the total amount of investment, where the banks will have to provide corresponding amounts of money to match such investment. In addition, government consumption can also be regarded as the arrangement of the planning system, which also requires banks to provide the corresponding amount of money. The money supply of these two aspects is not determined internally by banks but externally by the planning system (SPC and the Ministry of Finance). The third signal is the adjustment of the banks themselves according to the real situation of the money supply and demand. In order to stabilize the value of money (that is, to stabilize the price level), banks must manipulate the money supply and narrow the gap between money demand and supply.

The key for banks to regulate money supply is to control new loans. Cash issuance is in fact determined by the difference between deposits and loans, with little room for banks to regulate. In addition, adjustment of the required reserve ratio can also constrain the loan scale of various functional banks. This is because the planned loans of the central bank are lent to borrowers by those banks.

In addition to control the money supply, the banking system can impose impacts on the economy by adjusting the nominal interest rate. As long as the nominal interest rate rises faster than inflation, the real interest rate will rise, to shrinking aggregate demand and the demand for money.

[3] Refer to Refs. [35, 54].

9.5 Comprehensive Regulations

The planning system and the banking system are both independent, but their regulation and control processes are mutually influenced and constrained. Maladjustment between the planning regulation and banking regulation will be prone trouble to the economy. Therefore, the government should be responsible for coordinating the planning regulation and banking regulation to accommodate both.[4]

Stabilization of the price level is the common goal of government, the planning system, and the banking system. Therefore, it is easier to coordinate the regulations of the planning and the banking system from a perspective of stabilization of the price level. However, the goals of government economic regulation include not only stabilization of the price level but also an appropriate economic growth rate. Both the planning regulation and banking regulation will affect this economic growth rate. More precisely, the planning system affects the economic growth from the perspective of investment, while the banking system from liquidity. It thus becomes hard to reconcile the two.

In real economic life, banks often blame the planning system for its oversized initiatives, forcing them to issue extra money. On the contrary, the planning system also blames the banks for issuing too much money, forcing the planning system to increase the rationing limitations. In fact, as per the previous analysis, these two sectors are mutually influenced. Consequently, both the planning system(not only the State Planning and Development Commission) and the banking system (not only the head office of the People's Bank of China) must be jointly responsible for inflation in the macro economy.

If planned output Q_t^* is coordinated with money supply M_t^s to jointly determine Q_t^* and M_t^s , the economic development will be more harmonious and less contradictory. The prevailing problem is that these two variables have been independently determined by several various sectors, which are difficult to coordinate unless the government is required to intervene. How to manipulate these two main controllers Q_t^* and M_t^s of the economic system will become the research focus of the macroeconomic theory.

In modern economic life, due to the role of expectations, the demand for money becomes uncertain, which leads to the complexity of the relationship between Q_t^* and M_t^s. For example, with high inflation expectations, a certain amount of Q_t^* will require more M_t^s to support it, and vice versa. As a result, under the impact of expectations, the equilibrium between the commodity market and the money market is not stable. The equilibrium will change with the change of expectations. The impact

---

[4] Specifically,macroeconomic control can be divided into four sectors: the first is the SPDC (State Planning and Development Commission), the second is the Ministry of Finance,the third is the State Economic and Trade Commission, and the for this the banking system. The pricing sector can be added to this list. Policy coordination among these sectors is critical for macroeconomic regulations, which is in need of further theoretical study. The research in the comprehensive equilibrium theory in this aspect is worth inheriting.

Fig. 9.4 The relationship between output and demand for money with expectations

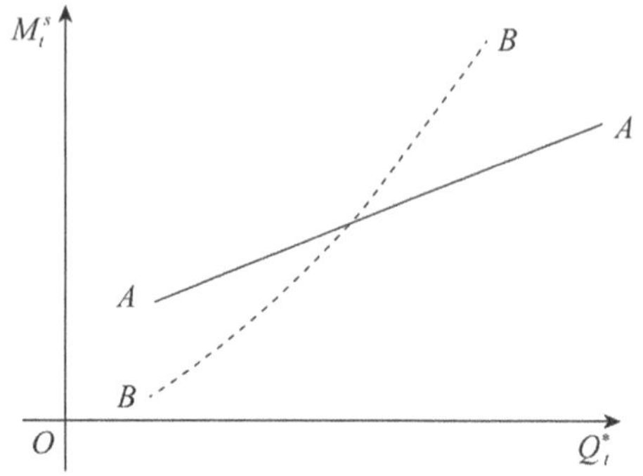

of expectations upon the equilibrium of the commodity market and the money market can be illustrated in Fig. 9.4.

In Fig. 9.4,assuming that the equilibrium between the money supply M_t^s and the planned output Q_t^* without expectations is represented by line *AA*, the new equilibrium between the money supply M_t^s and the planned output Q_t^* with expectations will be represented by curve *BB*. It shows that when the planned output Q_t^* or the money supply M_t^s exceeds a certain point, more amount of money supply M_t^s will be needed to support a certain amount of Q_t^* if there is an increase in inflation expectations and vice versa. However, it is difficult to accurately describe *BB* because of the uncertainty of expectations, which leads to the ambiguous relationship between M_t^s and Q_t^*. Specific measures to reduce such ambiguity will be analyzed in Chap. 11.

It is worth noting that when inflation expectations are particularly high and also particularly low, the relationship between M_t^s and Q_t^* is presented as a straight line perpendicular to the Q_t axis, as shown in Fig. 9.5.

In Fig. 9.5, when Q becomes Q_t^1 , since the real output level is far lower than the potential quantity supplied, the inflation expectations will be very low, and the quantity of money corresponding to Q_t^1 will be infinite. This is the expectation trap as analyzed in the previous sections. That is, an increase in M_t^s carries no impact on Q_t because M_t^s is absorbed by the low expectations and converted into inventory of product capital. When Q_t equals Q_t^2 , since the real output level has reached the

Fig. 9.5 Expectation traps and expectation impulses

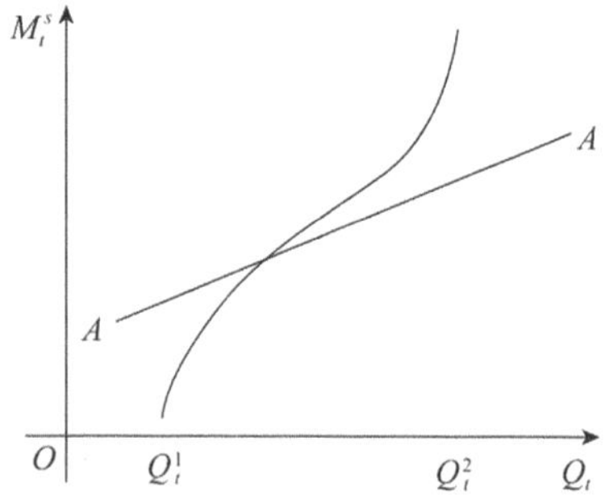

upper boundary of supply and inflation expectations are high, there will exist an expectation pulse.

Namely, the money required by Q_t^2 is infinite, which is the phenomena when hyperinflation occurs.[5] At this point, the increase in Mt^s carries no impact upon Q_t.

9.6 Determinants of Output Level

In the general model, the real output level is determined by the smaller side of aggregate supply and aggregate demand in the short-run, where aggregate demand will be influenced by the following three variables: the real interest rate r_t, the money supply M_t^s, and the planning variable $\left(Q_t^* - Q_t\right)/Q_t$. Aggregate supply will be influenced by only two variables: the money supply M_t^s and the planning variable $\left(Q_t^* - Q_t\right)/Q_t$.

Therefore, when aggregate supply is greater than aggregate demand, the real output level is determined by three factors affecting aggregate demand. When aggregate demand is greater than aggregate supply, the level of real output is determined by two factors affecting aggregate supply. The real output level which is influenced little by the rate of interest is mainly determined by the money supply M_t^s and the planning variable $\left(Q_t^* - Q_t\right)/Q_t$ no matter aggregate demand is greater or smaller than aggregate supply. At the same time, it should be noted that there exists an upper boundary for the expansion of real output levels in the short-run, which should not be surpassed.

On the surface, the real output level in the short-run mainly depends on the planned output from the planning system. However, it is in fact jointly determined by the planning system and the banking system. During periods of extreme economic expansion, the real output level is determined by the money supply as rationing constraints decline. This is the simplified disequilibrium model introduced earlier.

$$D_t = D\left(M_t^s\right)$$

$$S_t = S\left(M_t^s\right)$$

$$Q_t = \min(D_t, S_t)$$

When the economy is in a period of extreme contraction, the real output level in the short-run will be more determined by the rationing levels. That is:

[5] An expectation impulse is a theoretical abstraction, or a hypothetical extreme. When expectation tends to increase expectation impulse, on one hand, the velocity of money circulation is accelerated; on the other hand, rising prices cause an increase in the demand for money, and the interweaving effect of these two circumstances will further worsen inflation, which absorbs all the increases in it.

$$D_t = D\left(\frac{Q_t^* - Q_t}{Q_t}\right)$$

$$S_t = S\left(\frac{Q_t^* - Q_t}{Q_t}\right)$$

$$Q_t = \min(D_t, S_t)$$

In the general model, the real output level and money supply M_t^s are not linked by a single chain because Q_t is not only determined by M_t^s . In turn, Q_t also affects the demand for money M_t^d, which will to a certain extent affect the money supply M_t^s .

From the perspective of current economic development, the money supply is carrying more and more impacts upon the real output level, while the role of rationing is gradually shrinking. But this does not rule out the possibility of rationing expansion at a certain period of time, or for a particular industry.

So the theory herein is to some extent that the theory regarding money supply determines output level, and the applicability of this theory is based on the assumption that the real output level fluctuates near the potential aggregate supply level. In the case that the real output level reaches or is near the upper boundary of aggregate supply, the money supply will carry no impact on Q_t.

The output level being determined by the money supply does not mean that it is merely determined by the banking system per se because a proportion of the money supply is given by the plans of the planning system. However, in light of the final regulation, banks are still entitled to enlarge the money supply after identifying the actual quantity of the money supply required by the planning system. As the head office of the People's Bank of China becomes more and more independent, the role of the money supply in determining the output level will be further enhanced.

9.7 Determinants of Inflation

The formation process and the internal structure of the general inflation gap have been analyzed in Chap. 6 and 8 respectively. In this section, the contents of these chapters will again be summarized in light of the general model.

Since the general inflation gap is determined by (D_t-S_t), naturally, it will also be influenced by all the factors determining D_t and S_t. However, when S_t reaches its upper boundary, M_t^s will play a particularly critical role in shaping the general inflation gap. In essence, rationing per se is unable to bridge the general inflation gap, but the level of planned output Q_t^* can affect the enterprise expectations and thus shape the size of aggregate demand D_t. Consequently, rationing based on the planned output level can have an impact on the general inflation gap through alternating D_t and S_t. However, the role of rationing constraint will be invalid once the general gap is established. Thus, an increase in rationing will result in a reduction in the price rise gap while expanding the shortage gap at an equal size.

After the reform of the economic system, M_t^s carries more and more impact on the economy. Therefore, the theory of general inflation gap determinism can also be viewed as a theory of money supply determinism. The money supply determinism can be further divided into three stages: (1) when aggregate supply is lower than its potential, an increase in M_t^s will cause Q_t to rise but not the general inflation gap. (2) When aggregate supply is higher than its potential but not exceeding its upper boundary, an increase in M_t^s will cause aggregate supply to rise and enlarge the general inflation gap. Moreover, the general inflation gap will become larger and larger as M_t^s increases. (3) When aggregate supply reaches its upper boundary limit, the increase in M_t^s willfully work on the expansion of the general inflation gap.

Therefore, the general inflation gap is tightly related to the output level, without which it is impossible to analyze the relationship between the money supply and inflation. Consequently, the analysis on inflation should rely not only on the analysis of the money supply but also on aggregate demand and aggregate supply as well as integration with the analysis on the product market and the money market.

The internal structure of the general inflation gap cannot be interpreted by the money supply itself but by price rigidity and rationing. Rationing has been playing a more critical role than that of price rigidity in current economic life, endowing new features to the shortage. This point has been explored in detail in Chap. 8 and will not be further covered here.

9.8 Forms of Policy Rule

Both the planned output Q_t^* and planned money supply M_t^s are generally regarded as exogenous variables. Because of the inclusion of policy rules, Q_t^* and M_t^s will change according to these rules in this chapter, so that Q_t^* and M_t^s become endogenous variables, which are defined by other variables within the economic system.

In short, the following functions theoretically hold

$$Q_t^* = f_1(D_t - S_t)$$

$$M_t^* = f_2(D_t - S_t)$$

And

$D_t - S_t > 0$, Q_t* decreases,

$D_t - S_t < 0$, Q_t* increases;

$D_t - S_t > 0$, $M^t{}_s$ decreases,

$D_t - S_t < 0$, $M^t{}_s$ increases.

In real decision making processes, since D_t and S_t are not measurable, $Q^*{}_t$ and $M^t{}_s$ will be determined by the following rules

$$Q_t^* = f_1(P_t) \;\; M_t^s = f_2(P_t)$$

And
P_t increases, $Q^*{}_t$ decreases,
P_t decreases, $Q_t{}^*$ increases;
P_t increases, $M^t{}_s$ decreases,
P_t decreases, $M^t{}_s$ increases.
Policy rule only analyzes the change direction of both $Q_t{}^*$ and $M_t{}^s$ and the directive signals they follow, but it dose not analyze specific amounts and the length of such changes.

However, it is useful to include policy rule in the general model because it reflects the self-correction ability of the model. Especially when more uncertain factors are involved and the effect of expectations are amplified in the economic system, the influence of such uncertain factors can be effectively reduced if the government acts in accordance with the policy rule. In other words, the government must follow "the rules of the game" in formulating policies.

Policy rule treats policy variables as endogenous rather than exogenous as the traditional view since it focuses on the long-run effects of the policies, not just the effects of one-off policy changes.

It has been pointed out that the Chinese government is rational and has basically followed the policy rule in its economic regulation and control for more than 40 years. However, this does not deny the fact that the government might follow different preferences in prioritizing inflation and economic growth in different periods. In one period, it prioritizes economic growth and tolerates higher rates of inflation, while in other periods, it prefers to control inflation and tolerates lower economic growth rate.

The inconsistent preferences of the government in its discretionary decision-making process do not necessarily mean that the government violates the policy rule, let alone that the government is irrational. Such inconsistency can merely show that the government exerts different efforts in making policies as per the policy rule. In terms of the integration of policy objectives and policy tools, the government is still performing in accordance with these rules. Such integration is the theoretical foundation of the anti-inflation policy to be analyzed afterwards.

9.9 Economic Cycle and Inflation

The general model under scrutiny offers a fundamental theoretical analysis of the economic cycle, as well as the internal relationship between the economic cycle and inflation. In accordance with the theory, the general trend of economic development is that real aggregate supply will be higher than its potential when aggregate demand runs over aggregate supply so as to push up inflation. When inflation rises for a period of time, policy rule will trigger policies that drag down aggregate demand and thus

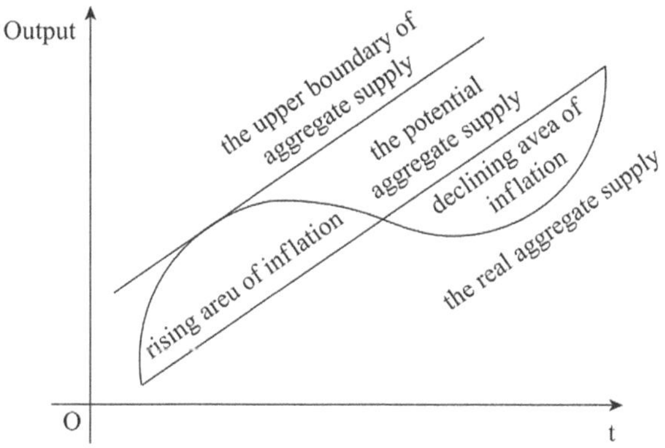

Fig. 9.6 The economic cycle and inflation

suppress inflation, which in turn causes aggregate supply to fall. Inflation will also fall if aggregate supply is below its potential level.

When inflation falls for a while, policy rule will again stimulate economic growth. Thus, an economic cycle is completed. The turning point in this cycle is policy rule. It remains uncertain as for how long inflation will last before the policy rule takes effect to drive down inflation since it is more influenced by factors external to the economic system per se. However, when the real aggregate supply has reached its upper boundary, the continuous increase in aggregate demand can no longer cause the real supply to rise. However, when all turns into increased inflation, the government will face the pressure of public demand to pull down inflation, and the policy rule will thus take effect. Such a theory of the economic cycle can be demonstrated by a graph, as shown in Fig. 9.6.

It seems that the causes of the economic cycle have been satisfactorily explained theoretically. However, showing the ability of a theory to explain an economic cycle in principle is different from showing its ability to explain an economic cycle in practice. This theory explains how changes in aggregate demand lead to changes in aggregate supply and inflation and denotes the internal causes and mechanisms of economic cycle. However, in reality the economic cycle is complex and subject to many factors. The theory herein is only a high level of abstraction, and it is impossible for it to accurately explain the amplitude and duration of a real economic cycle. Only when it can explain the trend of a real economic cycle will the theory be justified to stand the test of reality. In fact, because of the stickiness of both prices and expectations, inflation will lag behind real economic growth but uncertainly, which complicates the issues and obscures theoretical explanations. A theoretical explanation is not a snapshot of reality. A theoretical explanation can be meaningful only when it is able to detect the essence of issues through the phenomenon. However, there exists at times a gap between the essence and the phenomenon, the essence ultimately determines the change of the phenomenon. For instance, due to the stickiness of expectations, inflation will keep increasing for a period of time and not immediately decline with a decrease in the real aggregate supply.

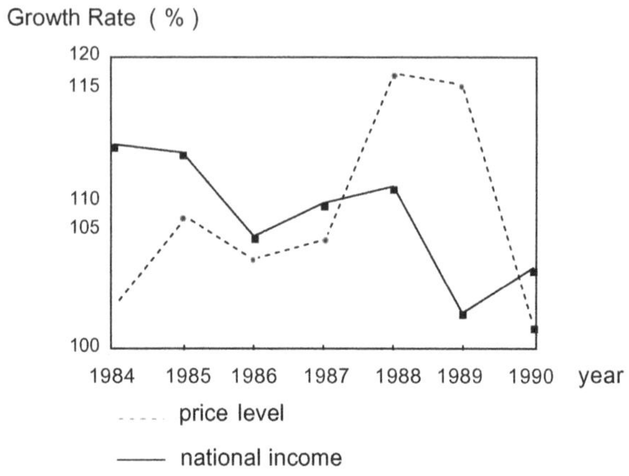

Fig. 9.7 The relationship between the price level and the growth rate of national income

In order to compare the price level (retail prices) with the growth rate of national income on the same graph, the growth rate of national income has been used to replace aggregate supply and a referencing period from 1984 to 1990 (which includes a complete cycle) is employed to identify if there is an approximate cycle relationship as above-mentioned. Fig. 9.7 is derived on the basis of real data.

As can be seen from Fig. 9.7, 1985 to 1990 can be regarded as a cycle. From 1985 to 1988, economic growth declined and then increased, while the same pattern of economic growth is followed by the price level. However, even when the economy reached a trough in 1989 and then began to recover in 1990, the price level was still decreasing in 1990. Thus, over the entire cycle, the real relationship between price level and supply was consistent with the theoretical relationship previously discussed.

Chapter 10
The Theory of Sticky Expectations

In previous chapters, a repeated emphasis has been put upon the influence of expectations on the economic system, and the term "expectation" has been used to explain the economic phenomena that are hardly ever possible to be decoded by traditional economic theories. Expectation is so pervasively used in this book that no analysis of every important concept and no explanation of every critical issue will do without it. However, in all previous chapters, no efforts have ever been made to systematically present how expectation comes into being and how it changes over time. As uncertainty of expectation is highlighted here, this term seems to become a ghost independent of the economic system. Though its influence upon the economic system is tremendous, its presence on the other hand remains veiled in mystery.

In this chapter, we will systematically analyze the formation process and variations of expectation, attempting to unveil its mysteries. A set of behavioral rules will be proposed so that expectation can be managed as an endogenous variable in the economic system in order to minimize its uncertainties.

After the reform of the economic system, progress has been made in the field of economic theory in China. Economists in China have been urged by new practices and problems to constantly update their theories in order to better explain the economic issues in practice. As a new research topic in China's economic world, the introduction of expectation theory indicates that China's economic theory is tending towards a higher level. Though it is still hard to measure the impacts of expectation theory on the development of economic theory in China, economic theoreticians in China will be shocked by the research in the field of expectation. The traditional theories, methodologies, and arguments will be thoroughly re-estimated by Chinese economists eventually, which will gradually facilitate the birth of a new theory and methodology.

L. Li, *The Inflation Mechanism and Expectations*, Understanding China,
https://doi.org/10.1007/978-981-97-2570-0_10

10.1 Information Foundation of Theory of Expectation

Expectation is defined as the anticipation of the future value of economic variables relevant to current decisions. Expectation is essentially subjective. However, people do not formulate their expectations out of thin air. Their judgments about the future have to rely on a comprehensive analysis of information gathered from the past, the present, and the future. The correctness of such judgments depend not only on the critical information in hand but also on the methodological appropriateness in analyzing comprehensively such information.

Expectation used to be primarily initiated by a particular individual. A general expectation can then be reached by aggregating all those individual expectations. For instance, the consumer's expectation of price is viewed as the sum of all individuals' expectations of the future price. However, the expectation of each individual can differ because the information collected and analytical ability might not be identical. It is therefore becoming a primary concern to establish how to aggregate all these different aspects to converge on a general expectation.

Multiple approaches such as an arithmetic average or geometric average will be applied to such an aggregation. From the perspective of probability distribution, expectation from economic actors of the future is treated herein as a distribution, the mathematical expectation of which will then be defined as their general expectations. It is safe then to maintain that the distribution of expectation is approximately a normal distribution. This is because that for most people, neither the information collected nor the analytical methodology adopted is too differentiated.

In addition, for each independent individual, his or her anticipation of the future value of a variable (such as price) is not limited to a single value but a distribution. For instance, what might be the probability for a price to increase by 5% or by 10%? Consequently, the expectation of such a distribution is counted as the anticipated value of the future variable.

There is currently a prevailing method of collecting expectation data directly from households and enterprises in the international academia. This method is very simple by asking individuals to answer a "yes" or "no" question. For instance, a "yes" would be responding to an expectation of a price rise while "no" to a price fall—these answers will then be summarized; or the households may only be required to provide a potential price rise figure, which will be accordingly aggregated to compute mathematical expectations. Originated in the late 1940s, this method has been common in Western countries since the 1950s. The expectation data collected through this method powerfully supports the expectation research in the field of economic theory as well as assisting in policy decisions.

If we treat the imputed value of the future variable of each individual as a trial, it is impossible to confirm the size of such imputed value prior to the trial (before answering the question). This can be regarded as the uncertainty inherent in a random trial. On the contrary, in case a random trial is repeated and its distribution tends to be stable, the uncertainty magnitude of such a random trial should then be measurable, and vice versa. Two types of uncertainty criteria are hence established. One is measurable with a stable distribution; the other is immeasurable with an unstable distribution. Uncertainty in economic theory refers to the later, i.e. the uncertainty in random trial with unstable distributions.

As for a measurable uncertainty, if we assume that there are only a limited number of incompatible results of A_1, A_2 … An in a random trial a, their corresponding probabilities are $P(A_1)$, $P(A_2)$,…, $P(A_n)$, respectively. It also satisfies then we have

$$\sum_{i=1}^{n} P(A_i) = 1$$

$$H = -C \sum_{i=1}^{n} P(A_i) \ln P(A_i)$$

This formula depicts the specific value of an uncertainty. It is named the Shannon Formula. Where H represents the entropy in random trial a . Coefficient C depends on the unit of measurement, which would be either binary or decimal. Base 2 is used for the logarithm of a binary unit, while a common logarithm would be applicable for a decimal unit.

Further study of entropy is ignored here since it relates to the theory of information. It is predicted that more and more relevant contents in the information theories will be absorbed in the future development of economic theories attributing to the importance of expectation.

10.2 Assumptions of Expectation

Since any expectations about the future are relevant to current decisions, economic actors will endeavor to anticipate the future accurately in order to reduce losses from current decisions. Such behavior demonstrates the rationality of economic actors. Therefore, the rational assumptions of economic actors should be the primary assumptions underpinning expectations. Additionally, the following assumptions should be considered by economic actors whenever expectations are involved:

1. The assumption of the black box and the gray box. What most economic actors employ to anticipate the future on the basis of the gathered information is the blackbox model. Since exploration of the relationship between inputs and outputs is their sole concern regardless of a particular structure, the model finally turns out to be merely a blackbox for economic actors. The relationship between inputs and outputs might potentially be identified based upon the actors' experiences which also might be modified in accordance with their judgments about the future. People with professional economic educational backgrounds are to a certain extent acquainted with the variable relation of economic issues as well as with the model structures. Therefore, the models they utilize could partially reflect the

reality despite the certain gap between the models and reality. These models are accordingly referred to as the gray box.

Differing from the assumptions of the blackbox and gray box, the assumption of the white box is what rational expectations rely upon. Rational expectations assume that all economic actors in the market comprehend the model structures which are further believed to be accurate. Nonetheless, even economists themselves endlessly debate which theoretical models truly reflect the objective world, and it is much more impossible for these model structures to be understood by ordinary individuals. As a result, the white box assumption of rational expectations appears to contain too many idealized flavors to match the real world, which is imperfect itself.

The assumption of the blackbox we have determined appears to be more inline with the predictive power of ordinary people. Since the input end represents the information gathered, while the output end denotes the value of prediction, the relationship between input and output can then be determined on the basis of personal experiences. Such a relationship can constantly be further adjusted in practice or in accordance with new circumstances. The foundations of the relationship between inputs and outputs remain unknown to most ordinary people. As a consequence, even an illiterate person would be able to conduct his or her own anticipation based on the existing information at their disposal.

2. The assumption of the marginal cost (MC) of information equals the marginal revenue (MR) of a decision. Economic actors must spend time, money, and other resources on collecting information. The outlays for these resources finally become costs, namely, the costs of achieving information. Though, the more information is collected, the more accurate the expectations are. The cost of information collection also positively correlates with the increase of the quantity of that information collected. It becomes unworthy if the cost of information collection exceeds the benefit generated by a correct decision. As a result, a rational economic actor will definitely cease further efforts in information collection once a certain quantity is gathered.

Let q be the quantity of information; $R(q)$ represents the revenue function from the decision made on the basis of such quantity of information; $C(q)$ represents the cost function of information collection; $\pi(q)$ represents the profit function generated by the aforesaid information, then we have

$$\pi(q) = R(q) - C(q)$$

Since rational economic actors aim at profit maximization, the following equation holds

$$\frac{\mathrm{d}\pi(q)}{\mathrm{d}q} = \frac{\mathrm{d}R(q)}{\mathrm{d}q} - \frac{\mathrm{d}C(q)}{\mathrm{d}q} = 0$$

Re-arranging the above, we have

$$\frac{dR(q)}{dq} = \frac{dC(q)}{dq}$$

Thus, the marginal cost of obtaining the information equals the marginal revenue of the decision. Therefore, this assumption is derived from the rational assumptions of economic actors. It requires

$$\frac{d^2R(q)}{dq^2} - \frac{d^2C(q)}{dq^2} < 0$$

$$\frac{d^2R(q)}{dq^2} < \frac{d^2C(q)}{dq^2}$$

The above discussions demonstrate that when profit is maximized, MC of information increases much more rapidly than that of MR of the decision.

Based on the foregoing assumption, economic actors are unlikely to chase all information prior to arriving at a decision. The consequence is that if parts of the critical information are missed, there may be systematic errors in the anticipations. This biases the results of the rational expectations.

Similarly with other economic variables, the acquisition of information herein is not determined by any external conditions, but rather by internal variables in the economic system.

3. The assumption of learning of expectations. All economic actors will learn from the expectations of others. That is, the expectations of a few are likely to become those of the majority. Panic buying could be used as an example of this. The panic-buying behavior of a few residents can lead others to join the queue so that a panic buying phenomenon occurs. When residents of one region learn that the residents of another region are rushing to purchase a particular commodity, the former often correspondingly panic buy the same. There exists a feature in the geographical distribution of the learning assumption of expectations: the rural person learns from the urban person, small cities from big ones, and the interior from the coastal areas. Such a feature helps to illustrate the rationality of economic actors who hold that expectations of people in coastal and large urban areas are generally more accurate than those of their counterparts in the interior, small urban and rural areas. This suggests that economic actors would be willing to learn from them to gain greater revenue at lower costs.

Owing to the learning behaviors associated with this assumption, the probability of a normal distribution of expectations will be enhanced.

Additionally, the variance in such a normal distribution will become lesser attributing to the learning behavior. The function of expectations will consequently be refined. The combination of a larger expectation with a smaller variance could better explain the concentration of the distribution. Meanwhile, the learning behaviors associated with the expectation can further accelerate the acceptance by the public of the expectation results from any Gray Box assumptions so that a general expectation is shaped. It could finally be concluded that the correct expectations of a few could result in widespread public consensus through the dissemination of the learning behaviors.

4. The assumption of unsustainable false expectations. Economic actors learn not only from others but also from practice. Once an expectation is found to be wrong, economic actors typically have it modified to match the reality. Therefore, a false expectation would not be sustainable in the long-run. The trial-and-error method adopted by economic actors will enable their expectations to move around the trends of accuracy. As a result, expectation becomes consistent with reality in the long-run. This is why we do not rely on the role of expectation when a long-run analysis is conducted. Nonetheless, an expectation can potentially deviate from reality in the short-run.

10.3 Formation Process of Expectation

Expectation itself is a psychological phenomenon, and so is immeasurable directly. However, such a psychological phenomenon is a reflection of the objective world rather than something out of the thin air or merely a kind of transcendence. Thus, the formation of expectation should also be an objective process. What we are attempting to accomplish is to grasp such a seemingly immeasurable psychological expectation through a measurable objective process.

The extrapolative expectation model was constructed by Metzler in 1941. Assuming that P_{t-1} represents the price during period of $t-1$, P_{t-2} represents the price during the period of $t-2$, the extrapolative expectation of the price at time t can be illustrated in the following formula:

$$P_t^* = P_{t-1} + \varepsilon(P_{t-1} - P_{t-2})$$

where, ε denotes the coefficient of expectation. The previous trend remains unchanged if ε is greater than 0; if ε is smaller than 0, the previous trend will move towards an opposite direction; in case ε=0, the anticipated price in current period equals the real price in previous period. The value selected for ε depends on the economic structure on which the model is based. A negative ε is considered to be more appropriate for the cobweb model. In that case, high price will stimulate production, thus increasing the supply of a product in the coming quarter and causing the price to fall. That is, the price will move towards the opposite direction rather than remaining unchanged as years go by.

However, economic actors will keep learning from their experiences to modify current expectations by applying errors from the past. That was the foundation for Cagan to construct his adaptive expectation model in 1956. With the same mathematical symbol as above, adaptive expectation can be expressed in the following formula:

$$P_t^* = P_{t-1}^* + \eta(P_{t-1} - P_{t-1}^*)$$

where, η represents the adaptive coefficient, which determines the adjustment speed of the errors in the past.

Since P_{t-1}^* can be expressed as

$$P_{t-1}^* = P_{t-2}^* + \eta\left(P_{t-2} - P_{t-2}^*\right)$$

Then, there is

$$P_t^* = \eta P_{t-1} + \eta(1-\eta)P_{t-2} + (1-\eta)^2 P_{t-3}$$

If later expectations are constantly adopted to substitute in the previous expectation formula, the following formula holds:

$$P_t^* = \eta P_{t-1} + \eta(1-\eta)P_{t-2} + \eta(1-\eta)^2 P_{t-3} + \eta(1-\eta)^3 P_{t-4} + \eta(1-\eta)^4 P_{t-5} + \eta(1-\eta)^5 P_{t-6} + \ldots$$

It can also be simplified as

$$P_t^* = \eta \sum^{\infty} (1-\eta)^{k-1} P_{t-k}$$

This is the sum of an infinite series. It converges when $0<\eta<1$, so the value of the assumption will be $0<\eta<1$.

If the extrapolative expectation is based merely on the information contained in the real values of the previous two periods, the foundation for adaptive expectation will include all the previous information covered in this sequence. However, both the extrapolative expectation and adaptive expectation employ only particular information from the past, such as the previous price and its relevant expectation. Whereas in reality, on top of the particular past information, other information currently available will also be utilized by economic actors to make their expectations. For instance, when a price expectation is formulated, other information such as government economic policy will be counted in addition to the price and expectation of the price in the past. This is because the economic policy of the government imposes substantial impacts on the future price changes, but the signals of price and expectation of the price in the past may not be fully embraced by the policy. It is obvious that both the extrapolative and adaptive expectation make use of only a fraction of the information available. It could be concluded that neither the extrapolative expectation nor the adaptive expectation is deemed to be the correct way of optimal resource allocation in case information is also counted as a commodity.

Targeting at such a critical weakness of the extrapolative expectation and adaptive expectation, Muth initiated the rational expectation model in 1961. In the 1970s, the view of rational expectation was introduced into the world of macroeconomics, which led to a new wave of research in this field, or in other word, it triggered a revolution in the world of macroeconomic theories.

Rational expectations can be expressed as

$$P_t^* = E_{t-1}\left[P_t/I_{t-1}\right]$$

The equation represents a conditional mathematical expectation, where I_{t-1} is used to denote the information attainable in the time period of $t-1$.

Some fundamental features of rational expectations are described as follows:

1. Economic actors make use of all relevant and accessible information in formulating their expectations.
2. The expectation value of the objective probability distribution is consistent with that of the subjective probability distribution. However, this does not ensure the correctness of the expectations of the consumers or producers. Economic actors will learn from their failures to eliminate the systematic errors in expectations.
3. The economic system can only be affected by unanticipated policies. In other words, government policy is ineffective. This is an important conclusion of the theory of Rational Expectations.

As mentioned in the previous chapters, expectation behavior has imposed substantial impact on China's economic activities. How to study the formation process of expectation in China becomes theoretically important and practically significant.

The author of this book maintains that both the extrapolative expectation and adaptive expectation are rather simplistic. Neither of these two expectations is able to explain the fact of sudden price jumps in 1988. It is impossible for producers and consumers to formulate rational expectations under the current economic environment in China. On one hand, the economic actors are unable to obtain adequate information to formulate a rational expectation. On the other hand, the economic actors are not equipped with sufficient ability to analyze such information rationally. Hence, in this book, we attempt to explore a theory of expectation lying in between the adaptive expectation and rational expectation.

The theory of sticky expectations proposed in this book is based on several expectation assumptions introduced in the previous section, which constitute the foundation and framework of this theory. Now a complete theoretical system of expectation will be accomplished once the formation process of sticky expectations is supplemented to the above.

The formation process of sticky expectations is as follows: the economic actors utilize the information attainable under cost constraints to anticipate the future value of the economic variables. Such expectations will be formulated by overlapping the following activities of the economic actors, i.e. (1) following experiences; (2) relying upon the newly existing phenomena; (3) learning from others as well as from their own errors in the past.

As per assumptions of the formation process of expectations above mentioned, the following characteristics are deemed to be inherent in the theory of sticky expectations:

1. Errors are possible in the short-run expectation. Firstly, the blackbox model employed by economic actors for expectation may lead to a failure; secondly, due to the cost constraints of gathering information, economic actors may miss some critical information, which will also produce errors in their expectations. Such errors may be random or systematic ones in the short-run (several years for instance). For example, from 1984 to 1987, expectations of inflation of individuals in China were lower than those of the real inflation rate because money illusions existed among these people.
2. Expectation is fundamentally correct with only random, not systematic errors in the long-run. It is not difficult to draw this conclusion from the learning assumption and unsustainable false expectation assumption.
3. Expectation is sticky, which would not change too quickly in the short-run. Due to the comparatively high costs of gathering information in China, especially the delay in the publication of information, which consumes a long time for economic actors to collect. Correspondingly, no significant change will take place in these short-run expectations because of little change in information collected by economic actors.

The theory of sticky expectations is fundamentally a kind of theory of rational expectations in the long-run. However, in the short-run, it is an irrational expectation. This corresponds to the theory of sticky prices, which holds that any price is sticky in the short-run but elastic in the long-run. Therefore, the theoretical model in this book can be referred to as a dual sticky model.

The analyses of the influences of expectations on the economic system in previous chapters do rely upon the theory of sticky expectations.

In contrast, there are certain differentiations between the theory of sticky expectations and the theory of adaptive and rational expectations. Rational expectations hold that expectations vary completely with the changes of economic variables and are consistent with the real changes of these economic variables. Meanwhile, adaptive expectations believe that expectations are determined by experiences. So as long as people summarize their experiences and constantly correct the deviations between expectations and economic variables, the variations in the expectations will generally be consistent with those of the economic variables. In short, both rational expectation and adaptive expectation exclude the nature of stickiness of expectations.

If expectations formulated from the gray box model are agreeable to the majorities, the formula for the formation of sticky expectations can also be expressed as

$$P^* = E_{t-1}[P]$$

However, this may not be consistent with reality. There may be systematic errors in the short-run, which indicate inconsistency with rational expectations. Nonetheless, in the long-run, the results generated from this formula are consistent with those from rational expectations.

10.4 Empirical Analysis of Sticky Expectations

As a psychological activity of the human beings, expectations cannot be directly measured. In this section, we will indirectly measure the variations of expectations by means of the relationship among expectations, money, and prices to prove whether expectations are sticky.

According to the analysis in Chap. 7, the following equation can be derived on the basis of the equation of exchange $MV=PQ$:

$$\frac{\Delta M}{M} + \frac{\Delta V}{V} = \frac{\Delta P}{P} + \frac{\Delta Q}{Q}$$

In the aforesaid two equations, we can only detect the relationship among money, the velocity of money circulation, prices, quantity of products, and so on without directly observing any relationship between the expectation, money, and prices. While the relationship between expectation, money, and prices is implicitly underlying in the fluctuations of the velocity of money circulation.

As a psychological activity, expectations can only influence the economy through certain transmission channels. One of these transmission channels is demonstrated by the behavior of consumers in seeking to preserve their existing monetary wealth. When anticipating a higher inflation rate than the interest rate of bank deposits, consumers would convert their monetary wealth into material wealth to avoid losses caused by the inflation. After running on bank deposits, consumers will panic buy in the market by giving up money for physical products. The second transmission channel lies in various behaviors of the producers to avoid losses. When anticipating a rise in the inflation rate, producers will take into account the pressure of pay-raise demands from their employees, as well as the pressure from escalation of raw material prices, which will signal them to increase product prices according to the anticipated inflation rate. On top of that, when the interest rate on bank loans is expected to be lower than the anticipated inflation rate, producers will seek more loans and rush to procure raw materials. As a result, when anticipating a higher inflation rate, both producers and consumers will attempt to give up their money as soon as possible, and rush to buy physical products in order to avoid losses caused by a devaluation of currency, which will speed up the velocity of money circulation. Accordingly, fluctuations in expectations can be indirectly measured by the fluctuations in the velocity of money circulation.

It should be pointed out that, as analyzed previously, the velocity of money circulation is influenced by multiple factors. In contrast with variations in expectation, the changes of these factors are relatively slow and stable, which will not result in a sudden acceleration or deceleration of the velocity of money circulation. Therefore, the variations in expectation can be measured indirectly from different phases of the velocity of money circulation. A feasible foundation is consequently established for the empirical analysis for the expectation theory in this book.

For example, data for $\Delta M/M$, $\Delta V/V$, $\Delta P/P$, $\Delta Q/Q$ in China for different years are shown in Table 10.1. Here, $\Delta Q/Q$ actually represents $\Delta GDP/GDP$. M represents the $M3$ defined earlier. For convenience, we also list the differences between the growth rate of the money supply (annual growth rate of $M3$) and the annual growth rate of GDP (at constant prices) in Table 10.1. Additionally, since GDP is used to replace Q, we hence substitute P by the GDP deflator so as to ensure consistency of measurement among the indicators.

As depicted in Table 10.1, the values of $\Delta V/V$ were negative from 1982 to 1987. This indicates that the velocity of money circulation is declining year on year. Furthermore, the money has been absorbed by such tardiness in the velocity of money circulation, which helps to weaken the impact of growth of money supply upon the increase of price level. However, over these periods, the values of $\Delta V/V$ varied from year to year, distributing within the range of −3.9–12.4. Among them, the highest $\Delta V/V$ value appeared in 1985 that is −3.9; the year 1986 witnessed its minimum that is −12.4. Such a phenomenon can be interpreted as follows: having experienced the economic overheating and substantial price rises in 1984, people's expectations of inflation increased in 1985 so that the velocity of money circulation accelerated. On the contrary, the economy contracted in 1986; GDP growth rate dropped back to 8.3%, which weakened people's inflation expectation and caused a decline in the velocity of money circulation.

Therefore, the variations in expectations of inflation can be indirectly inferred from the fluctuations in the $\Delta V/V$ values. The fundamental change in 1988 can also be found in Table 10.1, where the $\Delta V/V$ value changed from negative to positive. This indicates a significant acceleration in the velocity of money circulation in 1988. It did not absorb money but strengthened the impact of the money supply growth rate on the price level. In contrast with previous years, the difference (only 8.2 %) between the money supply growth rate and GDP growth rate reached the minimum in 1988, but it caused the price level to rise to the maximum point. Apparently, this was a consequence of a significant amplification of the expectations of inflation in 1988. Such a phenomenon could be evidenced through the soaring of retail prices

Table 10.1 China: indirect measurement of expectation fluctuations

Year Indicators	$\frac{\Delta M}{M}$	$\frac{\Delta V}{V}$	$\frac{\Delta P}{P}$	$\frac{\Delta GDP}{GDP}$	(1)–(4)
	(1)	(2)	(3)	(4)	(5)
1982	15.4	−6.6	0.0	8.8	6.6
1983	17.3	−5.7	1.4	10.2	7.1
1984	27.0	−7.6	4.9	14.5	12.5
1985	25.9	−3.9	9.0	13.0	12.9
1986	25.5	−12.4	4.8	8.3	17.2
1987	21.6	−5.4	5.6	10.6	11.0
1988	19.4	3.8	12.0	11.2	8.2

Table 10.2 Monthly Retail Prices

Month	Retail price index	Month	Retail price index
Jan.	109.5	Jul.	119.3
Feb.	111.2	Aug.	123.2
Mar.	111.6	Sep.	125.4
Apr.	112.6	Oct.	126.1
May.	114.9	Nov.	126.0
Jun.	116.5	Dec.	126.0

Source: *China Monthly Statistics*, No. 1, 1989

driven by panic-buying from the exacerbating inflation expectations in 1988. Details are shown in Table 10.2.

As can be seen from Table 10.2, panic-buying reached its climax in July, August, and September, 1988. The retail price index rose from 119.3 in July to 125.4 in September, and by 6.1 % in three months corresponding with about a 2% per month increase.

From both Tables 10.1 and 10.2, it can be witnessed that though China's inflation expectations did fluctuate in recent years, such fluctuations were not too severe until 1988 when they jumped to a higher level. It demonstrates that from 1984 to 1987, even though the money supply was growing too fast every year, exceeding the GDP growth rate by 11% and above, expectations of inflation had not accelerated following the faster growth rate of the money supply attributing to the money illusion. Instead, it moved at a slower pace than the growth rate of the money supply and stuck to a lower level. It was the stickiness of inflation expectations that led the growth rate of price levels to lag behind the growth rate of the money supply in the initial phase of inflation. However, such false expectation did not sustain indefinitely. After a while, the stickiness disappeared, and the expectation rose and again stuck to a higher level. At this point, the resistance of stickiness emerged once more if people attempted to pull down the expectations. Meanwhile, although growth rate of money supply had slowed down, the stronger expectations of inflation could still push up the price level, and the traditional relationship between money and prices would be destroyed.

As depicted in Table 10.2, in the second half of 1988, although a more severe contractionary policy had been implemented, the price level growth rate was still sticking to a higher level without declining with the contraction of the economy. Until 1989, the general retail price index still remained at 18%. At this stage, the growth rate of prices was synchronized with the growth rate of money supply or was rising even faster than the growth rate of money supply. This is because the expectations of inflation were still sticking to a higher level. In 1990, expectations of inflation fell again, sticking to a lower level. The growth rate of money supply in 1990 was not significantly lower than that of the previous year, but the retail price index dropped sharply to 2.1%. Although the government endeavored again to stimulate the economy in 1990, the results were not satisfactory. The powerful influences of the stickiness of expectation can thus be witnessed.

As for the common view about the lagging influence of money supply on the price level, the main reason lies on the stickiness of the expectation, which sticks to a lower level (that is, the anticipated price level is lower than the real one). When expectation sticks to higher levels, such a lag will disappear. Thus, the growth rate of the price level will be synchronized with the growth rate of money supply or even faster than the growth rate of money supply.

Both Keynesian and Monetary Schools recognize the stickiness of expectation. For example, the Monetary School theory maintains that after the change of the growth rate of money supply, it will take some time for the anticipated inflation rate to adjust to the real inflation rate. During this transitional period, the additional money supply will influence the change of the real interest rate. However in the long-run, the impact of the anticipated inflation rate on the nominal interest rate will eventually push the real interest rate back to its original high level. As a result, it is unreasonable and ineffective for the government to attempt to maintain a low interest rate by increasing money supply in the long-run. The European and American economists, however, have not yet explicitly put forward the proposition of sticky expectations. They are merely applying this concept unconsciously.

10.5 Uncertainty of Expectation

Expectation is stable owing to its stickiness; however, expectation is unstable because of its uncertainty. At present, it is still difficult for us to comprehend when and under what condition such expectation stickiness can be modified and a greater change appears.

The uncertainty of expectations originates from its counterpart in the real world. In contrast to a human being's cognition, the unknown realm is still very vast in reality. Our knowledge about the world is still very limited. For what we do not know, its law of change is beyond our control. For human kinds, the variations of the unknown will remain uncertain and unexplainable. Meanwhile, it is precisely because of the uncertainty of the objective world that economic actors realize that their expectations are not necessarily entirely accurate. Even so, economic actors will not easily alternate their expectations unless they realize that the established expectations are false and such falseness is caused by systematic errors. However, investigation of such falsehoods would be a time-consuming process. Therefore, in facing uncertainty in the real world, economic actors tend to explore carefully from the existing expectations and gradually adjust to reach some optimal points. Adjustment of expectations will thus appear to be relatively tardy. This trial and error method is regarded as a feasible approach for economic actors adjusting their expectations in the face of uncertainty in the real world. In the case of knowledge of the real world being certain, economic actors will be able to rapidly adjust to the optimal point through the determined model. Hence, expectations will no longer be sticky.

There are two main causes for economic fluctuations, i.e. the shock of uncertainty of the real world as well as the shock of uncertainty of expectation on the economy. The economy would be substantially influenced in case the two causes are combined. For example, in 1988, the slogan of "Breakthrough of Price Reform" did trigger people to sharply raise their expectations of the price level. Such a sudden change in expectations turned out to be uncertain and unpredictable in advance and had relatively huge impact upon the China's economy in 1988.

The uncertainty of expectation presents a major challenge to economic theory in explaining real economic phenomena. Due to the uncertainty in both the expectation and the real world, the anticipation ability of economic models constructed on the basis of economic theories becomes suspicious.

For instance, the world oil price used to be influenced by both political and military factors in the Middle East. The viability of employing economic models to estimate world oil prices will be weakened because it is hard to predict changes in political and military factors in the Middle East such as Iraq's invasion of Kuwait in 1990. This is why we maintain that it is both a science and an art to construct an economic model as well as rely on it to anticipate the future.

To a certain extent, although the formulation of economic policy used to be guided by theories, for fine-tuning the particular numbers, only the trial and error method is adopted, which indicates that we are still "looking before leaping". The role of economic theory is to turn the uncertain and unknown factors in the economic system into certain and known ones so as to lessen the influence of uncertain factors on the economy. Nonetheless, uncertainty always exists due to bounded cognitive ability.

10.6 Effects of Expectation

Expectation carry multiple impacts on economic activities but herein we analyze only some major effects of expectation on inflation.

1. Expectation is an important factor in inducing inflation. Because of the sticky nature of expectations, in the initial phase of inflation, the shock of an increase in the money supply on the increase of product prices becomes tardy, which creates a false prosperous phenomena with market prosperity, brisk trades, economic growth, and income rise. Consequently, when the economy enters the track of inflation, the government observes only the boom in the economy without taking actions to control inflation. On top of that, both consumers and producers are disguised by the money illusion so that they mistake the increase in nominal income for the increase in real income. They therefore live and work in peace without complaint. As a result, the sticky expectation plays a role in varnishing inflation. Such an effect has enabled the government to silently skip the phase of managing inflation with a relatively smaller cost. For instance, the last round of inflation in China can be viewed as starting from 1984. From 1984 to 1987, the growth rate of money supply in China was about 20%, while the growth

rate of price level was mostly about 5%, reaching 9% only in 1985. Since China has implemented a policy of freezing prices for a long time, people are still accustomed to constant prices even if liberalization of prices has been initiated. Expectations during this period were relatively sticky so that people maintained low inflation expectations for a period of up to four years. If the government determined to manage inflation earlier during that period, the economic problems encountered would have been relatively less later on.

2. The expectation of inflation will stick to a higher level when inflation has been rising for a certain period of time, which in turn prevents inflation from falling and which indeed helps to push up inflation. The role of expectation herein can also induces tagflation. Because of a high level of the expectation, prices will continue to rise for some time instead of falling with the decrease in money supply when the economy faces a contraction and the growth rate of money supply falls. Stagflation will occur in case the economy is depressed by severe contractions and inflation expectation remains high. The China's economy went through such a period in 1989.
3. When the economy touches the trough and expectations are finally driven down, the expectation trap effect emerges once again. At this point, the government attempts to stimulate the economy by increasing the money supply, however, all extra money will be absorbed by the expectation trap and turned into a backlog of inventory funds. Consumers tend to save more because of the lower inflation expectation, or hold money to buy. A sluggish market will hence be formed. The China's economy also faced such a situation in 1990.
4. Expectation is also an important factor in transforming a demand-pull inflation to a hybrid of demand-pull inflation and cost-push inflation. As long as expectations of inflation of both consumers and producers stick to a higher level, the consumers will demand an increase in nominal income while the producers will accordingly raise product prices as per an anticipated inflation rate. Both of the above behaviors will drive up the production costs so that a cost-pushed price level is born. Simultaneously, it becomes difficult to pull down the market demand due to the pressures from consumers receiving income increases, generating a hybrid inflation of both demand-pull and cost- push.

10.7 Policy Effectiveness under Expectation

There is a prevailing witty remark in the economic circles in China that "you have your policies, and I have my countermeasures of getting around them". The effectiveness of the policy from the central government may be substantially weakened or even counterproductive in face of the countermeasures of local governments, enterprises and consumers.

For example, the attempts by government to increase government revenue through issuing more money could only be achieved when the money illusion exists with both producers and consumers. Once producers and consumers find anticipations to be wrong, they will raise their expectations of inflation. Consequently, the government cannot enjoy any additional revenue through the injection of the extra money because consumers are ready to demand higher income while producers attempt to increase product prices. The only approach for the central government to increase fiscal revenue by issuing additional money will be by injecting more money into the economy to allow the real inflation rate to run higher than the anticipated rate of both producers and consumers. This means that governments can only win by a surprise move. Nonetheless, this approach is not recommended since it may lead to hyperinflation.

As has already been analyzed, when the economy reaches the trough, the effectiveness of the government's initiation of an economic policy will also be seriously weakened by the expectation trap effect. Thus, the government encounters a dilemma. Less money injection cannot stimulate the economy while more money injection may trigger a new round of inflation.

However, the existence of expectations in China does not necessarily invalidate the policy of the central government. For example, the government's anti-inflation policy eventually pulled down inflation as well as expectations of inflation. The critical point is that the government's policy should not be in confronting the public, attempting to deceive the public and rob some of public wealth in disguise. The government may only be able to deceive the public for a while, but not for long. The public will learn from their errors in the past and take countermeasures to offset the impact of government policy.

Since China has determined to adopt a system of a planned commodity economy, government policy will play a critical role in guiding and restricting economic activities. Accordingly, the government should consider the public expectation when formulating policies without underestimating public influences on policy effectiveness. It should be pointed out that there are potential conflicts of interest among the central government, local governments, and enterprises because the former represents the overall interests of a nation, while the later two only focus on regional and local benefits. For instance, when the central government orders termination of a local infrastructure project, the local government may not follow suit if it suspects the central government will soon permit the construction so that such an order would only be viewed as a temporary suspension. However, if the central government insists on tightening policy and establishing credit, there will no longer be such an expectation by the local government, so that the construction project will be terminated since continuing the project will not be profitable in a contractionary economy.

In summary, the credibility and sustainability of government policy are two critical factors able to weaken the influence of expectations. If the policy is capricious and low in credit, it will not be adequately effective under the influence of expectation. Therefore, intent and scope of policy rules of the central government turn out to be quite critical when the role of expectation is enhanced. Consequently, the adverse impact of expectation upon policy effectiveness can only be minimized when the economy is run in accordance and aligned with policy rules.

As long as the central government follows the rules of the game and unswervingly adheres to its own policy rules, rational enterprises will pursue their maximum benefits in accordance with the intentions of the government. In case the government is hesitant or ignores the rules of the game, enterprises will fail to know what course to take, which will consequently undermine the effectiveness of government policy. For decades, although a set of operational rules for government policies has been formulated by the central government, such a set of rules still remains somewhat vague with unnecessary flexibility in the process of policy formulation, which in turn makes difficult to the implementation of such policies. It is time to seriously analyze these policy rules. We maintain that the emergence of the theory of expectation will prompt us to transform the traditional formulation process of government policies.

Part IV
Policy Theory to Manage Inflations

Chapter 11
Anti-inflationary Policy

11.1 Introduction

Policy making should be based on theory, and theory should correspondingly serve policy making. This requires that theory must face economic reality and objectively analyze problems existing in practice to search solutions rather than avoid contradictions. Economic theorists should not only emphasize achievements but also strive to detect problems and have them solved in economic work.

From the above standpoint, this book analyzes causes for the inflation mechanism in China explores the quantitative relationship of various inflation factors, and attempts to lay a theoretical foundation for the formulation of anti-inflationary policy.

11.2 Theoretical Foundation for Policy Making

The mechanism for analysis of inflation in previous chapters of this book establishes a theoretical foundation for anti-inflationary policy making. In this section, the main conclusions of those theoretical analyses are summarized as follows:

1. The institutional theory. Under the condition of softness of budget constraints of businesses, the mechanism of pursuing an average profit retention level by enterprises and an average income level by employees will cause the income growth rate of employees to increase faster than the profit growth rate of the business. At the macro level, it is reflected that the proportion of households' income to the national income as well as the proportion of the households' new savings to the accumulation of national income are both increasing while the proportion of state fiscal revenue to national income is declining. This shows that savings and investment are borne by different economic actors: governments and producers determine the level of investment, while households largely determine the level

L. Li, *The Inflation Mechanism and Expectations*, Understanding China,
https://doi.org/10.1007/978-981-97-2570-0_11

of savings. Therefore, the potential intrinsic disharmony between savings and investments turns out to be a root cause of economic instability.

2. The demand theory. The aggregate demand function is $D = f\ (M, r)$. D increases with the increase of M while D decreases with the increase of r. The Short-run aggregate demand D^* is not only determined by M and r but also affected by expectations. The relationship between the short-run aggregate demand D^* and the long-run aggregate demand D is

$$D^* = D + \delta(P^* - P) + U$$

When the short-run expectation price level P^* sticks to a higher level (i.e.$P^* > P$), D^* will be greater than D; when P^* sticks to a lower level (i.e. $P^* < P$), D^* will be smaller than$D$. In the long-run, P^* will converge towards P, and hence $D^* = D$.

3. The supply theory. The short-run aggregate supply function is $S = f\ (M)$. It appears as a rightward sloping curve with an upper boundary (see Fig. 5.2 in Chap. 5). Expectation imposes a critical impact on the short- run supply. In case the enterprise believes that the output level S^* can be achieved when the real quantity of money supply is M^*, $S^* = f\ (M^*)$ will hold; if the enterprise is stuck with the money illusion, that is, when the nominal money M is larger than the real money M^*, the firm mistakes it as a real increase in money (in fact, because P increases, M/P equals M^* or even smaller than M^*). This encourages the firm to further expand production, resulting in a greater short—run supply S than S^*.The relationship is illustrated in

$$S = S^* + \eta(M - M^*)$$

The money illusion will disappear in the long-run, so $S = S^*$.The elasticity of increase in the short-run supply depends not only on the expectation stickiness but also on the idleness of fixed capital assets and labor force in the business. The upper boundary of short-run increase in aggregate supply is constrained by supply restrictions from the bottleneck sectors, constraints on increase of production rhythm as well as diminishing returns to scale, and so forth.

The long-run aggregate supply function is $S=f\ (K, L)$. The long-run aggregate supply is inelastic towards M. It is a vertical line as shown in Fig. 5.4 of Chap. 5.

4. The theory of money. Money is regarded as an asset, which bears not only an exchange function but also a wealth function. In the short-run, money supply affects not only the price level but also the output level. But in the long-run, money supply only influences the price level, not the output level. Therefore, the function of money is neutral in the long-run.
5. The theory of expectation. The expectation stickiness is an important factor triggering economic fluctuations in the short-run. The uncertainty of expectation stickiness obscures the quantitative relationship among various variables, especially the quantitative relationship among inflation, money and output. This

leads to difficulties in the process of policy making and the analysis of policy effectiveness.

6. The theory of regulation. Since prices are sticky, a firm's response to a demand change is reflected in regulating its output rather than price at the micro level. As at the macro level, the government's response to demand change is reflected in the rationing of quantity and regulating the quantity of money. The regulation of interest rates herein only plays an auxiliary role. Quantitative control is the main means of economic regulation in China, which can effectively regulate aggregate demand and aggregate supply, thus restricting the escalation of inflation. However, inflation will not be cured by quantitative control, and it further lead to waste of resources while the adjustment of money supply can drive both the product market and money market to equilibrium simultaneously.

Our theory demonstrates that there is an intrinsic mechanism that drives the aggregate demand to be larger than the aggregate supply in China's economic system. The government can restrain the aggregate demand by means of quantity control, but it will result in a non-optimal allocation of resources. Therefore, economic system reforms should be taken as the main instruments to cure inflation in the long-run, while in the near and medium run, quantitative control and structural adjustment are still the main means of managing inflation.

11.3 Effectiveness or Ineffectiveness of Policy

The theory of rational expectation derives a theoretical conclusion of policy ineffectiveness on the basis of policy rules and expectation correctness. As a stone disturbs the water, this conclusion caused great repercussions in Western economics world. A simple model is cited herein to illustrate how the theory of rational expectations has reached such a conclusion.

Assume that the following models hold

$$Y_t = \alpha X_t - \beta P_t (\text{the demand function}) \tag{11.1}$$

$$Y_t = y + \delta\left(P_t - P_t^*\right) + U_t^* (\text{the supply function}) \tag{11.2}$$

$$P_t^* E_{t-1}[P_t] (\text{the function formation of expectations}) \tag{11.3}$$

In the above models, Y_t stands for demand and supply (the equilibrium condition of supply equals demand implicitly holds here); X_t is the control variable for government to control demand; P_t is price; P_t^* is the expected price; Y is the natural output rate, that is, the potential supply level; U_t represents the random error ;α, β, δ are the parameters of the equation set.

Owing to equilibrium, there is

$$\alpha X_t - \beta P_t = Y + \delta\left(P_t - P_t^*\right) + U_t$$

By sorting out the above equation, there is

$$-\beta P_t - \delta P_t = Y - \delta P_t^* - \alpha X_t + U_t$$

Then

$$P_t = \frac{\delta P_t^* + \alpha X_t - Y - U_t}{\beta + \delta}$$

From $P_t^* = E_{t-1}(P_t)$ $P_t^* = E_{t-1}(P_t)$
The following equations are derived

$$\begin{aligned} P_t^* &= E_{t-1}(P) \\ &= E_{t-1}\left(\frac{\delta P_t^* + \alpha X_t - Y - U_t}{\beta + \delta}\right) \\ &= \frac{\delta E\left[P_t^*\right] + \alpha E[X_t] - E[Y] - E[U_t]}{\beta + \delta} \end{aligned} \tag{11.4}$$

Due to

$$E\left(P_t^*\right) = P_t^*, E(Y) = Y, E(U_t) = 0$$

There is

$$P_t^* = \frac{\delta P_t^* + \alpha E[X_t] - Y}{\beta + \delta}$$

By re-arranging the above equation, there is

$$P_t^* = \frac{\alpha E[X_t] - Y}{\beta} \tag{11.5}$$

This equation shows that rational expectations of the price level depends only on the "natural" output rate and the anticipated policy.

When equation (11.5) substitutes equation (11.4), there is

$$P_t = \frac{\alpha\beta X_t + \alpha\delta E[X_t] - (\beta + \delta)Y - \beta U_t}{\beta(\beta + \delta)} \tag{11.6}$$

Then, by subtracting equation (11.5) from equation (11.6), there is

$$P_t - P_t^* = \frac{\alpha(X_t - E[X_t])U_t}{\beta + \delta} \tag{11.7}$$

This is the equation of the error of the price expectation, which originates from two sources: the random error $U_t$and the inequality between the real policy X_t and the anticipated policy $E[X_t]$.

The equation of total output level is derived by substituting equation (11.7) into equation (11.2). It is

$$Y_t = Y + \delta(\frac{\alpha X_t - \alpha E[X_t] - U_t}{\beta + \delta}) + U_t$$

The following also holds

$$Y_t - Y = \frac{\alpha\delta X_t - \alpha\delta E[X_t] + \beta U_t}{\beta + \delta} \tag{11.8}$$

As price expectation is based on the equilibrium price, i.e. equation (11.4), the real output Y_t is deemed to be the equilibrium output, that is

$$Y_t = \text{Demand} = \text{Supply}$$

Equation (11.8) indicates that two reasons are applicable for why the real output deviates from the potential output (or natural output rate). The first is the random error in supply U_t, and the second lies in the deviation between government policy and the anticipated policy $(X_t - E[X_t])$.

The theory of rational expectations holds that due to the knowable government policy rules, $E[X_t] = X_t$ attributing to the nature of the rational expectations. There may be possibly random errors between $E[X_t]$ and X_t but no systematic errors will incur. Consequently, from this model, the conclusion of rational expectations could be drawn that not any kind of policy rules (different theories result in different policy rules) will be able to drive output $Y_t$to deviate from its natural output level Y. Therefore, no policy would systematically influence the output level, and the policy is ineffective.

The key point of whether a policy is effective or not depends upon whether the anticipated policy $E\ [X_t]$ is consistent with the real policy X_t. According to the theory of sticky expectations, not only the anticipated policy level in the short-run is unequal to the real policy level, but there also exists a systematic error (which is the key viewpoint of the theory of sticky expectations). Consequently, there will be a systematic error between the real output Y_t and the natural output Y. The policy will therefore be influential. This conclusion is completely drawn on the basis of the model of rational expectations theory. It can be inferred from this conclusion that as long as the expectations of the economic actors remain sticky, the government policy will carry impacts on the economy. Such impacts originate from the changes of an unanticipated government policy.

It should be pointed out that this model itself is hypothesized by the theory of rational expectations to explain its conclusion of policy ineffectiveness. However, the real economic process is far more complex than this. In China, the phenomenon of disequilibrium is obvious in the short-run, and it is also impossible to formulate expectation from the equilibrium prices. Therefore, Chinese economists should not blindly copy the conclusion of the theory of rational expectations on policy ineffectiveness, but its proposition deserves a high degree of concern. Chinese economists should accordingly analyze the applicability of this proposition to the China's economy by applying their own theories.

According to the previous theoretical analysis, since there is money illusion in the short-run, an increase in the money supply will stimulate the growth of real output and cause it to surpass the potential supply level. However, an increase in the money supply will only enhance the inflation rate because such a money illusion will disappear in the long-run. When the inflation expectations of both the firms and individuals are synchronized with the real inflation, the previous inflation policy used to stimulate supply will be ineffective, and supply will gradually return to its potential aggregate supply level.

In order to stimulate a sustained growth of aggregate supply, the inflationary policy adopted by government must not be foreseeable by the public, that is, government should try to induce the public to anticipate a lower inflation than reality. A consequence of this will be a worse inflation. Therefore, an inflationary supply-stimulating policy can only be effective in the short-run, not in the long-run.

When real supply is lower than its potential level, an expectation trap will appear when expectation sticks to a lower level, hence an increase in the money supply will not be able to propel the output level. This was reflected in China's economic practices in 1990. However, a period after an increase in the money supply, especially when money for investment explores, economic expansion will create a change in expectations due to the multiplier effect of investment. The role of monetary policy will be demonstrated at this time.

Consequently, whether a policy is effective or ineffective depends on the following factors, and different combinations of them may result in different conclusions.

1. The technical factors. Such as whether real supply reaches its upper boundary, whether it is under or above its potential level, and so forth.
2. The expectation factors. Does the expectation stick to a higher or lower level?
3. The policy rules. Is the policy made in accordance with certain rules or at will?

Whether a policy is effective or not mainly depends on two of these factors. The first is the technical factor. The change in policy will be unable to drive the real supply to breakthrough constraints of resources, technology and so on, which is rigid. The second is the expectation factor, which is a relatively soft constraint because of its stickiness in the short-run but not rigid and will eventually change. If we need to enable an effective policy, the direction of expectation should be consistent with the policy goals. When the direction is inconsistent, effectiveness of policy will be crippled or even invalidated. It is obvious that a clear set of policy rules should be required to align the change of the expectation direction with that of the policy goals.

The theory of this book also demonstrates that although China's economic system contains an intrinsic mechanism triggering inflation, the role of government policy in curbing this mechanism does actually exist, so inflation is not inevitable. The government policies can be chosen in between economic growth and inflation, or on a discretionary basis. Within a period of time, especially after János Kornai's *Economics of Shortage* was introduced to China, there has been inadequate research on the regulatory function of government policy so that interests of many scholars were pulled towards the research of the mechanism from which shortage is generated. Under the current circumstance, it is necessary to attach more attention to the effectiveness of regulatory function of the government policy.

11.4 Goals and Means of Policy

Multiple goals should be considered in making macroeconomic policy: curbing inflation, stimulating economic growth, maintaining the balance of payments, improving economic efficiency, and adjusting industrial structures, etc. These policy goals are not entirely compatible, such as the contradiction between curbing inflation and stimulating economic growth. In the short- run, stimulating economic growth will inevitably lead to higher inflation, and curbing inflation will hurt economic growth. The previous theoretical analysis has shown the incompatibility of these two targets.

To develop a policy outline, incompatible policy goals should be taken into account. For instance, the formulation of anti-inflationary policies must ensure a necessary speed of economic growth. The policy focus should be varied during a period of time. For instance, in order to control inflation, we should slow down the economic growth. However, it is not advisable to control inflation at the cost of collapse of the entire economy.

After we determine the policy goals, corresponding measures must be formulated to achieve them. Wrong choice of measures will not only hinder the achievement of the goals but also be counterproductive. At the same time, the side effects of policy should be accounted for. We should strive to avoid the situations where the loss outweighs the gain, which is possible in practice.

Feasibility should be prioritized in determining policy goals. Over demanding policy goals will inevitably encourage short-term unfavorable economic behavior to reduce the long-run benefits of economic development initiatives. Many factors do impose impacts on the establishment of policy goals by the Chinese government, which tends to pursue the target of relatively fast economic growth rate. As the saying goes "haste makes waste", the lessons of history are bitter.

The policy goals should be relatively stable once they are finalized. Stable and feasible policy goals can stabilize public expectations, reduce the influence of uncertain factors in the economy, and be conducive to sustainable economic growth. Frequent alternations of economic goals will only confuse the public and inject chaos into the economic system.

Determination of policy goals and means of implementation is huge systematic engineering. Generally speaking, the effect of multiple policies is better than that of a single one because the former can disperse the cost and reduce the risk of policy to achieve the goals safe and sound.

Based on the aforesaid knowledge and the theoretical analysis of this book, when making an anti-inflationary policy, it is advisable to aim at reducing inflation and maintaining the necessary economic growth rate, which are two incompatible but balanced targets. For example, the inflation rate can be targeted at 5% with an economic growth rate of 5%-7%, and regard them as the two main targets of the outline of the economic plan. Moreover, we need to maintain the stability of the targets without changing them in the near and medium term. Because of the uncertainty in the economic system and the expectation stickiness, there will be errors in achieving these targets. But as long as the targets remain unchanged, these errors will be merely random. In order to achieve these two goals, macroeconomic policies such as planning policies, price policies, fiscal policies, and financial policies should be coordinated attempting to minimize the incompatibility between policy instruments.

Our theoretical analysis has highlighted that there is an inherent mechanism of economic expansions in China's economic system. The above two goals we have determined are only artificial lines and should not be viewed as the red lines of any economic expansion. Policy measures should be developed to suppress economic expansion. According to the theory within this book, when aggregate demand expands, the economy overheats, and inflation rises, it is advisable to adopt a fiscal and credit tightening policy and, if necessary, a planned rationing policy to suppress aggregate demand; when aggregate demand is insufficient, a policy of easing rationing and increasing the money supply can be adopted; further fiscal policies should be implemented when an expectation trap emerges. In general, financial policy is more effective in suppressing aggregate demand, while fiscal policy is more effective in stimulating aggregate supply.

Due to the uncertainty of the economic system and the expectation stickiness, when implementing the policy, we should try to avoid eagerness for quick results and move towards the goals step by step by breaking down the process in reasonable stages and allowing the policy to become incrementally effective. Multiple stages can also betaken for controlling inflation, which can be pulled down step by step. Because of the expectation stickiness, it can be a little stronger at the initial stage, which is conducive to pulling down higher inflation expectations of the public, but afterwards the efforts must be evenly distributed so as to gradually pull down the inflation. When stimulating aggregate supply, the same approach should be adopted step by step. This will help to stabilize economic development. It is not desirable to rapidly alter the approach of implementation, which may cause severe economic fluctuations. It has been four decades[1] since the founding of the People's Republic of China. We must examine the recurrent severe fluctuations in our economic lives during these years. The phenomenon of a contraction following an expansion and an expansion followed by a contraction is triggered not only by the inherent mechanism of the economic system but also by the anxiety for quick success in any given policy implementation process.

[1] This book was first published in 1991 on which all timelines are based.

11.5 Policy Information Transmission and Policy Rules

Public expectations are influenced by government policy. An anti- inflationary policy can help to reduce inflation expectations of the public. The critical point is that, how can the government make the public aware of its targets as well as the measures to achieve these targets. Moreover, how can the government convince the public that the government is determined and able to achieve these targets without giving up halfway.

Over the years, China's economic growth plans have tended to be very ambitious. Although the plans of the national planning organs strive for stability, it is also true that the tendency of the government to pursue high indicators appears repeatedly in the economic life in China. In this trend, the government's anti-inflationary policy is likely to fail halfway, which may encourage the government to change its policy direction. In other words, in order to stimulate the economy, the government may be tempted to do something different from what it had promised. A case in point was the "Soft Landing" (this stands for incrementally decreasing the inflation targeting) in 1986. As a result, just after a slight contraction, the economy expanded significantly again, finally leading to a complete contraction in 1989 to halt the upward trend in inflation.

Because of the swinging nature of the formulation and implementation of government policy, the information transmitted to the public was confusing, which disturbed the formation of public expectations. Unpredictable policies will induce ambiguity to public expectations, which amplifies uncertainty in the economic system.

If the government follows an open set of policy rules and unswervingly implements them, the policy rules themselves will provide the public with more information about the process of government policy making, which in turn helps to reduce the uncertainty of public expectations. It can also prevent policymakers from changing their original intentions and improve the credibility of these policies. It should be said that over the past 40 years,[2] China's economic practice has proven that the Chinese government has developed a set of policy rules, but it has not yet been well organized and still remained arbitrary to some degree.

Policy rules will change the value of policy variables from exogenous to endogenous. To a certain extent, this increases the technical difficulty of economic simulation models while it can offer convenience for theoretical analysis. This is helpful to the analysis of economic turning points and the abrupt behavior of the economy.

Policy rules can be roughly divided into two types: feedback and no- feedback, which is similar to the closed-loop system and the open-loop system in cybernetics. Feedback policy rules will constantly adjust the strength of the policy according to the implementation and results of it, so that the goals can be achieved. Non-feedback policy rules follow a static approach. Once the policy is formulated, it will not be modified if nothing special happens so as to reduce the public uncertainty and stabilize the public expectations. For example, the law of the growth rate of money supply is stable and constant as emphasized by Milton Friedman and with the policy

[2] This book was first published in 1991 on which all timelines are based.

rules recently released by the Chinese government to maintain a 6% growth rate of its national income.

A good policy rule should be to stabilize the economy, not to trigger economic fluctuations. Due to the influence of uncertainty and the time lags between policy and action, unexpected events may be encountered in the process of policy implementation, which could make the role of policy contrary to the original plan.

For instance, it may be initially to stimulate economic growth by increasing the money supply to pull out the economy from the trough; however, when the policy comes into play, the economy had already recovered in achieving its potential aggregate supply level. Hence, such policy could only stimulate the supply to surpass its potential level, resulting in inflation. Therefore, we should never attempt to achieve a goal in only one leap even if the policy rules are followed. All should be accomplished gradually in order to avoid uncertainty.

11.6 Management Policy for Aggregate Demand

According to our theoretical analysis, because of price and expectation stickiness, an excessive money supply over economic growth will influence the growth of aggregate supply in the initial stage. Such an influence will gradually weaken when the real aggregate supply exceeds its potential level. When aggregate supply reaches its upper boundary, an excessive money supply over the economic growth will only push up inflation. Moreover, in the long-run, the money illusion the public holds will disappear, such an excessive money supply will again trigger higher inflation, and economic growth will return to its potential level. This is a main conclusion of our dual sticky model on the relationship between growth of the money supply and aggregate supply. It is also the theoretical foundation for our aggregate demand management policy.

When aggregate demand rises for whatever reasons (such as a sudden change in expectations, especially in 1988, or when the money supply increases as in 1984), the government formulates policies to stabilize aggregate demand and thus control inflation. The need to keep aggregate demand stable is now agreeable to most economists. The present question becomes what policies the governments should adopt to stabilize aggregate demand.

No one method can be called a countercyclical measure. Aggregate demand must be dropped down when it runs over aggregate supply. Aggregate demand should be otherwise stimulated in case it runs below aggregate supply. This is called "cutting high and filling low". There are three approaches to pull down aggregate demand: one is to control the money supply; the second is to raise interest rates; and the third is to increase rationing. Rationing is a means of planning, while controlling money supply and raising interest rates are both financial means. The way to stimulate aggregate supply is to relax rationing, drop the interest rates, and increase the money supply. Usually, stimulating aggregate demand will indirectly expand aggregate supply.

However, when the expectation is sticking to a lower level, a direct adoption of fiscal policy would be more effective. This involves increasing government investment and consumption in order to directly stimulate aggregate supply depending on the multiplier effect of these two instruments. In 1990, when the government started to stimulate the economy, the first two rounds all relied on money injections, and the effectiveness of them was not obvious. The reason for this was that public expectations stuck to lower levels or fell into the expectation trap. Fiscal policy was adopted in the third round to increase the government's investment and consumption, which turned out to be more fruitful. Hence, a mix of financial and fiscal policies is important. But countercyclical financial and fiscal policies are also problematic. The impact of the money supply on the economy unfolds over a period of time, the lagging of which is also influenced by expectation, and as that change of expectation remains uncertain, all of this may lead to a dislocated temporal reaction. This can be illustrated as the lag of money supply, causing a delay ineffectiveness on the monetary stimulus or on the restraining measures. The monetary expansion policy that attempts to push up the aggregate demand may only take effect when this phase of aggregate demand contraction has passed and the aggregate demand expansion has arrived. This acts as a stimulus to the expansion of economic activity, thereby exacerbating economic fluctuations. It shows that policies that were intended to stabilize the economy may actually turn out to be counterproductive and become policies exacerbating economic fluctuation.

In 1990, the government stimulated the economy for 3 rounds by injecting large quantities of money into the economy. It became a concern for many scholars in the economic circles whether such an injection would lead to a new round of inflation in 1991. The scholars shared similar emotional sentiments no matter what their theoretical differences were. Both the inherent uncertainty in the economic system and the enhanced influence of expectation imposed technical difficulties on the rule of countercyclical money supply. One way to reduce the difficulties is to adopt the trial and error method to gradually increase the money supply. Thus, once the problem is identified, it can be settled immediately without causing greater fluctuations. That is to say, whether we attempt to depress or stimulate the aggregate demand, we should avoid eagerness for quick results by allowing a transition period, so that policies gradually take effect. Although this may consume a bit more time, the implementation can be steadier, thereby avoiding a negative consequence. In a system where uncertainty still plays a critical role, the trial and error method is a relatively satisfactory basic adjustment method, or a fundamental regulation rule.

Another problem with the countercyclical measure is that when stimulating economic growth, the government tends to stimulate aggregate supply to surpass its potential level due to the effect of expectations and price stickiness, resulting in a sharp increase in supply, not the price level. If the government is addicted to this way, a new round of inflation may then occur. If the inflation in China had remained at an acceptable level in 1991, there would have been appeals for stimulus for aggregate demand so as to increase aggregate supply in 1992, which would accordingly have put stress on the government, and the government would have been confronting the test of this problem. When economic and political problems are mingled, the government may once again be misled by these issues and slide back into an inflationary orbit. There have been quite a number of rounds of inflation in China, but the lessons we have learned are never sufficient to resist new inflations.

Because of the potential risks in countercyclical policies mentioned above, Chinese economists are now turning to a negative approach to tackle with the constantly changing environments. This is what was discussed earlier—regulating the money supply and rationing on the basis of a constant and stable economic growth rate, which is also known as a medium growth rate, referring to a national income growth rate of 6%. This is the so-called rule of a constant growth rate. The advantage of this rule is that it clearly discloses the target of the government's policy to the public, which helps to eliminate the uncertainties in public expectations and guide people to arrange their own economic activities inline with this target, thus lessening economic fluctuations. Because the government's target remains unchanged, both the government and the public will be able to alleviate the negative impact of these problems. People will then anticipate and coordinate their economic activities according to this target. In order to follow such rules, the government must primarily be credible and reliable without abandoning its policy commitment halfway.

It is believed that to stabilize the speed of economic growth, we need to first stabilize the growth rate of the money supply. That is, stabilizing the growth rate of the money supply will stabilize economic growth rate. According to our theory, in the long-run, since the money illusion disappears from the public's concern and because of the neutral nature of money, a stable growth rate of money supply will bring about stable economic growth. Given the uncertainty and the role of the internal expansion mechanism in the economic system, we can also adopt both countercyclical planning policy and fiscal policy, integrating them with the financial policy for stabilizing the money supply so as to eliminate fluctuations in the economic system as much as possible. This is a macroeconomic management measure with a financial policy as the core, supplemented by planning and fiscal policy.

11.7 Management Policy for Aggregate Supply

The theoretical basis of aggregate supply management policy is that the economic structure in China is unbalanced with too large a proportion of processing industries but too small a proportion of basic industries. As a result, the effectiveness of supply has been weakened by the constraints of such a structural factor creating serious shortage of some products and prominent surplus of some products.

The goal of aggregate supply management policy is to adjust the economic structure, particularly to strengthen investment in basic industry, to close, suspend, merge, and transfer some enterprises in industrial sectors which are technologically and managerially backward and with considerable product backlog. However, it is not possible to accomplish such a structural adjustment overnight. It takes quite a long time. Furthermore, the structural adjustment itself also demands new investment, which contradicts the aggregate demand management policy. Therefore, the feasible approach lies in shrinking aggregate demand first, and then structural adjustment can be carried out to stimulate the economy when it hits the trough so as to pull the economy out of this.

According to Marx's theory of capitalist economic crisis, there is a general technological renewal and transformation following each crisis, and this renewal of fixed assets will help to bring the economy out of the trough. There is an intrinsic mechanism of technological renewal and transformation in the capitalist economies. Nonetheless, in socialist economies, such a mechanism is relatively feeble. As a consequence, we should attach importance to the characteristics that the ability of socialism to regulate the economy is stronger than that of the capitalism. The government intervention measure should accordingly be undertaken to adjust the economic structure from a macro-perspective to achieve the dual goals of pulling up the economy out of the trough and affecting the technological renewal and restructuring.

Chapter 12
Effect of Inflation and Costs for Managing Inflation

Since inflation carries both positive and negative effects on the economy and the control of them bears certain costs, governments have to weigh the tradeoffs when combating inflation. It then becomes especially difficult for governments to curb inflation at its mild stage because enterprises and households are used to indulging in money illusions. Rational governments, neither from the West nor the East, are in favor of inflation, as they all wish to maintain stable economic climates. The common problem bothering the governments lies in the costs to decrease such inflation. As a result, the evaluation of the positive and negative effects and the costs of controlling inflation will become a critical referencing index for governments to formulate an anti-inflation policy.

12.1 Analysis on Negative Effect of Inflation

Some economists believe that inflation merely distorts reasonable economic accountings without substantial harm to the economy. They hold that the most serious negative effect of inflation is the additional burden arising from the inflation taxes (viewing increased price level as a disguised government tax), which will cause widespread public dissatisfaction.

However, the author holds that the effect of inflation is far more negative than the above estimates.

1. Inflation exacerbates uncertainty in the economic environment.

As inflation is sustained for a certain period of time, public inflation expectations will extricate from sticking to lower levels. However, changes in public inflation expectations are difficult to predict. This adds hardship for governments to monitor the economy. Different public inflation expectations may lead to completely different consequences even under the same growth rate of money supply. For instance, in

L. Li, *The Inflation Mechanism and Expectations*, Understanding China,
https://doi.org/10.1007/978-981-97-2570-0_12

1988 and 1990, the money supply growth rate in China did not significantly increase or decline; nonetheless the economy was presented as overheating in 1988 and too cold in 1990. Such a situation was inseparable from the differences in public inflation expectations in these two years. Due to the uncertainty of the economic environment, the disorientated government operations can easily generate errors, thus causing harmful consequences. In China, the harm caused by these government mistakes is more serious than in the Western countries.

To eliminate and weaken the uncertainty in the economic environment, price levels must be stabilized so as to condition the public inflation expectations. As indicated in the previous analysis, the main means to stabilize price levels include stabilizing the growth rate of the money supply, and secondly, the economic growth rate. This countercyclical and so-called proactive intervention policy should not be overused.

2. Inflation is conducive neither to enhancing economic benefits nor to ameliorating the economic structure. Inflation generates a situation where demand exceeds supply, and causes less loss of physical product storage than money savings. Under such a situation, buyers prioritize quantity over product quality, which in turn eliminates the external pressures for enterprise to improve their product quality.

The purchases of consumers and producers under inflation circumstances result insubstantial inventories, thus idling away the substances that could be used for reproduction, causing a waste in resource allocation.

Low economic efficiency will then be induced by low product quality and waste in resource allocation.

The inventories of consumers and producers also disguise the contradiction of oversupply of long-term products. During a period of inflation, both long-term and short-term products have shortages, which eliminate the internal motivation for the economic structural adjustment.

3. Inflation stimulates consumer consumption, which reduces savings and is not conducive to the expansion of reproduction. Households are not willing to save money since money saving is not competitive with the storage of physical products. Households' deposits in the bank will not stay idle anymore. The money will be loaned out by the bank, so the "surplus" household income will be put into the reproduction process in a physical form. But if households choose to stock physical products, the products will no longer enter the reproduction process. In comparison, inflation is not conducive to the expansion of reproduction.

Higher interest rates may attract more household savings, but it will simultaneously stimulate the interest rate on enterprise loans. As a result, enterprises have to raise their prices which can easily encourage inflation to spiral.

4. Inflation distorts the distribution structure, equaling a type of redistribution. In such redistribution, employees in the public sector will be disadvantaged

because inflation erodes their relative fixed income or their real income is diminished, arousing their dissatisfaction. Even households with a constant income are dissatisfied with the shrinking purchasing power of their existing monetary revenue.

5. Inflation stimulates imports, while escalating costs of exports. Shortage caused by inflation is conducive to the import of more products to bridge the gap between domestic supply and demand. At the same time, inflation escalates the export costs. Export-oriented enterprises will encounter an unfavorable situation if the exchange rate is not adjusted accordingly. This will bring a decline in exports, and the gap between import and export can only be remedied by foreign debts. Therefore, inflation may also aggravate the debt burden.
6. Inflation makes accounting even more troublesome. Due to inflation, deviations exist not only between the current price and original price of the fixed assets, but also in the circulating assets, which generate difficulties in cost accounting. The various income and expenditure items on the accounting ledger will deviate from reality. Western countries have tried to implement an inflation accounting system after a long time of suffering from inflation, but such a system has not yet reached the practical stage.

At the macro level, inflation is also not conducive to national economic accounting. The annual statistical investment and accumulation will be different from reality, and the computation of real GDP will also be problematic. The causes of these problems are consistent with the ones in accounting.

12.2 Analysis on Positive Effect of Inflation

Besides the negative effect, inflation also carries a positive effect.

1. When real aggregate supply is below its potential, inflation is conducive to pulling up aggregate supply and thus stimulating economic growth. This has been analyzed earlier and no need to repeat here.
2. Inflation is also conducive to mitigate the government's domestic debt burden. When the inflation rate is higher than the debt rate, the government's public debt is relatively lessened. Such debt mainly consists of two categories: one is the fiscal loan from the public, which is used to cover the gap in fiscal revenue and expenditure; the other is the public deposits in the bank, which will be turned into loans for investment by the bank. For the time being,[1] banks are in fact an integral part of national institutions. The imbalance between the revenue and expenditure will not cause bankruptcy of the banks. Such imbalance would be covered up by more money supply. Therefore, the bank deposits are viewed as a disguised treasury debt, which is different from Western countries. In fact, methods such as increasing treasury bonds are similar to robbing Peter to pay

[1] This book was first published in 1991.

Paul by stealing part of the bank deposits to bridge the gap between fiscal revenue and expenditure. Debt originated from deposits may constitute a heavy burden on the national economy. If the investment from debt can generate more revenue, then borrowing is conducive to the economic development; on the contrary (for instance, new investment cannot generate new production capacity due to a long-run economic recession), debt reimbursement will become a serious problem. Such debt may ultimately be cancelled (or reimbursed) only through the means of inflation. The problems of taxing the public as well as of cancelling or reducing the government's public debt by means of inflation are actually two sides of the same coin.

3. Inflation can also turn a batch of "dormant accounts" into "living accounts". According to the accounting system in China, as long as products are produced, their values will be counted as national income, and the relevant profits and taxes are all included in fiscal revenue. If the products remain unsold and backlogged in the warehouse, the funds corresponding to these products will become a "dormant account" on the bankbooks. Therefore, while the national income is virtually increased, it in fact becomes a deficit. Under inflation, the public panic buying behavior will procure all these products, thus making the "dormant accounts" into "living accounts". This, though beneficial for the banks, is economically unfavorable for the long-run interests of the country.

12.3 Trade-Off Between Negative and Positive Effects of Inflation

The trade-off between positive and negative effects of inflation focuses on whether moderate inflation is necessary.

The Keynesian school believes that moderate inflation is acceptable because it can balance the two major macroeconomic objectives—boosting employment and stabilizing prices. However, this basic Keynesian policy proposition has been severely attacked by the Monetarist school for the latter holds that zero inflation should be taken as the policy target. Under zero inflation, employment levels will return to natural unemployment as long as the money supply is stabilized and the market thoroughly functions. These two different sets of policy propositions rely upon their respective theoretical foundations. In Western countries, in fact, price levels have continued to rise in recent years but remain within the scope of an acceptable moderate inflation level (below 5% is generally regarded as a moderate inflation rate).

In China, only very few people advocate hyperinflation. The theoretical debate is whether to pursue a moderate inflation target. Actually, the government is also hesitant in formulating such a moderate inflation policy.

If we follow the theory of this book, both the economic system and economic structure in China inherently propel inflation. Opposite to Western countries, demand in China is not insufficient but excessive. Insufficient demand only occurs after a tightening policy in case government implements an emergency policy to regulate the economy. Such insufficient demand is the consequence of external policy coercion not from the interior of the economic system. Therefore, in China, there is no need to artificially stimulate aggregate demand. As long as macroeconomic policy is deregulated, aggregate demand will naturally be overheating. As a result, controlling overheating aggregate demand should be the basic standpoint of China's macroeconomic policy.

The problem is that there is an inherent driving force of inflation in China. Does it substantially slowdown the economic growth rate (e.g. below 5%) in case the government suppresses aggregate demand to equalize it to aggregate supply? Or, on the contrary, should there be an accompanying inflation if the growth rate is maintained between 5% and 7%? And how big will this inflation then be? This is still the trouble facing both the economic theory circles and the government sectors currently.[1]

This issue has been discussed separately in previous chapters. The fundamental standpoint is that there is no constant relationship between the economic growth rate and inflation in the short-run. Higher inflation may also be experienced during a period of slow economic growth due to factors such as uncertainty and expectations or vice versa. Similar situations can be found internationally. Cases of a simultaneous low or high in both inflation and economic growth rate or where one is high but the other low can be found in reality. Here, through the phenomena of uncertainty and expectations, the author attempts to reveal the wax and wane, however far inconstant correlations are between inflation and economic growth rate. On the basis of theoretical analysis, growth in money supply functions differently in stimulating economic growth when it is above, equal to, or below the potential growth rate. Even when the economic growth rate is higher than its potential, inflation can also function differently at different phases (when it is closed to the growth potential or closed to the upper boundary of such a potential).

As a developing country, it is necessary for China to maintain a certain economic growth rate, which is also constrained by various factors. Taking into account China's historical experience and the experience of other developing countries, it is possible for China to maintain a growth rate between 5% and 7%. China's money supply level can thus be based on such a growth rate, and gradually be constant. After a period of time, a concrete inflation rate can be identified under such an economic growth rate. If the inflation rate is fluctuating around 5%, moderate inflation is deemed to be acceptable when the economic growth rate is slightly higher than its potential rate; if it rises above 10% in the long-run, a reduction in economic growth rate becomes necessary; in case it runs below 5% in the long-run, the corresponding economic growth rate would be ideal or even be slightly increased. In conclusion, the appropriateness of the economic growth rate is tightly related to its accompanying inflation rate. However, such a relationship is only stable in the long-run, not in the short-run. That is why a stable money supply rate has been emphasized in the preceding chapter. A stable money supply rate should be maintained to achieve a stable economic growth rate in the long- run, and meanwhile to control the inflation rate within a low level (5%).

12.4 Costs for Managing Inflation

In case inflation has already occurred, managing inflation should be at the cost of economic growth. This has been illustrated in previous discussions. According to our theory, when inflation already occurs, real aggregate supply will exceed its potential. In order to decrease inflation, real aggregate supply should run below its potential level. The gap between real aggregate supply and its potential level will be the cost for managing inflation as shown in Fig. 12.1.

The shadow in Fig. 12.1 shows the cost for managing inflation. Prior to year t_1, the real aggregate supply is higher than its potential, thus triggering inflation. In order to decrease the inflation, real aggregate supply has to drop below the potential level. After year t_2, real aggregate supply is gradually returning to the potential level since inflation has been curbed. Till year t_3, a new inflation is triggered because real aggregate supply exceeds its potential.

The declining rate of inflation essentially depends on the decreasing rate of real aggregate supply (caused by tightening money supply), therefore, a reduction in real aggregate supply can be an alternative for managing inflation as shown in Fig. 12.2.

As indicated in Fig. 12.2, real aggregate supply can be manipulated in two paths: path *A* and path *B*. Path *A* declines faster than Path *B* but it also recovers quicker. Path *B* declines slower and it also recovers slower. Both path *A* and path *B* can be employed to control inflation. However, path *A* is like a dose of an intensive pill,

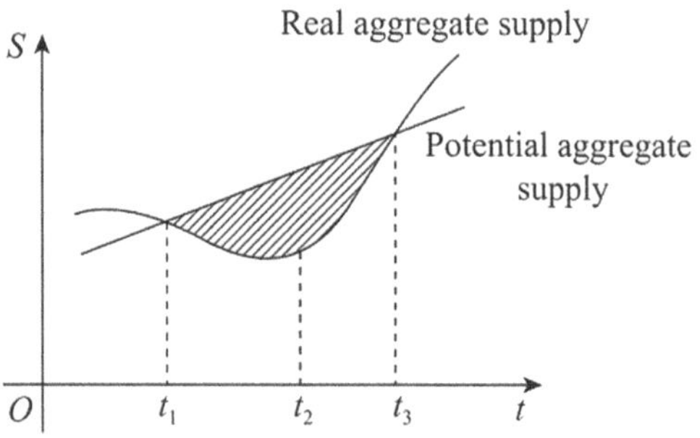

Fig. 12.1 Costs for managing inflation

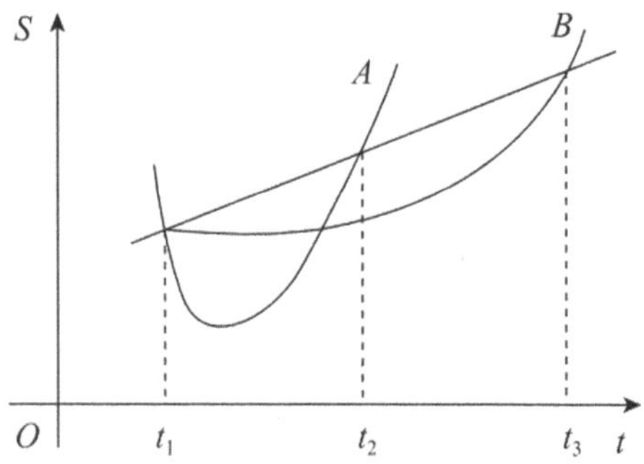

Fig. 12.2 A Comparison of Costs for managing inflation

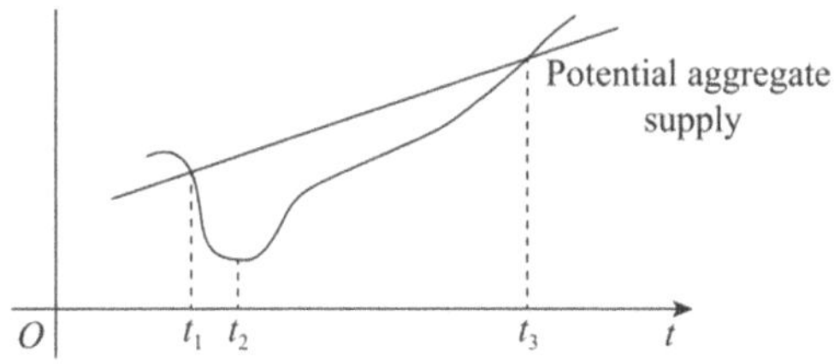

Fig. 12.3 Means for decreasing inflation expectation

which requires the public to tolerate the bitter fruits of declining economic growth; path B is relatively moderate but time- consuming and requiring relative better public patience.

Due to the impact of sticky expectations, it is necessary to decrease inflation by more severe means as soon as possible to weaken the inflation expectations of the public. Once such expectations are decreased, a more moderate means may be applied to manage the inflation so that it can be cured at a minimum cost. This is demonstrated in Fig. 12.3.

As shown in Fig. 12.3, since more severe means is implemented to reduce real aggregate supply in year t_1, the inflation expectations of the public have been decreased in year t_2 when a moderate approach can be adopted to drive real aggregate supply to gradually return to its potential level.

In the early stages of managing inflation, the government should express accurately its determination to the public and adopt necessary emergency measures to weaken inflation expectations of the public. However, such emergency measures should not last too long as it may otherwise bring about adverse consequences. Only when public inflation expectations are decreased will a moderate approach be more desirable.

It is still a subject for research as for what kind of policy can help to decrease inflation while the costs can be simultaneously minimized. Similar subjects have been explored in Western economic theories, whose research findings can be referred to by Chinese scholars.

12.5 Static and Dynamic Discussions on Minimum Costs

Two factors should be mainly prioritized as the optimal policy for managing inflation. The first is the cost factor, which must be as low as possible; the other is the time factor, which should not be too lengthy. In addition, factors such as adjustability of the economic structure and enhancement of economic benefits will also be included, however they may greatly complicate the problem. Therefore, only the minimum cost and time factors will be focused on here while ignoring the rest.

The gap between real aggregate supply and potential has been deemed as the cost for managing inflation in previous discussions. The minimum cost can be achieved by the smallest area between real aggregate supply and potential. This is viewed as the first reason for the optimal managing policy.

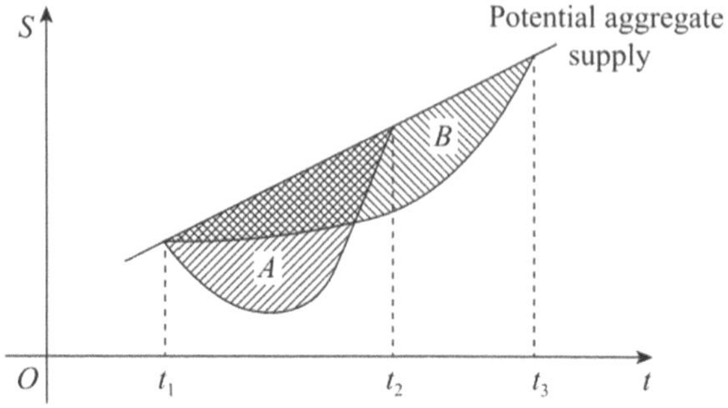

Fig. 12.4 A contrast of optimal policies

Even if equal areas, they would shape differently on the time dimension. Hence, the shortest time dimension under the equal areas should be considered as the optimal policy, which is viewed as the second reason for the optimal managing policy.

Based upon the above two reasons, different policies can be contrasted, and then the best be chosen. As shown in Fig. 12.4, *A* is preferable to *B*.

In Fig. 12.4, although the cost of policy *A* equals that of policy *B* since *A* shares the same area with *B*, policy *A* is preferable to policy *B* because the former enjoys a shorter time than the latter.

If the area of *B* is smaller than that of *A*, policy *B* is believed to be more preferable to policy *A* though policy *B* takes a longer time than policy *A*. That is to say, of the two criteria employed for judging optimal policy alternatives, a minimum cost is prioritized over a shorter timeframe. The time dimension is contrasted then on the basis of minimum cost.

Of course, public affordability should be considered when determining the length of time since implementation of a good policy requires public cooperation.

The above discussion on the optimal policy alternative is merely from a static perspective. In the following section, a more dynamic perspective will be further applied in the discussion. However, it should be noted that the mathematical tools adopted in the methodology are relatively complex and still present a challenge for practical applications. It is therefore viewed as a tentative theoretical analysis, or it is just at its initial stage of theoretical research work.

Considering optimal policy alternative from a dynamic perspective should begin with a study on the decreasing path of the price level. As stated in the previous theoretical analysis, the decreasing path of the price level can be determined by the quantity of the money supply. Accordingly, the dynamic optimal policy alternative can then be transformed into an issue of manipulation of an optimal money supply.

Assume t_0 is time of the initial stage of managing inflation and T_1 as the quantity of the market money supply, namely $X(t_0) = T_1$. Based on the theoretical analysis, at the end of the managing period t_1, in case the quantity of market money supply equals T_2, namely $X(t_1) = T_1$, then inflation will fall within the targeting level. The pre-requisite is that during the course when the market money supply increases from T_1 to T_2, the new money supply should be accumulated at a minimum level so as to decrease inflation as much as possible.

The change rule of $X\ (t)$ (quantity of market money in t period) can be represented by the following differential equation

$$\dot{X} = -kX + U$$

where, $X\ (t)$ is shortened as X; $\dot{X}$ the derivative of X; k is the constant coefficient; and U is the new money supply.

There is an economic background for the above equation. On one hand, the change in the quantity of money supply in the economic system, there is a withdrawal of money (that is, money returns to the banking system); on the other hand, there is an increase in the money supply (new money injection), and there is a positive relationship between the rate of withdrawal and the prevailing quantity of money in the economic system. As a result, the change rate of the money supply should be the algebraic sum of the rate of change of these two aspects above-mentioned.

Such a statement can be translated into the following mathematical languages.

Under the following constraints

$$\dot{X} = -kX + U$$

$$X\left(t_0\right) = T_1$$

$$X\left(t_1\right) = T_2$$

A proper U^* should be selected to minimize

$$J = \int_{t_0}^{t_1} U^2 \mathrm{d}t$$

where, U stands for the money injection, and it is the function of t, namely $U(t)$, shortened as U.

If U is the minimum, U^2 should be the corresponding minimum and vice versa. The choice of a minimized cumulative U^2 here is just to make it easier for computation. The U^*, which can generate a minimized accumulative U^2, will naturally be the one to generate a minimized accumulative U.

The above equation can be solved as follows.

The Hamiltonian function is then as follows.

$$H = -U^2 + P(-kX + U)$$

The canonical equation is

$$\dot{X} = -kX + U$$

$$\frac{\partial H}{\partial U} = -2U + P = 0$$

$$\dot{P} = \frac{\delta H}{\delta X} = -(-Pk) = Pk$$

And

Therefore $U = \frac{P}{2}$

and $\begin{cases} \dot{x} = -kX + \dfrac{P}{2} \\ \dot{P} = kP \end{cases}$

Therefore $\ddot{X} = -k\dot{X} + \frac{\dot{P}}{2}$

$$\ddot{X} = -k(-kX + \frac{P}{2}) + \frac{1}{2}kP$$
$$= k^2X - \frac{1}{2}kP + \frac{1}{2}kP$$

As well as $\ddot{X} = k^2X$.

And $X = C_1 \cdot e^{kt} + C_2 \cdot e^{-kt}$.

Substituted by boundary conditions

$$\begin{cases} C_1 + C_2 = T_1 (\text{Assuming } t_0 = 0) \\ C_1 \bullet e^{kt_1} + C_2 \bullet e^{-kt_1} = T_2 \end{cases}$$

Then

$$C_1 = \frac{T_2 - T_1 e^{-kt}}{e^{kt_1} - e^{-kt_1}}$$

$$C_2 = \frac{T_1 e^{-kt} - T_2}{e^{kt_1} - e^{-kt_1}}$$

Because $P = 2\left(\dot{X} + kX\right)$

$$P = 2\left(C_1 \cdot ke^{kt} - C_2 ke^{-kt} + kC_1 e^{kt} + kC_2 e^{-kt}\right)$$
$$= 2\left(2C_1 ke^{kt}\right) = 4C_1 ke^{kt}$$

Then

$$P = \frac{4k(T_2 - T_1 e^{-kt_1})}{e^{kt_1} - e^{-kt_1}} e^{kt}$$

Therefore

$$U = \frac{P}{2} = \frac{2k(T_2 - T_1 e^{-kt_1})}{e^{kt_1} - e^{-kt_1}} \cdot e^{kt}$$

Where, U is the required optimal control variable and U^* under the initial conditions of $X(t_0) = T_1, X(t_1) = T_2$.

Obviously, the optimal money supply U^* is a complex function which should not be followed by the banks to inject money. However, the theoretical curve of U^* can be used as a reference for banks to determine their own money supply so that the real money supply will fluctuate around such a theoretical curve or at least not deviate too far away.

It is necessary to point out that the dynamic optimal method introduced above is also a dynamic optimization idea commonly used in economic theory. For example, in research of the accumulation rate, it is well-known that a high recent accumulation rate will lead to a low recent consumption, but more consumption will be stimulated after a period of time; a low recent accumulation rate will generate a high recent consumption, but after a period of time, the consumption it brings will be a bit smaller than the corresponding previous accumulation rate. Obviously, the proportion between accumulation and consumption is a dynamic optimal problem. If it is required to maximize the total amount of annual consumption during a planning period, then the choice of the annual accumulation rate during such a planning period becomes an "optimal control" problem. The general result is that the accumulation rate will be high in the beginning and low afterwards during a planning period.

The solution to this optimal control is exactly the same as the mathematical method described above, which is also known as Pontryagin's Maximum Principle.

This idea of dynamic optimization can then be regarded as a natural result of the dynamic optimal as stated by the dynamic general equilibrium theory, which is developed on the basis of the static optimal held by the static general equilibrium theory. It is still a research area deeply rooted in the economic theory circles of Western countries. Chinese economists started similar research early in 1983, but the idea of a dynamic optimal has not yet been adequately developed in economic theories. This issue is pointed out here in a view to draw more attention to similar problems so that any purely theoretical analysis can be transformed into practical applications.

Bibliography

English Works

1. Charles H Whiteman. Problems in Macroeconmic Theory [M]. Academic press, 1987.
2. Eduard J Bomhoff. Manetary uncertainty-Elsevier [M]. Science Publishing Company, 1983.
3. David H Papell. Hall and Taylor's Macroeconomics Study Guids [M]. Second Edition, W. W. Norton and Company, 1988.
4. Geoffrey Whittington. Inflation Accounting [M]. Cambridge University Press.
5. G S Maddala. Limited-dependent and Qualitative variables in Econometrics [M]. Cambridge University Press, 1983.
6. Jan C Siebrand. Towards Operational Disequilibrium Macro Economics [M]. Martinus: Martinus Nijhoff, 1979.
7. Jean-Pascal Benassy. The Economics of Market Disequilibrium [M]. Academic Press, 1982.
8. Jean- Paul Lambert. Disequilibrium Macroeconomic Models [M]. Cambridge University Press, 1988.
9. K Holden, D A Peel and J L Thompson. Expectations: Theory and Evidence [M]. Macmillan Publishers LTD, 1985.
10. Laurence R Klein. The Economics of Supply and Demand [M]. Basil Blackwell, 1983.
11. Oliuter Jean Blanchard and Stanley Fischer. Lectures on Macroeconomics [M]. The MIT Press Cambridge, Massachusetts, 1989.
12. Otto Ectstein. Core Inflation [M]. Prentice-Hall, 1981.
13. Richard E Quandt. The Econometrics of Disequilibrium [M]. Basil Blackwell, 1988.
14. Robert E Hall, John B Tarlor. Macroeconomics [M]. W. W. Norton & Company, 1988.
15. Robert E Hall. Inflation, Causes and Effects [M]. The University of Chicago Press, 1982.
16. Roger J Bowden. The Econometrics of Disequilibrium [M]. North- Holland publishing Company, 1978.
17. Stanley Fischer. Indexing, Inflation and Economic policy [M]. The MIT Press, 1986.
18. Takeshi Amemiya. Advanced Econometrics [M]. Harvard University Press Cambridge, Massachusetts, 1985.
19. Thomas J Sargent. Macroeconomic Theory [M]. Second Edition, Academic press, 1987.
20. Volker Bohm. Disequilibrium and Macroeconomics [M]. Basil Blackwell, 1989.

L. Li, *The Inflation Mechanism and Expectations*, Understanding China,
https://doi.org/10.1007/978-981-97-2570-0

English Thesis

21. G S Maddala and Forrest D Nelson. Maximum Likelihood Methods for Model of Markets in Disequilibrium [J]. Econometrica, 1974, 42(6).
22. John P Burkett. Slack, shortage and Disconraged Consumers in Eastern Europe: Estimates Based on Smoothing by Aggregation [J]. Review of Economic Studies, 1988(LV):193–506.
23. Portes R and Winter D. Disequilibrium Estimates for Consumption Goods Markets in Centrally Planned Economies [J]. Review of Economic Studies, 1980, 47:137–159.

Chinese and Chinese Translation Works

24. 马克思恩格斯全集 [M]. 第23、第24、第25、第26卷.
25. [美]布坎南·瓦格纳. 赤字中的民主 [M]. 北京:北京经济学院出版社, 1988.
26. [英]布赖恩·摩根. 货币学派与凯恩斯学派——它们对货币理论的贡献 [M]. 北京:商务印书馆, 1984.
27. [加]戴维·威廉·莱德勒. 货币需求:理论、证据和问题 [M]. 上海:上海三联书店, 1989.
28. 戴园晨. 社会主义宏观经济学 [M]. 北京:中国财政经济出版社, 1986.
29. 邓乐平. 中国的货币需求——理论与实证的考察 [M]. 北京:中国人民大学出版社, 1990.
30. 樊纲. 现代三大经济理论体系的比较与综合 [M]. 上海:上海三联书店, 1990.
31. 樊纲, 张曙光, 等. 公有制宏观经济理论大纲 [M]. 上海:上海三联书店, 1990.
32. [美]Fraklin M Fisher. 微观经济学 [M]. 武汉:武汉大学出版社, 1988.
33. 符钢战, 等. 社会主义宏观经济分析 [M]. 上海:学林出版社, 1986.
34. 郭树清. 模式的变革与变革的模式 [M]. 上海:上海三联书店, 1989.
35. 黄达. 财政信贷综合平衡导论 [M]. 北京:中国金融出版社, 1984.
36. [美]霍华德·J. 谢尔曼. 停滞膨胀——激进派的失业和通货膨胀理论 [M]. 北京:商务印书馆, 1984.
37. [英]凯恩斯. 就业利息和货币通论 [M]. 北京:商务印书馆, 1983.
38. 厉以宁. 非均衡的中国经济 [M]. 北京:经济日报出版社, 1991.
39. 李扬. 财政补贴经济分析 [M]. 上海:上海三联书店, 1990.
40. 刘国光. 体制变革中的经济稳定增长 [M]. 北京:中国计划出版社, 1990.
41. [澳]迈克尔·卡特, 罗德尼·麦道克. 理性预期:八十年代的宏观经济学 [M]. 上海:上海译文出版社, 1988.
42. [美]米尔顿·弗里德曼. 论通货膨胀 [M]. 北京:中国社会科学出版社, 1982.
43. [美]米尔顿·弗里德曼. 失业还是通货膨胀——对菲利普斯曲线的评价 [M]. 北京:商务印书馆, 1982.
44. [美]M. 克莱因. 古今数学思想 [M]. (第1—4册). 上海:上海科学技术出版社, 1979.
45. 钱伯海. 国民经济综合平衡统计学 [M]. 北京:中国财政经济出版社, 1982.
46. 饶余庆. 现代货币银行学 [M]. 北京:中国社会科学出版社, 1983.
47. 汤学义. 利息率研究 [M]. 上海:上海三联书店, 1988.
48. 田源, 王育琨. 治理通货膨胀的思路和政策 [M]. 哈尔滨:哈尔滨出版社, 1990.
49. 外国经济学说研究会. 现代外国经济学论文选 [M]. (第七辑). 北京:商务印书馆, 1983.
50. 吴敬琏. 经济改革问题探索 [M]. 北京:中国展望出版社, 1987.
51. 吴敬琏, 胡季. 中国经济的动态分析和对策研究 [M]. 北京:中国人民大学出版社, 1988.
52. 薛暮桥. 中国社会主义经济问题研究 [M]. 北京:人民出版社, 1979.
53. [匈]亚诺什·科尔内. 短缺经济学 [M]. 北京:经济科学出版社, 1986.
54. 杨坚白. 国民经济综合平衡的理论和方法论问题 [M]. 北京:人民出版社, 1984.
55. 杨坚白. 社会主义宏观经济论 [M]. 大连:东北财经大学出版社, 1990.
56. 杨坚白. 社会主义社会国民收入的若干理论问题 [M]. 北京:中国社会科学出版社, 1983.
57. 钟朋荣, 吴同虎. 宏观经济论 [M]. 北京:经济科学出版社, 1990.

Chinese Thesis

58. 戴睿. 合理预期与宏观管理 [J]. 中国经济体制改革, 1989(2).
59. 董辅礽. 关于我国社会主义所有制形式问题 [J]. 经济研究, 1979(1).
60. 樊纲. 论公开宣布的通货膨胀计划 [N]. 理论信息报, 1988-09-19.
61. 国家信息中心、中国社会科学院经济研究所"通货膨胀问题"课题组. 我国通货膨胀的综合治理问题 [J]. 经济研究, 1989(3).
62. 李剑阁. 也谈当前宏观经济政策问题 [J]. 经济研究, 1987(5).
63. 李拉亚. 货币对经济的三大影响途径 [J]. 中国社会科学院研究生院学报, 1985(4).
64. 李拉亚. 货币动力学研究 [J]. 中国社会科学院研究生院学报, 1987(3).
65. 李拉亚. 使经济增长从非均衡向均衡转轨 [N]. 经济参考, 1990-10-22.
66. 李拉亚. 投入产出表的拓展及其在国民经济核算体系中的应用 [J]. 数量经济技术经济研究, 1987(10).
67. 李拉亚. 通货加剧是预期影响, 物价上涨有心理因素 [N]. 经济参考, 1989-03-28.
68. 李拉亚. 我国通货膨胀的几个问题 [J]. 中国社会科学院研究生院学报, 1989(2).
69. 李拉亚. 我国通货膨胀治理的战略思考 [J]. 江西大学学报(经济学版), 1989(2).
70. 李拉亚. 预期理论对我国经济学未来发展的影响 [J]. 经济研究, 1989(5).
71. 李拉亚, 张曙光, 杨仲伟, 樊纲, 左大培, 刘永强. 我国通货膨胀预期研究 [N]. 经济日报, 1989-03-10.
72. 李晓西. 预期与通货膨胀 [J]. 数量经济技术经济研究, 1990(2).
73. 马建堂. 通货膨胀和通货膨胀预期 [N]. 经济参考报, 1989-05-09.
74. 田江海, 李拉亚. 医治需求膨胀的政策处方 [J]. 三不月刊, 1988(11).
75. 乌家培, 李拉亚. 当今中国通货膨胀的特征分析 [J]. 财经问题研究, 1989(11).
76. 吴敬琏. 把国民经济的增长速度控制在适度的范围内 [N]. 人民日报, 1985-05-17.
77. 杨仲伟, 等. 我国通货膨胀的诊断 [J]. 经济研究, 1988(4).
78. 杨仲伟, 等. 我国通货膨胀的治理 [J]. 经济研究, 1988(6).
79. 张宝群. 论通货膨胀预期 [J]. 金融研究, 1989(2).
80. 张其佑, 贾渠平. 通货膨胀预期是加剧通货膨胀的重要诱因 [J]. 国内外经济管理, 1989(2).
81. 张曙光. 我国的通货膨胀预期 [J]. 财政经济, 1989(3).
82. 张曙光, 李拉亚. 我国预期理论研究评述 [J]. 经济学动态, 1989(12).
83. 李拉亚. 通货膨胀与不确定性 [M]. 北京:中国人民大学出版社, 1995.
84. 李拉亚. 宏观审慎管理的理论基础研究 [M]. 北京:经济科学出版社, 2016.
85. Bank of England. Monetary Policy Trade-off and Forward Guidance [R/OL]. http://www.bankofengland.co.uk/monetarypolicy/Pages/forwardguidance.aspx.2013.
86. Barro R J. Interest-Rate Smoothing [R]. NBER Working Papers, No. 2581, National Bureau of Economic Research, 1988.
87. Blinder A S, Ehrmann M, Fratzscher M, De Haan J & Jansen D J. Central bank communication and monetary policy: a survey of theory and evidence [R]. ECB Working Paper, No. 898, 2008.
88. CœuréBenoît. Inflation expectations and the conduct of monetary policy [C]. Speech given at an event organised by the SAFE Policy Center, Frankfurt am Main, 2019-07-11.
89. Carroll C. Macroeconomic expectations of households and professional forecasters [J]. Quarterly Journal of Economics, 2003, 118(1):269–298.
90. Carroll C. The epidemiology of macroeconomic expectations [M]//Blume & Durlauf. The Economy as an Evolving Complex System, III. Oxford University Press, 2005.
91. Clarida R, J Galí & M Gertler. The science of monetary policy: A New Keynesian perspective [J]. Journal of Economic Literature, 1999, 37:1661–1707.
92. Coibion O, Gorodnichenko Y, Kumar S. How Do Firms Form their Expectations? New Survey Evidence [J]. American Economic Review, 2018a, 108:2671–2713.
93. Coibion O, Gorodnichenko Y, Kumar S, Pedemonte M. Inflation Expectations as a Policy Tool? [R]. NBER Working Paper, No. 24788, 2018b-06.
94. Coibion O, Gorodnichenko Y, Weber M. Monetary Policy Communications and their Effects on Household Inflation Expectations [R]. NBER Working Paper, No. 25482, 2019.

95. Cruijsen Carin A B Vander and Sylvester C W Eijffinger. The Economic Impact of Central Bank Transparency: A Survey [R]. CEPR Discussion Paper, No. 6070, 2007.
96. Cukierman Alex and Allan Meltzer. A Theory of Ambiguity, Credibility and Inflation under Discretion and Asymmetric Information [J]. Econometrica, 1986, 54(4):1099–1128.
97. Evans G, S Honkapohja. Learning and Expectations in Macroeconomics [M]. NJ:Princeton University Press, 2001.
98. Francesco D'Acunto, Ulrike M Malmendier, Juan Ospina, Michael Weber. Exposure to Daily Price Changes and Inflation Expectations [R]. NBER Working Paper, No. 26237, 2019-09.
99. Fuster A, Perez-Truglia R, Wiederholt M, Zafar B. Expectations with endogenous information acquisition: an experimental investigation [M/OL].(2019)Social Science Electronic Publishing. http://www.nber.org/papers/w24767.
100. Gali J, M Gertler. Inflation dynamics: A structural econometric analysis [J]. Journal of Monetary Economics, 1999, 44:195–222.
101. Hagedorn M, Luo J, Manovskii I and Mitman K. Forward Guidance [J]. NBER Working Paper, No. 24521, 2018.
102. Krugman P R. It's baaack: Japan's slump and the return of the liquidity trap [M]. Brookings Panel on Economic Activity, 1998.
103. Levy D et al. Asymmetric price adjustment in the small: An implication of rational inattention [D]. Discussion Paper Series No. 04–23, Tjalling C. Koopmans Research Institute, Utrecht School of Economics, the Netherlands, 2005.
104. Mankiw G N, R Reis. Sticky information versus sticky prices: A proposal to replace the new Keynesian Phillips curve [J]. Quarterly Journal of Economics, 2002, 117:1295–1328.
105. Morris S, H S Shin. Coordinating expectations in monetary policy [R]// J-P, Touffut. Central Banks as Economic Institutions, Edward Elgar, 2008.
106. Nakata T, S Schmidt. Gradualism and liquidity traps [J]. Review of Economic Dynamics, 2019, 31:182–199.
107. Reis R. Inattentive consumers [J]. Journal of Monetary Economics, 2006, 53(8).
108. Roberts J M. Inflation expectations and the transmission of monetary policy [R]. Federal Reserve Board FEDS Working Paper, No. 1998-43.
109. Sheedy, Kevin D. Structural Inflation Persistence [R]. working paper, Cambridge University, 2005.
110. Sims C A. Stickiness [C]. Carnegie-Rochester Conference Series on Public Policy, 1998, 49(1):317–56.
111. Sims C A. Implications of rational inattention [J]. Journal of Monetary Economics, 2003, 50(3):665–690.
112. Svensson, Lars E O. Inflation Forecast Targeting: Implementing and Monitoring Inflation Targets [J]. European Economic Review, 1997, 41:1111–1146.
113. Svensson, Lars E O. Inflation Targeting [R]. NBER Working Paper, No. 16654, 2010–12.
114. Woodford M. Optimal Interest-Rate Smoothing [J]. Review of Economic Studies, 2003a(70):861–886.
115. Woodford M. Interest and Prices: Foundations of a Theory of Monetary Policy [M]. Princeton Univ. Press, 2003b.
116. Woodford M. Bank communication and policy effectiveness [R]. Paper presented at Federal Reserve Bank of Kansas City Economic Symposium at Jackson Hole, 2005–08.
117. Woodford M. Methods of Policy Accommodation at the Interest Rate Lower Bound [R]. Symposium, Jackson Hole, Wyoming, 2012–08.
118. Yellen J. Macroeconomic Research After the Crisis [G]//Speech given at "The Elusive'Great' Recovery: Causes and Implications for Future Business Cycle Dynamics" 60th annual economic conference 42 sponsored by the Federal Reserve Bank of Boston, Boston, Massachusetts, 2016.

SPRINGER NATURE

GPSR Compliance

The European Union's (EU) General Product Safety Regulation (GPSR) is a set of rules that requires consumer products to be safe and our obligations to ensure this.

If you have any concerns about our products, you can contact us on ProductSafety@springernature.com

In case Publisher is established outside the EU, the EU authorized representative is:

Springer Nature Customer Service Center GmbH
Europaplatz 3
69115 Heidelberg, Germany

The manufacturer's authorised representative in the EU is Springer Nature Customer Service Centre GmbH, Europaplatz 3, 69115 Heidelberg, Germany. If you have any concerns regarding our products, please contact ProductSafety@springernature.com

Printed and bound by CPI Group (UK) Ltd, Croydon, CR0 4YY
01/10/2026
02225849-0006